TO: The Korean War Veterans
of Galloping Hill Golf Course.

with the compliments
of the publisher

Gene. S. Rhie 8-9-97

www.hollym.com

The Forgotten War Remembered
Korea: 1950–1953
A War Correspondent's Notebook and Today's Danger in Korea

Published by
Hollym International Corp.   **www.hollym.com**
18 Donald Place
Elizabeth, New Jersey 07208
Tel: (908) 353–1655 Fax: (908) 353–0255

Library of Congress Catalogue Card Number: 96–76407
ISBN: 1– 56591–131–8

Manufactured in the United States of America

To my mother and father, left behind
when I fled Soviet-occupied North Korea fifty years ago
and whose fate remains unknown

CONTENTS

Chapter Two

NORTH KOREA STRIKES SOUTH

Chapter Three

U.N. COUNTEROFFENSIVE

MacArthur's Gamble Succeeds
Seoul Recaptured
MacArthur and Rhee at Dramatic Ceremony
Scoop on Inchon Landing
General Chung's False Account
Lost Family Found in Seoul
Indescribable Sufferings
Communist Brutality
Execution of Communist Sympathizers

U.N. Forces Break out of Pusan Perimeter
Marching North of the 38th Parallel
President Rhee Enters Pyongyang
Optimism Shattered

Chaos on Two Fronts
Eighth Army Withdrawal
Bloody Retreat from Changjin
Reminiscences of Changjin

General Walker Killed in Accident
Strategic Pullback
Counteroffensive Launched
Chipyong-ni Victory Turns the Tide
Seoul Retaken for the Last Time
MacArthur Relieved
Van Fleet Takes Eighth Army Command
New Defense Line
Washington Seeks Truce

Chapter Four

ARMISTICE TALKS

Chapter Five

A POTENTIAL FLASH POINT

PREFACE

The Korean War launched by North Korea on June 25, 1950 ended inconclusively on July 27, 1953. Not until long afterward was it even dignified by the name of war — the U.S. governmental euphemism was Korean Police Action — and it rapidly became the most forgotten war in American history. Because they could not look back on it with any sense of satisfaction, Americans preferred not to look back at all.

Dot Schilling, former Army private first class, wrote:

"Even when politicians gave a speech, they go right from World War II to Vietnam. They forgot us. You just want to stand up and say, 'What about Korea?' The Korean people never, ever think the Korean War was a forgotten war."

A total of five million human beings from all sides, military and civilians, young and old, were killed or wounded in the battles that raged up and down the Korean peninsula: One and a half million Americans left home to defend freedom in Korea and 54,246 died.

The unsung but proud veterans of the bloody war finally received recognition and gratitude on July 27, 1995, when U.S. President Bill Clinton and South Korean President Kim Young Sam dedicated the Korean War Veterans Memorial on the Washington Mall.

The Korean War is one of the most important and dramatic conflicts of the 20th century. Korea remains the only battlefield on which two great powers — the United States and Communist China — have met since World War II. The Korean War retains a special fascination as the only conflict in which troops of 17 nations fought under the flag of the United Nations for the defense of freedom against Communist aggression.

The Korean War never really ended. Tensions continue to bristle along the 156-mile demilitarized zone (DMZ), with 1.7 million armed forces facing each other. Forty-three years after the inconclusive armistice was signed in July 1953, none of the issues that started the war has been settled. It left only a legacy of hatred and division, and today more than 10 million Koreans are still separated from their families — as in my own case — by the DMZ.

What is most disturbing to Seoul is the fact that Pyongyang is maneuvering to neutralize the Armistice Agreement of 1953 by concluding a separate peace treaty with Washington, excluding South Korea. Pyongyang's ultimate goal is to realize its long-sought withdrawal of U.S. troops (now 37,000) from South Korea, whose presence was a critical factor in deterring a North Korean re-invasion in these past four decades.

Moreover, by December 1995 North Korea had moved troops, tanks and warplanes closer to the DMZ, indicating that the Stalinist regime, fearing famine-induced unrest, could try to restart the war in a reckless effort to keep its 23 million people in line.

Thus, Korea remains a potential international flash point. In order to build a foundation for peace in Northeast Asia, it is expedient to gain an understanding of the international dangers that center on the Korean peninsula today and that will continue for years to come.

I thought about those things as I wrote this book, reliving my memories of the war's endless fights and the murder of those who were its innocent victims. To understand the magnitude of the Korean War and its origins as well as its legacy — a strategic factor in world peace — requires an accurate knowledge of Korea's historical past as well as its present needs and the aspirations of its people.

This book closely examines the causes of the Korean War in an attempt to put an end to the arguments of some historians that America instigated the war, using the South Koreans as puppets. These revisionist arguments are based on North Korea's false propaganda. As recently as August 19, 1995, North Korean envoy Pak Gil Yon, protesting what he claimed were distortions in the 88-page booklet "The United Nations at 50," wrote in a letter circulated at the U.N: "In June 1950 the United States unleashed a war against the Democratic People's Republic in order to achieve its strategy for world domination and utilized the United Nations to justify its aggression in Korea.''

This book also delves into impoverished North Korea's problems and the prospects of South-North reunification.

It is sincerely hoped that this book will present an objective and comprehensive survey of the Korean War — its origins, bloody battles, long-dragged-out truce talks, its inconclusive ending, its legacy of controversies and the agony of the Korean people. Korea showed that freedom is not free. The lesson of Korea should not be forgotten.

Bill Shinn
Los Angeles
January, 1996

CHAPTER ONE

ORIGINS OF
THE KOREAN TRAGEDY

A SHRIMP IN A BATTLE OF WHALES

Korea My Country

As a native of Korea, I have lived with Korean misfortunes, undergoing ruthless oppression of the 36-year Japanese colonial rule and the tragedy of the Korean War. What I attempt here is a background glance from the current uncertainty and controversy to see whether some reflections on the past would help general readers understand the Korean question.

First, some fast facts by way of background: Korea is a mountainous peninsula located in the heart of the strategic triangle of Northeast Asia, bounded by China, Siberia, and Japan. The peninsula — 575 miles in length, averaging 150 miles across — comprises 84,300 square miles. The portion that is South Korea now covers 37,000 square miles (45 percent of the total).

Combining a ruggedly independent spirit with a taste for art and respect for individuality, Koreans are a distinctive race unified in language and culture. Their language is a unique achievement in the Orient, consisting in its *han-gul* form of ten vowels and fourteen consonants. During its long history, Korean cultural achievements were considerable. The oldest existing brass, iron-work and pottery show exquisite workmanship. Korea is credited with the earliest astronomical tower, the first use of movable metal type, and the successful employment of iron-clad warships.

The mythical founder *Tangoon* is said to have established the first civilization in Korea in 2333 B.C. Kija, a Chinese noble who is thought to have fled for sanctuary to the Paekdu Mountain in North Korea, is credited with the founding of the first kingdom of the Chao-hsien in 1122 B.C. Kija and the 41 kings who succeeded

3

him reigned for nearly 1,000 years. In peacetime, the country is as attractive as its poetic name, "The Land of the Morning Calm," denotes.

Subsequently, there flourished the great period of Silla civilization, lasting for 1,000 years, with its capital in the southeastern city of Kyongju, where still stands the oldest existing solar observatory in the world, and relics of the great seven-story pagoda and other evidences of a magnificent city that then contained over a million enlightened inhabitants. Following the fall of Silla, the capital was moved to Kaesong, just south of the 38th Parallel, and from the new ruling dynasty, Koryu, came the modern name Korea. In 1392, General Yi Sung-ke revolted and established his own family as ruling monarchs of the Yi dynasty in the present capital city of Seoul.

A brief chronology of Korean history comprises the following periods:

Tangoon (mythical)	2333–1122 B.C.
Kija (quasi-historical)	1122–193 B.C.
The Three Kingdoms	
Kokuryo (north)	73 B.C.–668 A.D.
Paekje (southwest)	18 B.C.–660 A.D.
Silla (southeast)	57 B.C.–935 A.D.
Koryo (capital at Kaesong)	935–1392
Yi Dynasty (capital at Seoul)	1392–1910
Japanese rule	1910–1945
U.S.-Soviet division and occupation	1945–1948
Republic of Korea	1948–
Democratic People's Republic of Korea	1948–

The tranquil "Land of Morning Calm" suddenly was invaded by Japan in April 1592 and fought a seven-year war costing hundreds of thousands of lives and the virtual destruction of the nation's cultural and productive resources. The war waged by Japanese warlord Toyotomi Hideyoshi resulted in the eventual defeat of the invader. The Korean victory was won by Admiral Lee Sun-shin, who fought with turtle-shaped iron-clad vessels he had invented. He crushed the Japanese naval force in the southern sea, blocking the supply route to the enemy troops fighting on the land. Thus Japan's first attempt to conquer Korea was defeated and turned back. But Japan made other attempts to control Korea.

Korea has been one of those few nations with the misfortune to lie at a crossroads of world power politics, repeatedly stomped over, brutalized, and occupied by stronger neighbors — China, Japan, and Russia. As an ancient Korean proverb aptly laments, "A shrimp is crushed in the battle of the whales."

Assassination of Queen Min

Both Russia and Japan realized that the Korean peninsula was the military key to control of northeast Asia, and commenced maneuvering for its conquest. In a whirlwind war in 1894, Japan forced China to withdraw its support from Korea, and the island of Formosa (Taiwan) was ceded to Japan. Victorious Japan was now determined to take over Korea as its colony by any means. The first blows were struck by the Japanese in 1895 when they murdered Korea's Queen Min.

Minister Miura Goro, a lieutenant general who was in charge of the Japanese Legation in Korea, set the stage for one of the most despicable plots in modern history. He was busy preparing to oust the pro-Russian group from the Korean government by force. Queen Min and her kinsmen were behind the new policy of reliance on Russia to counter Japan, for their power had been weakened as Japan's pressure had grown stronger. Miura's plan was the same as that which had overthrown Queen Min's faction just before the Sino-Japanese War, by occupying Kyongbok palace, seizing the King, and then placing lackeys of the Japanese in the government. This time, however, the Queen and her followers were to be eliminated permanently.

At dawn on October 8, 1895, a group of Japanese soldiers and civilians reached Kyongbok palace and opened fire on the royal guards, who were no match for them. There was no escape for Queen Min this time. The Japanese ransacked the palace, and, when they found her, immediately stabbed her. She was carried, dying, into the courtyard and there, even before she was dead, her assassins poured kerosene over her body and set it aflame and buried it to hide the evidence of how she had been killed.

The commander of the Training Unit, Hong Kye-hun, was killed while struggling to protect the Queen, and the Minister of Household Affairs, Yi Kyong-jik, was cut down when the Japanese found him. The Japanese troops occupied the palace and seized King Kojong and his crown prince. Thus the nation's Queen met a cruel death at the hands of foreign assassins.

Fearing an outcry of condemnation from abroad, Japan recalled Miura to stand trial in Hiroshima, Japan, but in the end he and his cohorts were declared not guilty on grounds of insufficient evidence.

Japanese Consul Uchida Sadatsuchi, who had taken part in the slaying of Queen Min, in a lengthy, secret report to his government, dated November 9, 1895, said: "The Queen was slain by a Japanese army officer first, and then by Nakamura *[sic]*. At that time Nakamura's right hand was wounded by the officer's sword." [1]

Within a few days the king was coerced into appointing pro-Japanese individuals to key posts in the government and issuing a decree that demoted the (late) Queen to commoner status. At the time no mention of her passing was made. The king became a prisoner in his own palace and lived in daily fear of his life.

In February 1896 Korean leaders loyal to the king succeeded in smuggling the king and the crown prince out of the palace; the Korean sovereign sought and received asylum at the Russian legation in the capital of his own kingdom. Immediately reaching the safety of the Russianl legation, the king decreed death sentences for several leaders of the pro-Japanese regime, particularly those who controlled the army and the police. Overnight, the political tables were turned; Japan lost its tenuous hold on the Korean government while the Russian legation suddenly became host to the royal family and the government of Korea.

Fearing the sudden surge of Russian influence, Japan proposed later that year to divide the sphere of influence of the two countries at the 38th Parallel roughly at the midriff. But Russia rejected the Japanese proposal.

In 1897, the nationalistic reformists and the conservatives decided to elevate the royal title from that of a king *(Wang)* to emperor *(Whangje)*. The name of the country was also changed, in

October, from Chosun to Taehan (Great Han); the new official name of the nation thus became Taehan Cheguk (the Empire of Great Han). For a decade, (1894–1904), Korea enjoyed a period of fitful independence as the Korean Empire, Taehan Cheguk, while Japan and Russia jockeyed for superior positions in Korea, preparing for the next war.

Russo-Japanese War

The Hermit Kingdom, as Korea was then called, was opened by American Commodore Robert W. Schufeldt and was assured of fair treatment by the Treaty of Amity and Commerce, known as the Chemulpo Treaty of 1882. By this action the United States placed itself in the middle of a rivalry that was soon to dominate northeast Asia — the struggle for power between Japan and Russia with Korea as the focal point.

By 1893 Korea had concluded treaties with the United States, Great Britain, Italy, Russia, Germany, France, and Austria. Diplomatically speaking, Korea had now emerged from her seclusion. However, the nation's leaders, artless in the business of diplomacy and modern power politics, squirmed and floundered in the net that was inexorably closing around them.

U.S. President Theodore Roosevelt gave his support to Japan, and the Japanese launched a surprise attack against Russia in 1904. Roosevelt then sent his Secretary of War, William Howard Taft, to Tokyo to conclude a secret agreement with Japanese Prime Minister Katsura Taro, offering American concurrence in the seizure of Korea in return for a Japanese promise not to harbor aggressive designs against the Philippines. Not only was the treaty of 1882 forgotten, but Roosevelt in effect told the Korean King that the matter was "none of his business" when he sought to send an emissary [Syngman Rhee] to the September 1905 Portsmouth treaty session that formalized the Japanese acquisition of a Protectorate over Korea. [2]

The British government also recognized Japan's "right to guide, to control and protect" its special interests in Korea in exchange for Japanese support for British interests in India. The two Western nations did not realize they had unleashed a dragon they would soon be unable to control; nor that their duplicity would be long remembered by Koreans.

Japan and Russia tried without success to settle matters pertaining to their conflicting interests in Manchuria and Korea, and Japan declared war against Russia on February 5, 1904. The Russian Far Eastern and Baltic fleets were destroyed by the Japanese fleet commanded by Admiral Togo Heihachiro; the Russian Army was beaten and driven into northern Manchuria; and Port Arthur, an important naval base, fell to Japan.

The Japanese Third Army commanded by General Nogi Maresuke and the Russian troops by General Mikhailovich Stessel fought a decisive battle at Russian-held Hill 203 at Port Arthur in 1905, which resulted in Japanese victory.

In the summer of 1937, when attending Yongsaeng High School in Hamhung, North Korea, I traveled to Port Arthur on a school excursion. At that time, we visited "Suishiei" where Nogi accepted Stessel's surrender, and then went up the historic Hill 203 to see the Russian fortress on its peak. The "impregnable" stronghold fell to the Japanese Army at the cost of innumerable soldiers. The fortress was girded by a huge open trench — about 20 feet wide and 30 feet deep — with a forest of lance-shaped iron bars planted on the concrete bottom.

A guide told us: "Russian soldiers holding this stronghold mowed down Japanese troops climbing up the hill with machine-gun fire. The Japanese had no machine-guns. When surviving Japanese soldiers reached the trench they fell into it and died. The remainder stepped over the corpses that had filled up the trench, and finally seized the fortress."

Japan defeated Russia with the moral and material aid of the United States and Britain, who had watched the Russian advance to the Pacific with unconcealed dread. Japan, cherishing far greater ambitions than the declining Czarist Empire ever had, now became the dominant power in northeast Asia.

Without sensing that Japan, in time, would upset the existing world order, the United States and Britain welcomed Japan's hegemony. At the Treaty of Portsmouth, signed in New Hampshire in September 1905 under the good offices of U.S. President

In 1937 Korean high school students (the author: second from right in front) visit the ruins of Russia's last fortress on historic Hill 203 at Port Arthur which fell to the Japanese army in 1905.

Theodore Roosevelt, the Russian interest in Manchuria was thoroughly checked. Besides the lease of Kwangtung Province, transfer of the Manchurian Railway and cession of South Sakhalin, Japan secured its long-sought foothold for Manchurian advance by winning the recognition of its political, military and economic supremacy in Korea.

Illegal Protectorate Treaty

The most important provisions of the Treaty of Portsmouth were Russia's acknowledgment that Japan possessed paramount political, military, and economic interests in Korea, and Russia's pledge not to hinder Japan from taking whatever actions it deemed necessary for the "guidance, protection, and control" of the Korean government.

Having won recognition from Russia, Britain, and America of its paramount interests in the peninsula, Japan moved immediately to establish a protectorate over Korea.

Marquis Ito Hirobumi was assigned to negotiate a protectorate treaty with the Great Han Empire (Korea). He arrived in Seoul on November 9, 1905, with a letter from Japanese Emperor Meiji advising Korean sovereign Emperor Kojong to come to an agreement with Ito, "as it is essential for maintenance of peace in the Far East."

General Hasegawa Yoshimichi, commander of the Japanese army in Korea, had been ordered to follow Ito's instructions. The Korean Emperor, pleading illness, declined to receive Ito in formal audience. When the delayed audience was finally granted on November 15, Ito presented a draft treaty of protection and demanded immediate acceptance by the Korean government. The Emperor wanted no part of Japan and thereafter the Emperor refused to grant another audience to the Japanese envoy. Ito then decided to persuade the members of the Korean cabinet. He told the cabinet ministers, "Your Emperor has commanded you to settle this matter with me now," and urged Prime Minister Han Kyu-sol to obey. But Han flatly refused.

One of the officials of the Japanese Legation accompanying Ito pressed a revolver barrel to Han's side. "Obey, or I shall kill you!" Han did not reply. He was dragged from the chamber by the Japanese soldiers. Ito shrieked at them: "Han (Korea) is dead. The Chinese are gone; the Russians are defeated. America is too far away to help, in spite of your Treaty of 1882. You are all alone. Agree with us and be rich — oppose us, and die!"

General Hasegawa came in. Beating on the table with his sword, he threatened to turn his soldiers loose upon the city, unless the cabinet signed a treaty of protection with Japan. No one was allowed to leave; soldiers with bayoneted rifles guarded every exit.

Japanese troops under Hasegawa's command were staging an impressive display of military might on the main street leading to Doksu Palace where the dramatic event was taking place. An American eyewitness reported, "Half of a regiment of artillery, three batteries with eighteen guns, were maneuvering, dashing to and fro, unlimbering their pieces....The street was full of excited people with an unusually large number of Japanese police and gendarmes about." [3]

Long past midnight November 17, tears streaming down his face, Foreign Minister Park Che-sun told the keeper of the seal to deliver the government's official signature. Because he refused to hand it over, the seal was seized by Japanese officials to be used to approve the "Japan-Korea Protectorate Treaty."

Ito, who thus served as the principal instrument of the Japanese aggression against Korea, became the resident general of Korea in March 1906. But he was assassinated by a young Korean patriot, Ahn Chung-kun, at Harbin, Manchuria, on October 26, 1909. Ahn was arrested by the Japanese police and executed in 1910.

A German diplomat's report, testifying to the invalidity of the Treaty of 1905 that Japan forced upon Korea to "protect" it, was discovered in May 1992 in an archive of the Austro-Hungarian Empire in Budapest by a Hungarian historian.

Karoly Fendler, the Hungarian scholar who brought the diplomatic report to light, said that the 15-page political report on the Korean situation was written by Emil von Saldern, who served as the charge d'affaires of the German Embassy in Seoul at the time of the signing of the treaty.

Von Saldern wrote the report to then Chancellor Furst von Bulow on November 20, 1905, only three days after the illegal treaty was concluded. Von Saldern pointed out that Emperor Kojong had never signed the Treaty of 1905.

The German diplomat unequivocally stated in his hand-written report: "The treaty was signed by Japanese Minister Hayashi [Gonsuke] and Korean Foreign Minister Park Che-sun....The Korean Foreign Minister, Park Che-sun, did not sign it in person, but his official seal had been seized by force and put on the treaty by officials of the Japanese Legation in Seoul....The treaty, which will serve Japan's aggression into Korea, is proof of the Japanese use of outright force." [4]

Von Saldern's report confirmed the assertions put forward in April 1992 by Professors Lee Tae-jin and Shin Yong-ha, both of Seoul National University, that the so-called "Protectorate Treaty" of 1905 and the subsequent Annexation Treaty of 1910 were "null and void," as they both lacked the seals of the Korean Emperor.

The illegally signed 1905 treaty first of all authorized the transfer of the administration of foreign affairs to Japan. Also a Japanese resident general was put in a position directly under the Korean Emperor. In sum, Japan had completely divested Korea of its sovereign power to maintain relations with foreign governments.

Annexation by Japan

In August 1910, Japan annexed Korea with the conclusion of the Japan-Korea Annexation Treaty, which provided the complete transfer of Korean sovereignty to Japan. Soon after this annexation Japan changed the name of Korea from Taehan to Chosun.

The Korean people had harbored strong antagonism toward the Japanese because of the savage wars of aggression waged by Toyotomi Hideyoshi for seven years from 1592 to 1598. Now that Japan's aggressive ploy was again brought to light, the masses of Korea arose to fight against the Japanese by launching nationwide struggles. But such movements were mercilessly crushed by the well-equipped Japanese army and police forces.

Japan's new resident general in Korea, General Terauchi Masatake, and pro-Japanese Korean Prime Minister Yi Wan-yong signed the Japan-Korea Annexation Treaty on August 22, 1910. And on August 29, Emperor Sunjong, heir to Kojong who had been forced to abdicate by the Japanese in 1907, was compelled to issue a proclamation yielding up both his throne and his country. Thus Korea, against the will of its people, was handed over to the harsh colonial rule of Japan.

Soon after the annexation, individual liberties of Koreans were systematically eradicated. Meetings could not be held without permission. Freedom of speech was abolished. Even personal names were ordered to be changed from Korean to Japanese. Koreans were urged to worship at Japanese *shinto* shrines and pledge to be faithful "imperial citizens." Japanese control was based on force, exercised by police power, particularly by military police. When trying to quiet crying babies, Korean mothers often whispered to the kids, "Be quiet! Japanese police are coming." Even little children were scared of sword-carrying Japanese policemen.

Frederick McKenzie, a correspondent for the *Daily Mail* of London dispatched to Korea in 1904, detailed in the book *Korea's Fight for Freedom* the terror of an unbridled police state that beat, tortured and killed Koreans at will, with techniques almost unimaginable in their cruelty. The Japanese took the best Korean lands, stole national treasures and controlled their lives down to the color of clothing they could wear and the ways they could spend their own money, he wrote. [5]

Korea's protest against the ruthless Japanese rule reached a climax with "passive revolution" on March 1, 1919, when 33 Korean leaders voluntarily subjected themselves to arrest by signing a declaration of independence, which was then read to the crowds at Pagoda Park in downtown Seoul. Demonstrations spread from Seoul to the countryside, marching crowds waving long-concealed Korean flags and chanting: *"Mansei!"* (May Korea live ten thousand years!)

The Japanese reaction to the Mansei uprising was swift and cruel. According to *Encyclopedia of Korean History* compiled by Dr. Lee Hong-jik, a total of 2,023,089 Koreans (15 percent of the Korean population) participated in the uprising, of whom 7,509 were killed, 15,961 wounded, and 46,948 imprisoned.

In the wake of the uprising, a group of independence leaders formed a Korean Provisional Government in Shanghai with Dr. Syngman Rhee as its president. The Provisional Government continued the anti-Japanese, independence movement abroad until Korea was liberated as a result of Japanese defeat in World War II.

After 36 years of enslavement under Japanese suppression, Korean patriots finally received encouragement from the outside world. In November 1943, American President Franklin Roosevelt, British Prime Minister Winston Churchill, and Generalissimo Chiang Kai-shek of China stated in their Cairo Declaration that "the three great powers, mindful of the enslavement of the people of Korea, are determined that in due course Korea shall become free and independent."

The Cairo Declaration, containing provisions requiring Japan's unconditional surrender and its territorial determination, was reconfirmed in the Potsdam Declaration of July 26, 1945. Soviet Prime Minister Joseph Stalin gave the Declaration his blessing at Teheran. Under the Potsdam Declaration, the United States, Britain, and China called on Japan to surrender, demanding the removal of leading forces of imperialism, punishment of war criminals, military occupation by allied forces, territorial limitation, disarmament, and thorough democratization.

Roosevelt, Churchill, and Stalin conferred at Yalta in February 1945, making the contents of their secret agreement public one year later in February 1946. The Agreement provided that the Soviet Union enter the war against Japan two or three months after the surrender of Germany under the conditions that Southern Sakhalin and the Kurile Islands be transferred to the U.S.S.R. and Chinese complete sovereignty in Manchuria be secured.

Based on this Agreement, the Soviets opened war against Japan on August 8, 1945, advancing into Manchuria and occupying the northern half of the Korean peninsula in lightning fashion. Thus Soviet expansion in the Far East was secured, causing instability in northeast Asia — a factor in the tragedy of the Korean peninsula.

PERSONAL STRUGGLES FOR FREEDOM

Dodging Japanese Army Draft

My own experiences living in Korea, Japan, and the United States during the years between World War II and the start of the Korean War reflect the life and mood of those nations in those days.

During World War II, the Japanese government mobilized more than one million Koreans for forced labor at the front and in munitions factories and mines. Japan also inducted a total of 4,385 Korean students from universities and colleges into the Japanese Imperial Army under the Student Volunteers Law promulgated on October 20, 1943. The volunteers system was changed to a conscription system in 1944 and about 200,000 Koreans were drafted. Japan also forced an estimated 20,000 women from Korea, the Philippines, Indonesia, China and the Netherlands into sexual servitude for Japanese.

In an attempt to dodge the military service, many Korean students purposely harmed themselves, for instance, by drinking large amounts of soy sauce that caused heart ailments, and many of those already inducted attempted to decamp only to be caught and court-martialed.

By registered mail, I, too, received an order to take a physical test. I was then about to graduate from Chuo University in Tokyo. As a Korean, I found no justifiable cause to join the Japanese Army for its war of aggression. So, I was determined to refuse the order by all means and hid myself in Itabashi ward. But later I received another registered letter. It was from my father in Korea. I opened the envelope with surprise and fear, for I had not let even my father know about my whereabouts.

"Please volunteer for *gakutoshiganhei* (student volunteer soldier)," my father wrote. "Should you fail to do so, a red line would be drawn by the Japanese authorities in our family register and we will be treated as traitors even to our remotest descendants," he added. It was obvious that the letter was written under Japanese police coercion.

I could not but obey my father. I went to the designated sixth floor of Chuo University in Surugadai, Tokyo. The large hall was full of volunteers. My number was Extra 19.

I was thinking of a lie tactic to escape the crisis by failing in the physical test. I had detected that pass or fail seemed to be decided at booth No. 4 where army physician Lieutenant Colonel Kawashima was making the final judgement.

A few minutes before my number was to be called, I sneaked out of the room through the back door as if I was going to a toilet. I ran up and down the idle stairs desperately. My heart was beating so fast that I felt almost fainting as I returned to the room.

In a minute my number Extra 19 was paged. After checking height, weight, and eyes, I proceeded to physician Kawashima's booth No.4. "Sink or swim. There'll be none the worse even if detected!" I told myself and decided to tell lies.

"Any previous disease?" The army doctor asked, examining my body with a stethoscope.

"Heart trouble, sir." (My heartbeats were still very fast.)

"How bad was it?" The doctor asked inclining his head.

"I had severe headaches everyday, could not sleep well, and could not see things well because of dizziness. I was short of breath whenever I walked fast or went up a slope."

In fact, this was only a partial lie; an exaggeration of a real story I had experienced when I was a freshman of Chuo University. Seized by serious headaches and dizziness I could not sleep nor walk by myself. So, my friends took me to Tokyo University Hospital. "You have a serious heart trouble. You had better enter the hospital at once," the doctor told me. But I could not even think of doing so because I, as a self-supporting student, could not afford to pay the hospital expenses. I could not but be resigned to die. However, I got well miraculously while staying at a four-and-a-half *tatami* (8 sq. ft.) room rented by my bosom friend Lee Chong-pil. As I repeated simple but sincere prayer, "God help me!...," a huge pillarlike image seemed to have appeared before my eyes making me feel relieved, and I gradually recovered my health. I recalled this experience while being questioned by Kawashima.

Examining with the stethoscope very carefully, the army doctor asked: "Any other previous illness?"

"Piles, sir"

"What kind?"

"Internal fistula, sir."

"What kind of treatment did you get? And where?"

"I was treated with salves and suppositories at Joto Hospital at Maki-cho, Ni-chome, Kyobashi-ku, Tokyo. I was told to have soft feces, to keep the body warm in the bath, and to rest as much I could."

I could reply like this without a hitch because I had learned a lot about piles while, as a student, I was working part time at the Joto Hospital, which was famous for treating anal diseases. The hospital was run by Doctor Sakai Ichiro, a graduate of a Tokyo high school I was attending. How could I think of using piles for my lying tactics? About one hour before the physical checkup began on the sixth floor, I went down to the basement for an X-ray examination, and overheard the doctors, saying, "Guys suffering from piles are absolutely no use for military service because they cannot march at all."

I knew that there were different types of piles such as internal and external fistulas, internal and external hemorrhoids, split hemorrhoids, and hemorrhoidal protrusion. In the case of internal fistulas, doctors cannot detect the disease unless they insert a finger into the anus to examine because no outside symptom is shown. I thought the army doctor, Kawashima, would not do that much, and I was glad that my guess was right. He was writing something on a prescribed report form marked with triangles, squares, and circles.

At the fifth booth the officer asked, "Do you have any technical skill?"

"I have a driving license," I emphatically answered, meanwhile thinking, "In case I am inducted, I will work as a driver for a Japanese officer and then defect to the American forces at an opportune time."

At last, I stood in front of Lieutenant General Nakamura seated on a high dais at the sixth "barrier" I had to get over, anxiously awaiting his "verdict" on the physical examination.

General Nakamura said in a solemn voice:

"Your health is very bad. A man like you shall work in the home front. Shinn is Grade C."

At this point, one had to recite the general's verdict.

"Shinn is Grade C," I repeated it with (pretendedly) rueful countenance. Those who received Grade C were ineligible for military service. I felt as if I were in a dream.

Those who had received General Nakamura's verdict went to a table attended by two soldiers to write down addresses where they were going to live during the coming one month.

"Do I have to write too?" I asked.

"Your kind of fellows cannot go to the army," a soldier said arrogantly.

I hurriedly left the university building and sent a cable to my father informing him that I had taken physical examination for a student soldier. "I volunteered for military service and took a physical examination today. Unfortunately I received the C grade, ineligible to join the army. As an imperial citizen, I am ashamed of myself."

The purpose of sending such a cable was to leave evidence to the local police at home that I was "faithful to the Japanese Empire."

Escape from Japan

Determined to escape from Japan as soon as possible, I burned my books and other belongings and hurried to Shimonoseki by train. The ferry line between Shimonoseki and Pusan was jammed with Japanese soldiers bound for China. Fearing that I might be interrogated by the Japanese police if I returned by that route, I used a different ferry going to Yosu, a small port west of Pusan.

In those days, my family was living in the lonely village of Chinhung-ni, Hajichon-myon, Hamju-kun, Hamkyongnam-do, in the northeastern region of North Korea. The hamlet was at the foot of Whangchoryong Mountain (3,960 ft) on the southern border of Changjin-kun on the Kaema Plateau.

Upon arrival home, I was greeted by Suzuki Yoshio, the local Japanese police chief. He heartily welcomed me as "an excellent imperial citizen who volunteered for military service." As I thought, he had known the contents of my telegram sent to my father. My scheme had worked so well! My father, who was well aware of my hidden intentions, was of course very much gratified.

But still it was too early to have peace of mind. For those young Koreans who had not gone to the army were being mobilized for forced labor at the front, various military facilities, and mines.

I had to take the initiative in order to surmount this extra hurdle. Because people called for forced labor also had to take physical checkups, there was the danger that my previous lie might be detected should I wait until the mobilization order came.

Upon learning that near my village there was a mine that supplied zinc to the Japanese military, I wanted to be employed by the mining company so I could be drafted on the spot without being mobilized again and sent to a far-off place. The mine's parent firm, called Kobayashi Mining Company, was in Seoul (then called Keijo).

In order to be hired by the Japanese company, I thought it expedient to get a letter of recommendation from the local police chief, Suzuki. I was placed on the regular payroll when I visited the head company in Seoul with Suzuki's letter and was assigned to work at the Hungjin Mine on top of Mt. Whangchoryong. Those working at this mine became automatically "drafted laborers" without being taken away to other places.

Hungjin was a secluded place with an average temperature of −20° F in winter. So, regular staff members received a special "remote place allowance," and lived in houses with provisions against cold, drawing special rationing of sake (Japanese wine) every month. I, as a regular staff member, received all these privileges, and was assigned as an accountant because I was good at the abacus and bookkeeping.

While working at a mine on a freezing mountaintop for the first time in my life, I became very much sympathetic with the poor miners whose living conditions were so miserable. Their living quarters and dormitories were dilapidated, many froze to death in winter, while staff members lived a comfortable life in houses with double walls to protect against the cold.

I wanted to help the miserable miners by improving their living quarters. About one hundred miners were living in the ramshackle dormitory, and many of them fell to their death in long vertical pits because of fatigue and malnutrition.

With the approval of the chief of the mine firm, Saito Torata, I renovated the old miners' dormitory by having thicker walls and double windows installed, and adding reading and recreation rooms. I also volunteered to live with the miners in their dormitory, and acted as a consultant to help those miners who indulged in gambling.

On August 15, 1945, I danced, overwhelmed with joy to hear the good news of Japan's surrender to the Allied Powers broadcast by Emperor Hirohito. Now that Korea was liberated at last, I hurried to my parents' new home near the city of Hamhung, 32 miles south of the mountain, where I had attended a Presbyterian mission school. But my new hope for a liberated motherland soon faded away as I witnessed horrifying scenes of Communist brutality. I was shocked to see Soviet soldiers looting Korean private homes, Korean Communists mercilessly persecuting people they branded as propertied or intellectuals, and especially the abominable scene of forcing a group of Japanese women into a warehouse for outrageous acts.

Desperate Flight from Communist North

I came to realize that Communism was not the guardian of the proletariat as Marxists professed. Although I was one of the poorest Koreans, I could not envision any hope for my future in such a Communist society. I decided to flee south of the 38th Parallel despite my parents' pleas not to take such a risk. As I insisted on fleeing to seek freedom in the south, even at the risk of my life, my father, mother, brothers and sisters cried. I cried, too.

I bid farewell to them on August 30, 1945, and continued my lone flight, plodding along desolate mountain trails, in constant fear of being shot by the Communists; they were shooting anyone found going southward. When I barely managed to arrive in Seoul on September 6, I heaved a deep sigh of relief, thanking God. Two younger brothers and my youngest sister joined me in Seoul later, but for the next fifty years I had no way of knowing the fate of my parents and three sisters in Communist North Korea.

On September 8, 1945, 72,000 troops of the U.S. XXIV Corps, under Lieutenant General John R. Hodge, arrived in Inchon, and dispersed by truck and train around the country, to take up positions from Pusan to the 38th Parallel. From the moment the Americans boarded the train for Seoul, they were greeted with uninhibited rejoicing. A crowd of Koreans stood by the tracks in every village they passed, gleefully waving flags.

In Seoul, they were greeted by vast throngs of cheering Koreans, cramming the streets and sidewalks. I was one of the most exultant welcomers, especially because I had fled to Seoul from the Soviet-occupied North Korea only three days before.

On the morning of September 9, I was watching the events taking place in front of the Bando Hotel, which was being prepared for General Hodge's headquarters. An American army captain, who was with a Korean interpreter in his jeep, shouted, "Is there anyone who can speak English better than this guy?" As a man who had risked own life to cross the 38th Parallel, seeking freedom in the South, I was more than happy to help the American officer.

"Can I help you?" I said to him in English.

"Where is the Chosun Hotel?"

"I'm also a stranger here. But I can ask people around here for you," I replied.

He seemed pleased with my English. He let the interpreter off the jeep and let me in. A Korean onlooker told me to go around the left corner. There was the Chosun Hotel, a Renaissance-style red brick building. Helmeted American military police were standing guard along both sides of the path from the gate to the entrance.

In the afternoon, General Hodge and officers ranking above lieutenant colonels were billeted at the Chosun. I was shown to the kitchen in the hotel basement, where I was asked to interpret for the GIs and the Japanese cooks. "You're an excellent interpreter!" a chubby American mess sergeant praised me, and asked me to stay with him in the basement, preparing a cot for me.

General Hodge, who had led the American invasion of Okinawa during the Pacific War, was a brave battle commander, but he lacked a sense of diplomacy. On the first day of occupation, he made a blunder by assenting to a request from the Japanese army commander to keep Japanese police armed so as to protect his troops and 600,000 Japanese civilians in Korea from reprisals. But the Koreans bitterly protested, and General George Marshall, army chief of staff, ordered Hodge to disband the Japanese police.

The pressure on the Japanese to leave Korea became irresistible. In four months, 70,000 Japanese colonial officials and more than 600,000 Japanese soldiers and civilians were evacuated to their homeland. Many were compelled to abandon their properties and possessions.

At the Chosun Hotel, however, the entire Japanese staff, including General Manager Horiuchi Shizuo, stayed on because there were no Korean replacements; the Japanese had not allowed Koreans to rise higher than assistant waiter. The Japanese therefore were expecting that all Japanese staff would be flown to Japan by an American military plane after their faithful service to General Hodge and the officers staying there.

Chosun Hotel Episode

As time passed, however, trouble cropped up between Japanese and Korean employees at the Chosun Hotel. Deeply worried about the situation, General Hodge's aides asked me to take charge of the hotel management. But I refused the offer because I was already organizing a civil aid organization, the Korean Social Service Society, together with my former Korean schoolmates of Chuo University, for the purpose of helping refugees from Communist North Korea. We were even dreaming of elevating the Society to Korea's first Red Cross in the future.

Nevertheless, the American officers insisted I was needed at the Chosun. So I told them I preferred to become an assistant manager under an elderly general manager because I was only 26 years old. They agreed and I assumed the assistant manager's post entrusted with the entire management, including personnel affairs.

I convened a staff meeting in the Banquet Hall, and told Manager Horiuchi and other Japanese staff in Japanese: "Your roles here are over now. It's only an illusion to think that this hotel cannot run without you Japanese. Japanese people are proud of having so-called *yamato damashii* (characteristic Japanese spirit), comparing it to cherry blossoms which bloom and fall together. All Japanese are now hurrying back to Japan, many abandoning their properties and possessions. I hereby order you Japanese to leave this hotel within a week without fail." Japanese female employees were sobbing.

Then I told Korean employees in Korean: "From now on you are the masters of this hotel. I want you to let the Japanese leave here in peace with all their belongings, and to carry out your new duties with full responsibility."

Horiuchi and other Japanese staff left the hotel within a week with all their belongings. I quickly established a new management system with the cooperation of the Railway Bureau, a government supervisory body. Mr. Min Won-shik, then president of *Seoul Times* (predecessor of the present *Korea Times)*, was appointed as new general manager.

One of Seoul's first giant edifices, the Renaissance-style, red brick Chosun Hotel had witnessed history being made, intrigues played out, the country divided, a new nation born, and then the savage Korean War fought.

Designed by a German architect named Geothelande, the hotel opened in 1914. Situated on the top of King Kojong's former Altar to Heaven about 200 yards from his residence in Doksu Palace, Chosun provided a view looking over Seoul to the North Mountain (Pukaksan) or the South Mountain (Namsan).

On October 12, 1897, King Kojong stood at the Altar of Heaven and stated that he was henceforth to be called emperor rather than merely king. In the hotel's backyard there still stands the eight-sided Temple of Heaven where Emperor Kojong prayed for independence and security of his nation. (The monumental main building of the Chosun was pulled down in October 1967 and a new high-rise hotel, Westin Chosun, was erected on the same site in a first-time Korea-U.S. joint venture.)

General Hodge was billeted at the old Chosun's best quarters — the former Imperial Suite (Room 201). A few days before Dr. Syngman Rhee, who had worked for the cause of Korean independence in the United States since 1910, returned home on October 16, 1945, Hodge decided to give the luxurious Imperial Suite to Rhee and moved over to the Bando Hotel where he had his office. Far East Commander Douglas MacArthur had instructed Hodge that

Chosun Hotel's front gate, with U.S. military guards, viewed from Sogong-ro.

Chosun Hotel employees gathered at its octagonal pagoda to bid farewell to the author (fourth from right in front) before his departure for the United States for advanced study in 1947.

Rhee should be treated most cordially because he (Rhee) was considered the best candidate for president of a future government of Korea.

On the morning of October 20, General Hodge had taken Rhee in a closed sedan to the former Japanese government building for a "Liberation Ceremony." General Hodge presided. To the sound of a brass band and rolling of drums, the huge, ebony-lacquered, folding screen of many panels, with the traditional-type mother-of-pearl inlay of phoenixes, was rolled back with a flourish, and there stood the septuagenarian, white-haired Syngman Rhee. The flags of the United States and the Republic of Korea waved overhead. This was a pleasant autumn day; the large Seoul crowds were cheering.

Some 100,000 people lined up Sejong-ro as Rhee and Hodge proceeded down the avenue in a motorcade. They rode together toward the historic South Gate (Namdaemun) and then veered off to the Chosun Hotel.

Unexpected Help from Rev. Kim and Gen. Hodge

In the summer of 1947, Reverend Kim Kwan-shik, who was principal of Yongsaeing High School in Hamhung, North Korea — a Christian mission school that I had attended as a very young boy — visited me at the Chosun Hotel. I was surprised by Reverend Kim's unexpected appearance, for I had not seen him since I left Yungsaeng ten years earlier. Reverend Kim was the first Korean national to receive a Doctor of Divinity degree from Princeton University.

"Don't you want to go to America for advanced studies?" Reverend Kim asked.

"I cannot even think of it, sir," I said.

"I am going to America soon as a representative of Korean religious institutes. I might be able to get an admission permit from an American college for you."

Reminiscing about the days when I was attending his school, Reverend Kim said: "I am sure that you can earn a scholarship at an American college each year as you did at Yungsaeng. So, please prepare application papers for admission to an American college."

I prepared the necessary papers and handed them to Reverend Kim. Later he sent me an admission certificate issued by Hastings College, Hastings, Nebraska. He wrote me: "There was only one scholarship available, which I decided to give to Ms. Lim Ok-In who was a teacher at Yongsaeng Girls' High School [she later became a noted author]. So, I am sending you the admission certificate only because I am confident that you would be able to earn your scholarship by your own merit."

I took the English test required by the American Embassy to determine eligibility for college studies in America, and passed with an A grade. Imbued with high spirits, I went to meet a Captain Akin at the Education Department of the U.S. Military Government to be briefed on procedures for entry to the United States.

"Have you got a scholarship?" Akin asked bluntly.

"No, I don't."

"Have you prepared five hundred dollars in greenbacks?"

"Not yet, Captain."

"Your kind of a fellow can't go to the States," the captain said arrogantly.

I was so furious at the haughty attitude of the captain that I lashed out: "The way you talk is too rude. As an educational administrator, you could have spoken in a more gentle manner. Because people like you are working at the American military government, favoring only rich people, you fail to get cooperation from capable and conscientious Koreans. Though I was hoping to learn American democracy, if most of the Americans are like you, I should never go to such a country." Indignantly I rose and left the room, slamming the door.

Upon return to the Chosun Hotel, I came across Lieutenant Colonel Saville, an advisor to the management. Noticing my angry look, he said, "You seem to be in a very bad mood. Anything happened to you?"

Explaining what had happened with Captain Akin, I poured out harsh criticism against the military government composed of his sorts. Colonel Saville was listening quietly and consoled me: "Calm down, Bill. Akin was certainly wrong."

Meanwhile, something totally unexpected happened two days later. Colonel Saville came to my office and urged me to go to the office of General Hodge's aide-de-camp. "Why?" I asked. "You will find out pretty soon. Please go there right away," the colonel insisted.

To my surprise, there was a big gift prepared for me at the aide's office. "Here is a gift for you, Mr. Shinn. Six-hundred-fifteen dollars have been raised by General Hodge's staff officers for you at the General's special order. It's for your travel expense to the States," said the aide. I was thrilled to receive such an unexpected gift. The amount was $115 more than the $500 Captain Akin at the Education Department had demanded.

When I told the story to Colonel Saville at the Chosun, he quietly said, "General Hodge believed that you are the best qualified Korean young man to study in America. So, he ordered his staff officers to raise the money for you."

A travel order was issued from General Hodge's Headquarters after the judge advocate, Colonel King, had signed an affidavit of support. I sailed from Inchon on a U.S. Navy vessel for Seattle, Washington, on August 2, leaving my wife, Sally, and two-month-old son, John, under the care of my parents-in-law. While sailing across the Pacific Ocean, I wished I could report to my parents, who were left behind the iron curtain of North Korea, that I was able to go to America for advanced study.

As I had completed the four-year course of Chuo University in Japan, I was admitted to the senior class of Hastings College. Among the Korean students at the college were Yoo Chang-soon (later, Korean prime minister), and Hyun Woong (Peter Hyun; later, an author).

Four months after my arrival at Hastings I helped Reverend Kim Kwan-shik's son, Kim Yoo-chol, come to Hastings College with the admission permit and the $500 that I had sent for him. (The money was a collection of stipends I had earned for my speeches at PTAs and churches in Nebraska.)

I was so grateful to his father, Reverend Kim Kwan-shik, that I wanted to return his kindness by inviting his son to Hastings College. But after only one semester's study at Hastings, young Kim returned home, complaining that English was too difficult for him.

The Graduate School at the University of Nebraska granted me its regent's fellowship, a scholarship awarded to select students whose scholastic records placed them within the upper ten percent of the graduating class at colleges in the States. While studying international law at the graduate school, I worked at the Cornhusker Hotel in Lincoln as a part-timer.

Trans-U.S. Tour

In December 1949, I set out across the country driving my $196 1929 Model-A Ford from Lincoln, Nebraska. First I went to Washington D.C. via Des Moines, Iowa; Chicago, Illinois; Michigan City, Indiana; Cleveland, Ohio; Pittsburgh, Pennsylvania; and New York.

The purpose of my visit to Washington was to ring an alarm bell for the U.S. government about its racial discrimination against the colored people (African-Americans) and Asians. I called on Mr. Ralph Busik who was then in charge of Asian affairs at the State Department.

"While studying in America, I found the American people in general are very kind and nice. So I do not wish to say good-bye to American citizens. But I came here to say good-bye to the U.S. government," I told him.

"What do you mean?"

"My African-American friends at Hastings College told me that in southern states the black people are treated like animals. The buses, for instance, have seats for white people separated from those for the colored people and that the white driver would shoot any black passenger who sits in a vacant seat reserved for the whites if he fails to obey the driver's order to leave it.

"Not only that. Your government is pursuing a discriminatory immigration policy against the Asian people in favor of the Europeans. I think that your government's racial discrimination against the colored people violates the spirit of the U.S. constitution which proclaims equal rights for all people. The racial prejudice against the Asians spurred anti-U.S. sentiment among Oriental people, thus allowing the Communist takeover of China mainland by Mao Tse-tung forces. I have therefore lost confidence in your government. That's why I want to say good-bye to your country and go home."

After listening to my lecture, Mr. Busik quietly asked, "Where are you heading from here?"

"I will go to the House of Representatives to see Representative Dodd, who I understand is actively supporting the causes of the Asian people. I want to appeal for his help in raising immigration quotas for Asians."

Busik, facing his typewriter, said, "If you wish, you can work at Voice of America, I will write a letter of recommendation for you."

Since I was determined to return home, I had no intention of working for an American government organ. But I accepted Busik's letter written with good will.

I met Rep. Dodd at his office and explained what I had told Mr. Busik at the State Department. Rep. Dodd, who was once a missionary in China and then actively engaged in promoting the interests of the Asians, told me, "I wish you had come one hour earlier! I have introduced a new bill proposing to raise immigration quotas for the Asian people this morning. You could have testified to the need of its enactment." He promised that he would continue his efforts for the Asian people.

I visited Voice of America in New York and delivered Mr. Busik's letter to the chief of the radio station. I was told to take a voice test to see if my voice was suitable for shortwave broadcast. I passed the voice test as well as English and Japanese language tests with ease.

But I refused to work there because I was scheduled to return home. The staff at Voice of America said, "Many Koreans want to come to America and once admitted here they never want to go home. Why do you want to go back to your poor country despite the offer of a job here?"

I replied: "Suppose your house caught fire. If you as a young member of the family escape for your own safety while elder members and neighbors extinguish the fire, do you think you deserve to be a key member of the household afterward? The more my country is in trouble, the more I would want to return home to help."

"If you still insist on going home, you had better work at the USIS (U.S. Information Service) in Seoul," said the chief. He handed me a letter addressed to Mr. James Stewart, director of the United States Information Service in Seoul.

The major cities covered on the second leg of my solo journey, starting from New York and going west, were as follows:

Philadelphia, Pennsylvania; Columbus, Ohio; Indianapolis, Indiana; St. Louis, Missouri; Kansas City, Kansas; Denver, Colorado; Rock Springs, Wyoming; Ogden, Utah; Boise, Idaho; and Pendleton, Oregon. I spent one night at Sunrise Point on the hillside of Mt. Rainier, which looked like Mt. Fuji of Japan, before going into Seattle, Washington. I marveled at the gorgeous sunrise spectacle. It was indeed worthwhile to have spent the cold night in an old car.

I was filled with joy when I arrived in Seattle safely after the long motor trip driving a 20-year-old jalopy. Many people were struck with admiration when they saw the stickers on my car from the many places the car had taken me.

While staying at the Benjamin Franklin Hotel in Seattle, a Korean naval officer delivered to me a letter from Mr. Yoon Ho-keun, whom I had hired at the Chosun Hotel. He was my junior at Yungsaeng mission school in Hamhung, North Korea.

Yoon pleaded in the letter, "I am suffering from serious tuberculosis. The doctor says it cannot be cured unless a newly developed medicine in America called streptomycin is used. Please get that medicine for me if you wish to save my life."

The new medicine had been sold out at Seattle drug stores because it was in such a big demand. Druggists advised me to visit the company producing the medicine south of Seattle. I went there and bought it using all the money I had on hand, 196 dollars.

Because I was scheduled to return home by a ship sailing from San Francisco for Pusan, I drove my old car over the Cascade Range, a range of mountains in Oregon and California with the highest peak of Mountain Rainier (14,410 ft). I still believe it was God's Providence that I survived while driving the jalopy, without tire chains, through snow storms on the steep mountain range during the dark night.

A Feat of Model-A Ford

Those who learned of the long distance my antique Ford traveled in its trans-U.S. adventure commented, "Even a brand new car could hardly make it." During the long, risky journey, there were occasional flat tires and minor engine troubles. But my greatest concern, brake failure, never happened. The car's sturdiness was well demonstrated when a Yellow Cab bumped into my Ford parked on a Chicago street; the cab's bumper and fender were dented but the Ford was intact.

The biggest danger I experienced was in crossing the Cascade Mountain Range en route to San Francisco. When I left Seattle, the weather was fine and warm. But as I drove up the steep range, whose weather conditions I had not studied, the temperature dropped to freezing with heavy snow continuously falling on the narrow winding mountain road that had no guard rails. I was driving up the steep mountains without tire chains. On the right side there were deep gorges. Should the engine stop, the car would slip and fall off the cliff or be buried under the snow.

Without being able to distinguish road demarcations because of the white snow cover, I kept driving in low gear, soaked in sweat despite the –20° F weather, being careful not to kill the engine, and trying to keep to the left as much I could lest the car slide off the right side cliff. It was a desperate struggle to survive. I sometimes resigned myself to die. But my faithful Ford continued working. I, too, continued to hold out, leaving everything to God.

After the overnight struggle, I suddenly felt a subtle change of the car's movement, which indicated it was now moving downward. But the snow kept falling and road conditions remained the same. At dawn, while still driving in low gear, the snow on the road turned gradually thinner. I felt a touch of hope. Finally the asphalt surface of the road began to appear. The snow had changed to rain. "Now I can live!" I shouted to myself in great relief.

The engine suddenly stopped at about 5 a.m., luckily on flat ground. Some vehicles passed, but heartless drivers paid no attention to my hand signals for help in the drizzling rain. Finally a kindly middle-aged man stopped his car to help me. His car towed my Ford to a garage several miles away. The carburetor was choked. Strangely enough, the Ford had not gone out of order in a dangerous or desolate place.

The Ford was almost blown off the Golden Gate Bridge at San Francisco due to stormy weather. On a sloping street, the cement bags in which I packed my books, and put on the fenders because there was no room inside the car, were ripped open, scattering books all over the street. The cable car trailing behind the Ford stopped, and passers-by picked up my books for me.

I was to sail from San Francisco for Pusan, Korea, on the *Lakeland Victory* of the Far East Pacific Line. To my great regret, I was afraid that I would have to abandon the Model-A Ford, that had shared fate with me all along, because I could not afford to pay the freight charge for shipping it to Pusan.

When I drove the car to the shipping company to go through the usual procedures of my voyage, I came across an unexpected stroke of good luck. The officials at the shipping firm were so moved to see the numerous stickers pasted on the car displaying the many places it had toured that they made an unprecedented offer.

"This is a really historic car," they said to each other. They held an extraordinary meeting and decided to ship the car to Pusan free of charge! The car was put on the deck by crane together with its load of books, without the usually required crating; it was therefore not listed in the cargo manifest.

Evacuation of U.S. Consul General Angus Ward

The *Lakeland Victory*, which was sailing for Tientsin, was assigned by the State Department to evacuate American Consul General Angus Ward, who was under detention by the recently established Communist regime of the People's Republic of China. The ship arrived in Yokohama one week later than scheduled because of a typhoon which was said to be the worst in history. While in Yokohama for a day, the crew was busy unloading all sorts of foodstuff to feed the hungry Japanese defeated in World War II. Meantime, I looked around the nearby city of Tokyo and was startled at the miserable plight of the postwar Japanese.

Shortly before the ship's departure from Yokohama, a host of correspondents came aboard. They were assigned to cover Ward's evacuation. Though I was scheduled to disembark in Pusan, the skipper had been ordered by the State Department to sail to Tientsin directly via the Yellow Sea. So, I had to go all the way to China. Because of the shallow shore of Tientsin, the ship anchored at Taku on the Gulf of Chihli off Tientsin.

Communist soldiers escorting Ward to the ship seized film from reporter Gene Zenier because he had taken pictures without permission. Zenier and other correspondents strongly protested and got the film back. I admired Zenier for his professional integrity and courage.

Numerous barges and tug boats were busy transporting cargos from the ship to the shore. The cargo consisted entirely of sulphur, which could be used to manufacture firearms in the Communist nation. I was amazed by the commercial spirit of the Americans who exported such materials to a hostile country, which had illegally detained their consul general.

Now that the ship was sailing back with Ward aboard, I was getting ready to land at Pusan. To my surprise, however, the captain said he had been ordered to sail to Kobe, Japan, directly for Ward's physical checkup. I angrily protested that such an arbitrary decision was "a trampling on my personal rights." American correspondents, especially Gene Zenier, sided with me, lodging a strong protest. The skipper yielded and stopped his ship at Pusan, so that I and another Korean passenger, Mr. Choi Sang-jip, 71, returning home to Cheju Island, could disembark there.

Yoon Ho-keun (Hogan), who had asked me to buy streptomycin for his tuberculosis, welcomed me, waving his handkerchief from a boat off Pusan. (Yoon was cured of his tuberculosis after using the medicine. Later, he was hired by *New York Times* correspondent William Jorden at my recommendation. Much later, Yoon became a diplomat and served as consul general in New York and ambassador to Finland.)

My favorite Ford was unloaded from the ship to the pier. I immediately tested the motor. It started as usual. I was thrilled. That was my happiest moment, which I shared with my wife, who had been anxiously waiting for my homecoming, with baby son John.

Yet I had to overcome an unexpected hurdle. The Pusan Customs Office insisted that I had to pay an import duty for the old Ford. I explained: "This twenty years old car has been shipped here free of charge by an American shipping company, honoring its historic record of a trans-American tour. The car was shipped here not as a commercial cargo but as a part of my personal effects. That is why the car has not been listed in the cargo manifest. Now is the time even iron scraps should be brought to our homeland. Yet if you insist to impose an import duty on this old car, I would rather throw it into the sea."

The customs officials checked the manifest of the Lakeland Victory, only to find that my Ford was not listed there. "Sir, it is true that your car was shipped here free of charge, but there is no precedence of exempting duty on a car brought in from abroad. Therefore, please bring us a certificate issued from the Foreign Ministry stating that this car is a part of your personal effects moved from the United States. Until that time, we will keep the car in the customs warehouse."

I reluctantly agreed, and went to Seoul by train with Sally and John. I met Foreign Minister Lim Byung-jik, whom I had known intimately since my Chosun Hotel days because he was one of the most trusted aides of Dr. Syngman Rhee, staying in Suite 201 of the Chosun. He immediately issued a certificate as the Pusan customs had wanted. I got the car out of the customs warehouse two days later and drove it to Seoul.

Soon after my arrival in Seoul, a renowned Korean painter, Kim Yong-whan, popularly known as "Kojubu," was so moved by the epic story of my Ford that he published a picture book depicting the antique vehicle running through the major cities across the United States.

While driving the car around American cities, I had put a label on the car: "Not the Newest, but the Best." And the truth of this catch phrase was well proven!

My jalopy was the most popular car in Seoul, distinguishing itself from other cars with a unique old-style toot of its horn. It was called the Emperor's car by my friends because it resembled the car used by Japanese Emperor Hirohito in the old days.

The 1929 Model-A Ford, seen behind the author (right), was driven by him on his trans-U.S. tour in 1949 and during his coverage of the Korean War.

The author and his sons with a U.S. army jeep made available to the Associated Press.

I had to abandon the car when I was caught by Communist North Korean soldiers in an enemy-occupied zone south of Seoul on June 29, 1950, and narrowly escaped death. But I recovered it after Seoul was recaptured by the United Nations forces on September 28. I had it completely overhauled and dubbed it Liberated Lizzie.

Embarking on a Journalist Career

I called on the Director of the United States Information Service, James Stewart, to hand him the letter I had brought from the chief of the Voice of America requesting my employment at the USIS. After explaining USIS activity in Korea, Stewart said, "We have a job available for you. Would you like to work with us?"

Since I was not interested in working at a foreign government agency, I gave a vague answer, "I will think about it."

The Bank of Korea also offered me a job at its Tokyo branch, which was the first to be opened overseas. The reason why the bank wanted to dispatch me to Tokyo was that I had a good command of English and Japanese and I was good at accounting.

Meanwhile, Dr. Kim Whal-lan (Helen Kim), president of Ewha Women's University, whom I had known since I was assistant manager of the Chosun Hotel, asked me to teach at her school.

Despite these several job offers, I decided to embark on a career as a journalist. The opportunity came when Associated Press correspondent William Moore asked the AP head office in New York to hire me as a correspondent. I believed that reporting important events through the network of such a prestigious news agency as the Associated Press suited my nature and afforded me the opportunity to deepen world understanding of the unfortunate situation of my divided country.

I was very proud to become an AP reporter when I heard Mr. Moore explain: American newspapers are the shareholders of AP and news reports filed by AP correspondents are relayed by more than 4,000 newspapers and broadcasting stations throughout the world.

I recalled an unforgettable book that I had read while a student at Hastings College. It was the autobiography of Lincoln Steffens

(1866–1936) who, as a reporter, uncovered the deep-rooted corruptions of American state governments and earned the reputed title of a reformist.

I wanted to become a reporter like him. As to the cause of the corruption of the government officials he concluded: "It was not Adam or Eve to blame, but money was. Money is the source of all evil." I was convinced that money was indeed the source of all evil.

KOREA DIVIDED

38th Parallel Barrier

The surrender of Japan to the Allied Powers on August 15, 1945 meant to the Korean people liberation from the yoke of its ruthless colonial rule, and Koreans believed a free, independent government would soon be established. It was in this spirit that they so heartily welcomed the arrival of the American and Soviet forces as liberators.

However, they found to their incredulous amazement and dismay that, by an agreement reached between the United States and the Soviet Union, without the knowledge of the Korean people, their country was slashed in half along the 38th Parallel.

Before Japan's surrender, 120,000 Soviet troops under Colonel General Ivan Chistyakov entered North Korea on August 2, 1945, and rapidly advanced southward.

Alarmed by the speedy advance of the Soviet troops, Washington decided to participate in the occupation of Korea, and the State-War-Navy Co-ordinating Committee (SWNCC) held an emergency meeting in the Pentagon August 10–11 to adopt a Soviet-American demarcation line. The two officers assigned to do the job — Colonel Dean Rusk, an aide to Army Chief of Staff George Marshall, and another colonel, C. H. Bonesteel — chose the 38th Parallel that ran broadly across the middle of the country. Japanese soldiers north of the 38th Parallel would surrender to the Soviets; those to the south, to the Americans.

It was not until the issuance of General Douglas MacArthur's General Order No. 1 on September 2, the day the Japanese signed the surrender on the USS *Missouri* in Tokyo Bay, that the SWNCC decision was made public.

To the relief of Washington, the Soviets readily accepted the 38th Parallel as the limit of their advance. The U.S. government emphasized that the 38th Parallel was a temporary line of military expediency, but the Soviets took it as a political demarcation.

The artificial line dealt a crippling blow to Korea because it had divided not only the land but also the people. Hence, to break down the cursed 38th Parallel barrier became the most earnest aspiration of the 70 million Koreans at home and abroad.

Anti-Trusteeship Struggles

Kim Koo, Kim Kyu-sik, and other leaders of the Korean Provisional Government in Chungking, China, arrived in Seoul in November. They found Syngman Rhee, who had returned one month earlier, already leading the conservative independence forces with the blessing of the American occupation authorities. Although the Koreans tried to establish themselves with the aid of the occupying forces, they were under the handicap of a divided country and conflicting policies between the two occupation zones.

Following the inauguration of the Communist Party led by Park Hun-yung, the Korean People's Party of Lyuh Woon-hyung and the National Party of Ahn Jae-hong were organized. Opposed to these left-wing parties, the right-wing camp organized the Korean Democratic Party (Song Chin-woo) and the Korean Independence Party (Kim Koo). By June 1946, numerous small parties numbering more than 113 were born in succession. Syngman Rhee formed the National Society for the Rapid Realization of Independence, appealing for support from all ranks of the people. He firmly refused to have any relationship with the Communists.

Meanwhile, MacArthur's headquarters decided to set up a military government south of the 38th Parallel and appointed Major General Archibald Arnold as military governor.

In North Korea, the Soviet Army which had advanced to Pyongyang on August 24, inaugurated the Provisional People's Committee on September 8 with the appointment of Victor Romanenko, a political officer of the 25th Army, as military governor. Kim Sung-ju, who had been dispatched to Korea as Stalin's puppet, made his first public appearance before Pyongyang citizens on October 14, posing as the legendary anti-Japanese partisan hero Kim Il Sung, who had died long before. The Soviets infiltrated a large number of Korean Communists who had received political training in the U.S.S.R. to expedite the formation of North Korea as a Soviet satellite.

Under these circumstances, foreign ministers of America, Britain and the Soviet Union met in Moscow for ten days from December 17, and resolved to create a U.S.-Soviet Joint Commission to discuss the rule of Korea under a Four-Power (including China) "International Trusteeship" for five years.

The trusteeship plan was violently opposed by all parties, particularly the conservative group. Kim Koo formed an "Anti-trusteeship Struggles Committee" on December 29, and called for a general strike. Syngman Rhee further fired the anti-trusteeship torch declaring, "To support trusteeship is to abet a plot to ruin the country."

Kim Koo convened an "Emergency National Conference," calling for the rally of all anti-trusteeship forces. Students across the nation staged fiery demonstrations on January 7, 1946.

The Soviets, meantime, spread false propaganda claiming that (1) the trusteeship plan was originally proposed by the United States, not for five years but for ten years, and (2) the Soviet Union supported Korean independence — thus fomenting anti-American sentiment among the Korean populace.

In his report on the Soviet propaganda scheme to MacArthur in February 1946, Lieutenant General John R. Hodge, commander of U.S. occupation forces, said, "The Korean people feel that America has betrayed them again." It was the Soviet's calculation that there was the possibility of establishing a pro-Communist regime if anti-U.S. sentiment was further aroused because of wide-spread unrest in Korea.

Meanwhile, the left-wing camp convened a conference of provincial committee representatives on February 10 and resolved to support the trusteeship plan. The Korean Communist Party (Park Hun-yung) and the Central People's Committee (Lyuh Woon-hyung), which had opposed trusteeship, changed sides and supported it. This sudden change was due to directives from Pyongyang.

Amidst the severe confrontation between the "bantak" (anti-trusteeship) and the "sootak" (pro-trusteeship) groups, right-wing leader Song Chin-woo, founder of the Korean Democratic Party, was assassinated at his home on the morning of December 30, 1945. The assassin was a fanatic nationalist, Han Hyun-woo, who was said to have attempted but failed to assassin left-wing leaders Lyuh Woon-hyung and Park Hun-yung as well.

Despite the strong anti-trusteeship campaign of the right-wing, a U.S.-Soviet Joint Commission, represented by Major General Arnold and Lieutenant General Terenti Fomich Shtykov, convened a preliminary session in Seoul on January 16, 1946, and agreed to inaugurate a joint commission of five members from each side on February 6 to discuss the establishment of a provisional government in accord with the Moscow Agreement.

It became quickly apparent, however, that the Soviets were not interested in the new approach. The Communists insisted that anyone who had ever expressed criticism of trusteeship should be ineligible for consultation in connection with the proposed provisional government — an action which would exclude virtually all rightist leaders, including Syngman Rhee.

When the United States balked at any such broad expulsion, the talks adjourned indefinitely on May 20, resulting in the withdrawal of Soviet representatives led by Shtykov to Pyongyang. The Cold-War chill was cast on the U.S.-Soviet relationship. When the Soviets denied the United States the right to maintain consular representation in Pyongyang, the Soviet consular staff was forced in turn to withdraw from Seoul.

As if he had been waiting for such a situation, Syngman Rhee on May 11 announced a plan to establish a separate government in the south alone. But U.S. Military Governor Archer Lerch, a major general who had succeeded Arnold, restrained this move. On the left-wing side, the Communist Party, the People's Party and the

Shinmin Party agreed on September 5 to merge and to form the South Korean Workers Party (Namnodang), which was inaugurated on September 23 with Park Hun-yung as its leader.

On September 24, Namnodang ordered railway workers to go on general strike, followed by the massive walkout of the workers at printing plants and the Central Telegraph Bureau. In Taegu the Communists began a campaign of agitation and vilification against the police, killing 59 policemen.

I was then working at the Chosun Hotel in Seoul as assistant manager at the request of General Hodge's headquarters. Since the Chosun Hotel belonged to the Railway Bureau of the U.S. Military Government, the hotel employees were obliged to comply with the general strike orders from the Railway Workers Union. The strike of Chosun Hotel employees was especially called for by labor leaders because high-ranking officers of the U.S. XXIV Corps were billeted there. Because the officers kept their pistols in their rooms, it was feared that the hotel might be embroiled in an extremely dangerous situation should the hotel employees take part in the strike. Fortunately the hotel employees, 197 in all, heeded my persuasion and kept working as usual despite the threats by stone-throwing Railway Unionists. The American officers at the Chosun felt greatly relieved.

By the time the strike ended in mid-October, about 4,000 strikers were arrested. Cho Byong-ok, police director of the U.S. Military Government, was wounded on October 16 by a bomb explosion set up by leftist terrorists.

On the political scene, Rhee was consolidating his control of the right without dilution by leftist elements less responsive to his leadership. Spurned by Rhee, Lyuh Woon-hyung debated some form of coalition with the moderate rightist Kim Kyu-sik. But the coalition negotiations came to an abrupt halt on July 19, 1947, when Lyuh was assassinated in broad daylight while driving through the streets of Seoul. The assassin, 19-year-old Han Chi-keun, who was described as a fanatic anti-Communist, openly admitted his crime. The original death sentence for him was commuted later to life imprisonment because he was a minor.

Hostile Regimes Established

In the midst of intensifying anti-trusteeship campaigns in the south, America, which had given up dealing with the U.S.-Soviet Joint Commission, submitted the Korean question to the General Assembly of the United Nations. While the leftist camp protested that the American act was against the Moscow Agreement, the right wholeheartedly welcomed it.

The U.N. General Assembly on September 26 accepted responsibility, with a 41–6 vote, establishing a U.N. mandate over the divided Korea. On November 16, the Assembly adopted an American resolution calling for a United Nations Temporary Commission on Korea (UNTCOK) which could "travel, observe, and consult throughout Korea," and which would observe the election of a Korean national assembly no later than March 31, 1948. The specter of an unwanted trusteeship was finally laid to rest.

In accord with the U.N. resolution, the United Nations Temporary Commission on Korea, composed of thirty-four representatives from the Republic of China, France, Canada, Australia, India, El Salvador, the Philippines, and Syria, arrived in Seoul on January 7, 1948. Two days later the U.N. Commission issued a communique announcing that (1) South-North simultaneous elections would be held by March 31 to elect people's representatives in a secret ballot; (2) the representatives elected in the general elections would compose a national assembly to establish the national government; and (3) the national government, in consultation with UNTCOK, would take over the political power from the military government authorities, and promptly begin negotiations on the withdrawal of occupation forces with the occupation military authorities.

While the right camp welcomed the UNTCOK communique as contributing to bringing early independence to the fatherland, the left vehemently opposed it, claiming that it would ruin the nation. The Soviets refused UNTCOK's entry into North Korea on January 23, 1948.

The UNTCOK adopted an American proposal to hold elections in South Korea alone where free voting was possible. Accordingly the Commission, after allotting 200 seats for the south and 100 seats for the north in proportion to respective populations, decided to hold the elections in the south on May 10, forty days later than the original schedule for March 1.

The leftists in both the south and the north, to no one's surprise, bitterly opposed holding separate elections in the south alone. Even some right-wing leaders, like Kim Koo and Kim Kyu-sik, joined the opposing forces on grounds that separate elections would formalize the south-north division, making national unification more difficult. Kim Koo of the Korean Independence Party and six others, including Kim Kyu-sik, issued a joint communique denouncing the separate election plan and proposed North Korean leaders and Soviet military commander Shtykov to open a south-north conference.

The northern side agreed to this and sent invitations to Kim Koo and thirteen others. The South Koreans led by Kim Koo and Kim Kyu-sik went to Pyongyang on April 19. The conference turned out to justify the lawfulness of the northern position and Kim Koo's group members, who had gone to the north risking their political lives, were made a cat's-paw of the Communist scenario. The conference adjourned on April 24 after adopting resolutions as the Communists had contrived that charged that "separate elections in the south alone is a traitorous act to divide the fatherland and make it subject to a foreign power." Another resolution demanded the withdrawal of U.S. and Soviet occupation forces from Korea.

Despite the intense obstruction maneuvers instigated by the left, the election was held throughout the area south of the 38th Parallel on May 10, 1948 under the supervision of the United Nations Temporary Commission on Korea. When the votes were tallied, the result showed that about 72 percent of the 7,884,095 eligible voters went to the polls. In those days the population in the south was estimated at twenty million and that in the north at about ten million.

Nine hundred and forty-eight candidates, including 417 independents, ran and 197 were elected. Influential persons among those elected were Syngman Rhee, Shin Ik-hi, Chang Myon (John M. Chang), Cho Bong-am, Huh Chung, Kim Joon-yun, and Lee Shi-yung. Kim Koo and Kim Kyu-sik, upholding their position against the separate election, did not run. UNTCOK which had observed the election process confirmed the fairness of the election.

When the National Assembly convened for the first time on May 31, it recognized Rhee as the person most responsible for its existence by electing him chairman — a step to the presidency. Lee Shi-yung was elected vice president. The Assembly adopted an Assembly Law on June 10 and decided to call the country "Tae Han Min Kook" (The Republic of Korea). The Assembly then turned to the drafting of a constitution. Drafted by Professor Yu Chin-o, this document was finally adopted on July 17. It provided for a president elected by the Assembly but enjoying strong independent powers. Thus on August 15 the Republic of Korea government recognized by the United Nations was officially inaugurated.

On August 15, 1948, the American flag was lowered at the capitol building and the Korean flag (Taegukki) raised in its place, signifying the transfer of governing authority from the U.S. military government to the Republic of Korea. General Douglas MacArthur flew from Tokyo to witness the transfer of government. At the inaugural ceremony of President Syngman Rhee, MacArthur told Koreans, "Personally I will do anything I can do to help the Korean people and to protect them. I will protect them as I would protect the United States or California against aggression....An artificial barrier has divided your land. This barrier must and shall be torn down."

The United Nations Temporary Commission prepared its report. The Commission placed its weight firmly behind the new government. On December 12, the United Nations General Assembly declared that "There has been established a lawful government (the government of the Republic of Korea) having effective control and jurisdiction over that part of Korea where the Temporary Commission was able to observe and consult and in which the great majority of the people of Korea reside; and that this government is based on elections which were a valid expression of the free will of the electorate of that part of Korea and which were observed by the Temporary Commission; and that this is the only such government in Korea."

In North Korea, "The Democratic People's Republic of Korea" was established on September 9, and 36-year-old Kim Il Sung, who was originally Kim Sung Ju, emerged as premier. Wearing the proud name of Kim Il Sung, a legendary hero who had been famous for

President Syngman Rhee (right), General Douglas MacArthur, and Lieutenant General John R. Hedge observe the inaugural ceremony of the Republic of Korea government on August 15, 1948.

his guerrilla exploits against the Japanese, he was pictured all over North Korea on big posters, alongside of Joseph Stalin.

North Korea was organized as a totalitarian police state under the control of Soviet Russia. The Communists spread propaganda that the efforts by the United Nations to reunite Korea upon the basis of a free election was "the hypocritical mask of imperialism, seeking to enslave the free Korean people under the ruthless rule of American capitalists." The United Nations Commission on Korea, which had replaced the earlier Temporary Commission in December 1948, tried in vain to make contacts with the North Korean government to facilitate national reunification.

North Korean young men were subjected at once to conscription that soon reached a force of 150,000 men, armed with Soviet-made tanks, planes, and heavy artillery. The military strength in South Korea, meanwhile, was deliberately kept weak by America for fear that a strong South Korean army would be tempted to seek reunification of the country by an attack on the north — thereby risking another world war. As the price of providing light arms to the South Korean troops, the United States exacted a solemn promise that under no provocation whatever would they set foot upon the northern side of the 38th Parallel. South Korea had only 50,000 lightly armed troops, mainly for defense against North Korean guerrillas and Communist-instigated internal revolts.

With the emergence of the Soviet-controlled Communist regime in North Korea, Kim Il Sung initiated the tragic Korean War. The three-year war, triggered by Communist North Korea with the support of Soviet Russia and Communist China in June 1950, left almost five million dead or wounded.

The origin of the Korean tragedy goes back to Japan's illegal "Protectorate Treaty" of 1905 and its outright annexation of Korea in 1910. Had it not been for the Japanese army on Korean soil during its 40-year domination, there would not have been the 38th Parallel barrier created by the United States and Soviet Union for the purpose of disarming defeated Japanese troops in 1945.

Korea, until it was annexed by Japan, had retained its independence, although its political destiny was closely tied with neighboring China, Japan, and Russia. The Korean War has exposed the tremendous inadequacy of great-power policy in Asia. The inconclu-

border guard brigade, which shall be deployed in the western plain of Korea. The paramount task of this group shall be to deal a fatal blow to the South Korean forces in the vicinity of Seoul with surprise attacks, overrun Seoul and advance rapidly along the coast.

"In the first front of the group shall be the 6th, 1st, 4th and 3rd infantry divisions with strong combat ability, while the second front shall drive into two areas — the vicinity of Seoul via Kapyong and Kwangju, and the Hongchon area by way of Yanggu and Inje. The entire armored battle equipment, independent tank brigade and motorcycle brigade shall be concentrated on the operational forces groups.

"The key to lightning action is to break through the not-so-strong enemy defense positions along the 38th Parallel in surprise preemptive strikes, advance to the Seoul area, smashing the enemy's basic war capability, and to reach a line linking Suwon, Wonju and Samchok.

"According to the opinions of Soviet military advisers, it will take three to four days to achieve the goal.

"After the initial goal is accomplished, we shall keep driving to south, destroying the South Korean 2nd infantry division in the Taejon area, the 3rd division in the Taegu area, and the 5th division in the Kwangju area.

"The Korean People's Army shall completely smash the South Korean forces in two weeks, and liberate the entire Korean Peninsula."

Former Soviet Premier Nikita Khrushchev also divulged in his memoirs published in the West in 1970 that Kim Il Sung visited Stalin toward the end of 1949 and told him the "North Koreans wanted to prod South Korea with the point of a bayonet. An attack would touch off an internal explosion in South Korea and swiftly topple Syngman Rhee from power." [8]

According to Khrushchev's account, Stalin reacted cautiously, because he was worried that the Americans would jump in, telling Kim to come again to Moscow with a concrete plan. Kim visited Stalin again two months later and explained his invasion plan, assuring that "the attack would be swiftly carried out. So the American imperialists won't be able to intervene." The final decision came at a high-spirited dinner at Stalin's dacha outside Moscow.

Kim also talked with Mao Tse-tung at Stalin's suggestion. Mao, too, supported the invasion assuming that the Americans would not intervene in what he considered a "Korean internal matter." [9]

Meanwhile in Washington, Secretary of State Dean Acheson ticked off America's "defense perimeter" in Asia connecting Japan, Okinawa, and the Philippines. Thus South Korea and Formosa (Taiwan) in effect were placed outside that belt of nations against which aggression would automatically be resisted by the United States. The Acheson announcement, made on January 2, 1950 in a speech before the National Press Club coupled with the withdrawal of American troops from South Korea in late 1949, gave assurances to the Communists that Americans would not intervene in the North Korean invasion.

Having completed his invasion scheme with Stalin and Mao's support, Kim Il Sung set June 25, 1950 as the D-Day. On June 10, Korean People's Army (KPA) Chief of Staff Kang Kun ordered various army units, under the guise of an emergency drill, to advance to designated positions close to the 38th Parallel. Senior Colonel Lee Hak-ku, Second Army operations chief of staff, was charged with campaign details for the invasion. The devastating North Korean artillery and mortar barrage opened at 4 a.m. on the Sunday morning of June 25, 1950. Ten Communist divisions, supported by Soviet-made T–34 tanks, streamed over the 38th Parallel.

Only about one third of the South Korean Army, without heavy equipment, was deployed in the line confronting the assault by such formidable enemy power, and the South Korean front rapidly collapsed.

At 9:30 a.m. Kim Il Sung broadcast his concocted version of events along the 38th Parallel:

> The South Korean puppet clique has rejected all methods for peaceful reunification proposed by the Democratic People's Republic of Korea, and dared to commit armed aggression...north of the 38th Parallel....The Democratic People's Republic of Korea ordered a counter-attack to repel the invading troops. The South Korean puppet clique will be held responsi-

ble for whatever results may be brought about by this development.

Kim's fictitious statement became the basis of the public posture on Korea not only in the Communist world, but also in part of the free world even until now. Soviet documents, copies of which were handed over to South Korean President Kim Young Sam by Russian President Boris Yeltsin in June 1994, and other authoritative Russian sources have proved in effect that Kim Il Sung was the world's biggest liar.

If Kim Il Sung's claim that South Korea started the Korean War proved true, how could the United Nations forces have fought for South Korea to repel the Communist troops from the South? It would have meant that the peace-keeping world body had aided the aggressor.

To the surprise of many, some Western journalists and scholars held views sympathetic with Kim Il Sung's claim that South Korea initiated the war against North Korea. Well known for writing books advocating such views were American journalist I.F. Stone; Vanderbilt University professor D.F. Fleming; Robert Simmons, professor at Guelph University in Canada; and Bruce Cumings, Professor of East Asian history at the University of Chicago. Their books influenced Japanese media so much that even now many Japanese say, "The origin of the Korean War is still shrouded in mystery."

British journalist Max Hastings correctly pointed out in his book, *The Korean War:* "The miscalculation of Kim Il Sung was to launch so blatant an act of aggression that even the least bellicose spectators around the world found it difficult to take refuge in equivocation." [10]

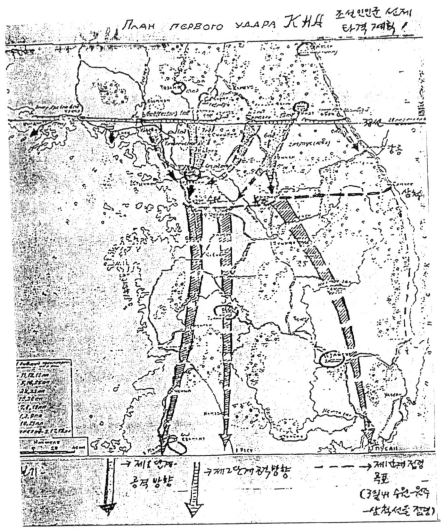

North Korean invasion plan presented to Moscow for Stalin's approval by Kim Il Sung on February 27, 1950, four months before North Korea provoked the Korean War. The war plan was divided into two phases; first to seize an area north of the Suwon-Wonju-Samchok line, including Seoul, in three days, and then to drive into Pusan, Kwangju and Yosu on the southern coast. The Communist conspiracy was revealed by Dr. Gavriil Korotkov, a senior fellow at the Institute for Military History at the Russian Defense Ministry, to South Korean news agency Yonhap in Moscow on August 28, 1992.

Principal leaders of the North Korean
People's Army in June 1950:

Supreme Commander	Kim Il Sung
Defense Minister	Choi Yong-kun
Chief of Staff	Kang Kun (Lt. General)
Field Commander	Kim Chaek (Lt. General)
First Army Commander	Kim Am (Lt. General)
Second Army Commander	Kim Moo-jung (Lt. General)

South-North Military Strength as of June 1950

	South Korea	North Korea	Ratio
Ground forces	67,416	120,880	1:1.8
Support Units	27,558	61,800	1:2.2
Navy	7,715	4,700	1:0.6
Air Force	1,879	2,000	1:1.1
Marines	1,166	9,000	1:7.7
Total forces	105,752	198,380	1:1.9
Mortars	960	1,727	1:1.8
Howitzers	91	552	1:6.1
Anti-tank artillery	140	550	1:3.9
Armored vehicles	27	54	1:2
Self-propelled guns	—	176	—
Tanks	—	242	—
Aircraft	24[*]	211[†]	1:8.8
Warships	28	30	1:1.1

[*]Training planes [†]Fighter planes

Source: General (ret.) Choung Il-kwon's memoirs
Chonjaeng-gwa Hyujon (War and Truce)

CHAPTER TWO

NORTH KOREA
STRIKES SOUTH

FULL-SCALE INVASION

June 25, 1950

On the morning of June 25, 1950, I was moving my household from Seoul's western district to the eastern area. It was a rainy Sunday.

While moving luggage at around 11 a.m., I saw two strange airplanes buzzing over the capital city. I called my boss, O.H.P. King, at the AP office in Ulchiro. He cried out: "Where are you now? Something very serious seemed to have happened. Come right away!"

I dashed to the office. King frantically showed me an urgent message from New York, relayed by Bill Jordan at AP's Tokyo bureau, saying UP, the opposition news agency, had reported North Korean troops striking south. This "rocket" was a query about a dispatch from United Press correspondent Jack James, reporting, "North Koreans launched Sunday morning attacks generally along the 38th Parallel...."

I rushed to phone my sources at the South Korean Defense Ministry, Army Headquarters, KMAG (American Military Advisory Group in Korea), the American Embassy, and Korean police.

Through frantic calls, I found out that Jack's report was a indeed a smashing scoop. Captain James Hausman, KMAG advisor to South Korean Army Chief of Staff Major General Chae Byong-duk, was the most reliable source for me. Hausman said that reports indicated the North Korean People's Army had launched an all-out attack at around 4 a. m. all along the 38th Parallel throwing in several divisions. He said he had received the first telephone report about 4:30 a.m.

Jack James, who now lives in retirement in Mill Valley, California, recounted later that he obtained a scoop on the news of the Communist attack by luck. On his way to the American Embassy press room to pick up his raincoat a few minutes after 8 a.m., he encountered an American intelligence officer at the corner of the Bando Hotel housing the embassy. Jack was asked, "What do you hear from the border?" Jack responded, "Not very much yet. What do you hear from the border?" The officer told him, "Hell, they're supposed to have crossed everywhere." Jack rushed to telephone his sources to confirm the North Korean attack, and sent an urgent cable around 9:50 a.m. reporting, "Fragmentary reports from thirty-eighth parallel indicated North Koreans launched Sunday morning attacks generally along entire border..."

The initial UP scoop dealt a devastating blow to the Associated Press, and I thought I would try my best for fast and accurate reporting, launching rockets (news agency slang for a message from the head office that you have been scooped by an opposition reporter) rather than receiving them. While covering the three-year Korean War I was lucky to get scoops on some important stories, as Al Kaff, then UP's Korean War correspondent and later a UPI vice president before leaving the organization in New York in 1985, indicated in a personal message to me on October 2, 1993. Congratulating me on the Japanese-language publication of my book on the Korean War, Al said:

> Bill, with your impeccable sources and your excellent reporting, you scooped us all on the Inchon landing. Your skill as a journalist in winning the trust and confidence of important people contributed to many of the rockets that we in the United Press received during the Korean War. In the middle of the night came the dreaded message: another exclusive from Rox, the code word that United Press used to identify The Associated Press.
>
> Now you've done it again, this time with your book *Bringing Down the 38th Parallel Barrier: Reflections on the Korean War and its Legacy*....I know that the archives of history would not be complete without a

memoir of the Korean police action written by Bill Shinn....

Lightning Attack

The North Korean lightning attack took the South Korean (ROK) army units by complete surprise. South Korean troops, after months of false alerts, had relaxed for a weekend vacation. Less than 40,000 men of four divisions, only one of the three regiments of each division, was actually occupying defensive positions. The remaining regiments generally were in reserve areas 10 to 30 miles south of the 38th Parallel or on leave. A large number of enlisted men were given 15-day leave to help farmers in the rice paddies, while some frontline commanders had gone to Seoul to attend a festive celebration opening a new officers' club at army headquarters.

Half of the 90,000 invading forces and most of the 240 Soviet T–34 tanks were concentrated in a 25 miles arc on the western front, launching the main attack on the Uijongbu corridor toward Kaesong — the historic invasion route to Seoul.

Lieutenant Kim Jin-hak of the South Korean 1st Division, stationed near Kaesong, related in an interview: "The war began with a sudden eruption of artillery fire, a barrage laid onto our lines all along our sector of the frontier....I was sleeping in a dugout, built into the side of a hill and with sandbags on the top. The impact of the first rounds knocked me off my cot, and sand dirt poured into the dugout. I managed to pull on my clothes and run outside. One of my sergeants was near the door, groaning and holding his shoulder. I reached down to move him out of my way. His arm fell off; it had been severed near the shoulder. He groaned again, and was dead."

Captain Joseph R. Darrigo, assistant KMAG adviser to the 12th Regiment, South Korean 1st Division, had quarters in a house just northeast of Kaesong. Half awake in his bed around 5 a.m., Darrigo heard the whine of shell fragments through the air and the slap of small-arms fire against the house.

Darrigo put on his trousers and, with shoes and shirts in hand, rushed out from his quarters. He drove his jeep into Kaesong, where he was shocked to see North Korean soldiers unloading from a long train at the station. Darrigo darted toward the South Korean 1st Division headquarters at Munsan south of the Imjin River. Division commander Colonel Paik Sun-yup had not yet returned from Seoul.

The Communist North Koreans, completely prepared for the offense, were armed with 242 Soviet T–34 tanks, noted for crushing the Germans advancing toward Moscow in World War II, 211 YAK fighter planes, heavy artilleries, 120–mm mortars, 122–mm howitzers, and 54 armored vehicles, compared with the totally unprepared South Koreans who had only rifles, machine guns, 81–mm mortars, 105–mm howitzers, 2.36–inch "bazookas," and 27 armored vehicles. They had no tanks or fighter planes.

North Korea's 14th Regiment of the 6th Division and the 3rd Constabulary Brigade attacking the Ongjin peninsula on the west coast met with death-defying resistance of the South Korean 17th Independent Regiment led by Colonel Paik In-yup. But the North Koreans brought that entire peninsula under control, forcing the South Korean regiment to withdraw to Inchon by LSTs after losing many men.

Meanwhile, two regiments of the North Korean 6th Division, spearheaded by the 206th Armored unit, marched toward Kaesong, just south of the 38th Parallel, and the main force of the North's 1st Division, with the 203rd Tank Brigade ahead, attacked Korangpo. The 12th Regiment of the South Korean 1st Division was defending the front of Kaesong while its 13th Regiment defended Korangpo. But they were no match for the vast enemy force surging forward with tanks. A suicide squad of volunteers at the 1st Battalion launched human bullet attacks using hand-made bombs jerry-built with TNT powder. The eight-man suicide corps hidden in ambush under a thicket sprang at the advancing enemy tanks one by one. Four of the men were killed by enemy machinegun fire before the assault, but the other four successfully blew up the enemy tanks. As the flames belched out of the tanks with deafening explosions, the enemy's tank company was forced to retreat, and did not show up until the next day.

The 12th and 13th South Korean regiments, which had fought so desperately, had to withdraw toward Munsan, and Kaesong fell at 9:30 a.m., June 25.

Uijongbu Falls

The North Korean People's Army (NKPA) threw its 3rd and 4th Divisions along with two tank regiments, the main force of the 1st Army, into the Uijongbu corridor. The 1st Regiment of the South Korean 7th Division desperately fought against the lightning attack of the North's 4th Division supported by the 107th Tank Regiment. But the South Koreans were forced to withdraw south of Tongduchon after all their ammunition was fired. The 3rd and 9th Regiments of the South's 7th Division defending Pochon 18 miles south of the 38th Parallel failed to check the attacks of the Communist 3rd Division and the 109th Tank Regiment, which made a triumphant entry into Uijongbu, 14 miles north of Seoul, at 1 p.m., June 26.

The 2nd Division of the North Korean 2nd Army advanced to Chunchon at the central front while the 7th Division broke through Inje in the east. The South Korean 6th Division headquartered in Wonju was defending the Hongchon-Inje route along the ridges of Puyong Mountain. The Communist 2nd Division marched southward along the valley from Hwachon at the upstream of the Bukhan River to 11 miles south of the 38th Parallel, while its 4th Regiment assaulted the front of the South Korean 7th Regiment and the enemy 6th Regiment was blocking the South Korean withdrawal route after its seizure of Chunchon City.

The South Korean 8th Division based in Kangnung was defending the east coast area of the 38th Parallel assigning its 10th Regiment and the 18th Artillery Battalion to guard the northern front and the 21st Regiment based in Samchock to mop up Communist guerrillas in Odae Mountain.

The North Korean 5th Division advanced south along the trails toward Odae Mountain while a task force made a surprise landing on Jungdongjin south of Kangnung and Imwon further south.

The South Korean forces, whose total strength at the front was less than a half that of the North, had to commit a considerable number of troops for the suppression of Communist guerrillas in Chiri and Odae Mountains.

The South Korean troops, overrun on all fronts, had to fight the onrushing enemy tanks with small arms which were soon exhausted. Meanwhile, Soviet-made YAK fighter planes strafed Seoul's Kimpo airfield at 4 p.m., damaging gasoline storage tanks and C–54 transport planes. The Yoido airstrip was also struck and several training planes were destroyed.

The North Korean 3rd and 4th Divisions, which had captured Uijongbu in the early afternoon of June 26, were the first Communist troops to approach the capital city of Seoul. The 25th Regiment of the South Korean 2nd Division, which had withdrawn from Uijongbu, and South Korean Military Academy cadets and the Logistics Unit in Seoul joined in the defense of Miari Pass, the gateway to Seoul. At about five o'clock in the afternoon of June 27 the North Koreans started striking the Miari defense line.

After sunset, rows of frightened refugees were flowing south and distant explosions were heard. Most of the three million Seoul citizens had remained in the city believing a false radio broadcast that "Our armed forces have stopped the advance of the North Korean puppet army, whose troops are being driven back." But they panicked when they heard of the advance of the enemy troops to Miari on the 27th.

Frantic Evacuation from Seoul

President Syngman Rhee learned that Kaesong and Tongduchon, gateways to Seoul, fell to enemy hands on the first day of the North Korean invasion and that the South Korean armed forces were in critical condition. Rhee telephoned General MacArthur in Tokyo at about 2:30 a.m., June 26, appealing for immediate help.

MacArthur promised he would send fighter planes, howitzers, and anti-tank artillery as soon as possible. Rhee and MacArthur had been friends from before World War I when Rhee was studying in America and MacArthur was working at the War Department.

President Rhee also phoned Ambassador Chang Myon (John M. Chang) in Washington instructing, "You will see President Truman at once and tell him that the enemy is at our threshold. Please ask him for immediate supplies of arms, for help of any kind."

In the early afternoon of June 26 (local time), Ambassador Chang and First Secretary Han Pyo-wook were shown into the Oval Office at the White House to meet President Truman. "We admire your people and their struggle in adversity," Truman told the visitors. "Your soldiers are fighting bravely. Please convey my appreciation of this to President Rhee."

Early the next day, Chang and Han were jubilant to hear that Truman had promised immediate U.S. air and naval support for the South Korean forces. The two Korean diplomats hurried to the United Nations to meet Secretary-General Trygve Lie and request U.N. assistance as ordered by President Rhee.

In Seoul, U.S. Ambassador John Muccio called on Rhee at the presidential mansion, Kyungmudae, in the evening of June 26 and advised the president to leave Seoul as soon as possible. Because Rhee obstinately refused to leave, Muccio asked Rhee's Austrian-born wife, Madame Francesca Rhee, to persuade her husband to leave in a hurry.

At dawn on June 27, Defense Minister Shin Sung-mo knocked on the door of Rhee's bedroom at Kyungmudae and pleaded with him to leave the capital "because the enemy troops are approaching."

Rhee refused to leave saying, "I must defend Seoul to the last." Soon after, the president's chief bodyguard, Kim Chang-hung, reported to Rhee that enemy tanks had reached the outskirts of Seoul. The president, along with principal Cabinet members, left for Taejon by a special train at 7 a.m., June 27.

Fearing that South Korean troops might lose their fighting spirit if they knew the government had evacuated the capital, Defense Minister Shin Sung-mo broadcast a false radio announcement that the government was still working in Seoul. At the strong protest of government spokesman Ryee Chol-won (Clarence Ryee), who was incensed to hear such a lie, Shin admitted on an HLKA radio broadcast at 11 a.m. that part of the government had left Seoul.

At the National Assembly, some lawmakers complained that the hasty evacuation of the government was an act of deserting the people. But the majority of the legislators supported the government's early evacuation, pointing out that "We can continue to fight under the leadership of President Rhee by moving the government out of Seoul. Our Republic would die should the president be captured by the Communist army."

Of the total of 210 assemblymen, 55 did not leave Seoul, and 28 of them were kidnapped later by the Communists and taken to North Korea.

At midnight, Muccio, through Radio Station WVTP, ordered all dependent American women and children (682 in all) to assemble at designated locations to be picked up by embassy busses for the trip to Inchon. From there the small Norwegian freighter *Reinholt* would take them to Kokura, Japan.

Remaining embassy staff and family along with foreigners (about 2,000) were evacuated to Japan by American transport planes. Muccio and his suite left Seoul for Taejon via Suwon in the afternoon of June 27. AP correspondent King also flew to Tokyo together with American embassy staff members.

The French charge d'affaires, who decided to stay, had sent his wife and children out with the American women. British Minister Vyvyan Holt and many French, including Catholic priests, also declined to leave. They were captured and sent to Pyongyang by North Korean agents on June 28.

As the sounds of guns could be heard closer and closer, rows of refugees and wounded South Korean soldiers were streaming into Seoul passing Miari Pass from the Uijongbu area. Amidst this panicky situation, many Koreans — young and old, men and women — began fleeing southward carrying their meager belongings on their heads or backs.

Toward dusk, I, too, decided to flee. I went to the AP office from the Chosun Hotel, where I was covering the war news, to collect important papers, and rushed home.

My wife, who had been anxiously waiting for my return, reported that two men calling themselves "members of a security unit" had come about an hour earlier and searched for my Ford car. "They shouted at me, 'Where is the dark-blue old car?' They left because I declared that we don't have any car at all," she said.

If I had been at home at that time, I would have been taken away by them. The so-called "members of a security unit" must have been either North Korean agents or members of the South Korean Workers (Communist) Party who became active in preparation for the entry of the North Korean army into Seoul. What they were looking for was not the Ford car; it was me working as a correspondent for AP, an "American imperialist news agency," as the Communists would call it. I was saved thanks to the fact that the Ford car was then at the parking lot of the Chosun Hotel where I was gathering war information.

At about 8 p.m., when I had finished my first meal at home in three days, I heard a big explosion outside. A bomb had been dropped. Since my house was on a hill near the Miari Pass, there was no doubt that the bomb had hit in that direction.

We had to flee at once. We hastily packed our essential belongings and fled in the old Ford. Amidst sporadic whines of small firearms, I drove desperately, without headlights on, toward the Han River bridge, the only exit from Seoul to the south. We felt relieved when we reached the bridge shortly after 10 p.m., believing that we would be able to save our lives once we safely crossed the bridge. But to our consternation, we were stopped at gunpoint by South Korean military police at the entrance and ordered not to cross the bridge. "No one is allowed to cross!" the MP shouted.

Reluctantly I drove to the ferry at Kwangnaru about three miles east of the bridge. It took forty minutes to get there because the road was so jammed with panic-stricken refugees. With so many refugees and wounded South Korean soldiers trying to board the ferry, we gave up using it. I drove back to the Han River bridge and tried again to cross, but MPs stopped my car again at gunpoint. "If you don't obey, we'll shoot you!" they cried.

"I am a correspondent of the Associated Press of America, reporting to the world on the North Korean invasion and the gallantry of the South Korean army fighting against the invaders. I want to come back after I send my family to Yongdungpo on the other side of the river. Shoot if you will!" I exclaimed and kept on driving across the bridge, defying the MP orders. My family was trembling in fear in the car. But we reached the other end of the bridge safely. We had narrowly escaped death! It was 11:45 p.m., June 27.

We were heading for a hamlet called Shingwon-ri about six miles south of the Han River, where Kim Jong-wook, a close friend of my younger brother Shinn Wha-boong, was living. It was slow driving on a narrow unfamiliar country road, which was muddy and slippery due to rain. But we did not have to hurry now that we had safely escaped from Seoul before the approaching enemy troops. We were scared when we were checked by club-carrying young men a few times on the way, but we felt relieved to know that they were South Korean youths guarding against Communist infiltration.

Shinwon-ri was a small farm village with some twenty straw-thatched houses. When I managed to reach Kim's house, I was on the verge of collapse from fatigue after the past few days of covering the North Korean invasion and fleeing the onrushing Communists.

Han River Bridge Blown Up

Well after midnight, I was roused by deafening explosions. I suspected they were artillery fire from the enemy approaching the village. But later I learned from refugees that the Han River bridge was blown up at 2:15 a.m., June 28, and scores of vehicles and hundreds of civilians crossing the bridge fell into the water and drowned. It happened two and a half hours after I had crossed it with my family.

The bridge, then the only span for vehicles and pedestrians to cross the Han River, was blown up by Colonel Choi Chang-shik, South Korean army chief engineer. He succeeded in demolishing the highway bridge, but the separate railway bridge was only partially destroyed, thus enabling enemy tanks to cross the river later.

General Chae Byong-duk, South Korean Army chief of staff, had promised KAMG officers that he would not blow up the bridge until after the South Korean army officers and men still engaged in street fights in Seoul had crossed it. But he did not keep his promise and had left for Shihung south of the Han at the suggestion of his men.

There were three South Korean divisions still holding Seoul, with all their arms and military transport. It did not appear that the enemy could reach the center of the city before noon of the 28th.

Deputy Chief of Staff Brig. Gen. Kim Paik-il was now in charge after Chae left. Brig. Gen. Lee Hyung-keun, commander of the 2nd Division, rushed to Kim and pleaded with him, "At least let me evacuate my troops, with their equipment, to the south of the river!"

Moved by Lee's plea, Kim turned to Brig Gen. Chang Chang-kook, "Drive to the river and tell the chief engineer to stop the demolitions!" Chang headed for the highway bridge, but by now the streets were so clogged with refugees and frightened civilians that he made only slow progress. At 2:10 a.m., Chang arrived at a point just 150 yards from the northern end of the three-lane bridge, which was jammed with refugees and vehicles.

According to eyewitnesses of the tragic destruction of the Han River bridge, a sheet of orange fire burst across the dark night, and the ground shook. With an ear-shattering roar, two long spans on the south side of the river dropped into the swirling dark water. No one would ever know how many soldiers and civilians died in the explosion or were hurled screaming into the river to drown.

The untold number of people who were unable to flee Seoul across the bridge were killed or kidnapped to North Korea by the Communists.

South Korean 7th Division Commander Yoo Jae-hung reached the south side of the river with 1,200 men, and 2nd Division Commander Lee Hyung-kun and remnants of his troops also crossed the river by boats or by swimming. Colonel Paik Sun-yup, whose 1st Division soldiers had fought tanks with hand-made bombs, brought less than half of his men across the river, leaving his artillery behind.

At Chunchon to the east, the gallant 6th Division heard the news, and prepared to abandon its pillboxes and bunkers. At Samchok, the 8th began its own retreat. Several days later men of these divisions assembled beyond the river with most of their weapons, equipment, and transport intact, bringing the South Korean fighting force to 54,000.

The gallantry of the South Korean Army was widely acclaimed, but it was no match for the onrushing enemy tanks. The South Koreans fought with hand-made bombs or suicide squads. During the first three days, 44,000 men were killed, captured, or missing. To the Korean people, the first three days of the war were days of great determination, fear, confusion, and ordeals beyond description.

Civilian refugees flee southward with their meager belongings before the onrushing North Korean army.

Soldiers of the North Korean 3rd Division triumphantly enter the South Korean capital city of Seoul on June 28, 1950, the fourth day of the Communist invasion.

ORDEALS IN ENEMY ZONE

Family Lost

I experienced nightmarish ordeals in a Communist occupied zone during the first week of the war — my family getting lost and myself being captured by enemy troops.

On June 29, I went to Suwon 15 miles south of Shinwon-ri to find out what was going on. Because it was so risky to drive a car, I went on foot posing as a refugee carrying a bag of rice on my back. At Suwon airstrip I saw two U.S. transport C–54s burning after being strafed by North Korean YAK fighter planes. The airplane *Bataan,* which had carried General MacArthur from Tokyo, and four Mustang escort planes also could be seen. MacArthur had gone to the Han River front for an inspection.

A little later President Rhee and U.S. Ambassador Muccio arrived in separate planes. Rhee was waiting for MacArthur at Suwon Agricultural College. Upon MacArthur's return, the two old friends hugged each other and held an hour-long conference.

In view of repeated strafings by YAK fighters, I thought it more important to rush back to Shinwon-ri to evacuate my family than to gather news in Suwon. The liaison officer at the newly set up Advanced Command (ADCOM) told me, "The situation here is getting worse. We will have to move out of here."

I met Seoul Mayor Kim Tae-sun at Suwon City Hall. Kim said, "Now I am getting ready to leave for Taejon. Mr. Shinn, you too had better go to Taejon where the government is now."

"I am worried about my family left in Shinwon-ri. I must evacuate them without a moment's delay," I said.

"Numerous people are fleeing southward. Should a young man like you go northward, you would be suspected as a Communist element," Mayor Kim cautioned and kindly issued an "emergency pass" for me.

Seized with drowsiness while walking northward in the dark, I fell asleep at a barn of a roadside farmhouse. I was roused by a shout, "Who is there?" I was questioned by a young man. I showed my AP reporter's ID card and the emergency pass given by Mayor Kim to prove that I was not a Communist.

Walking wearily at dawn, I could see South Korean soldiers limping along with their rifles upside down. As I moved further north, gruesome dead bodies lying in the roadside ditches greeted my eyes.

When I got to Shinwon-ri at last, not a soul could be seen in the village. Kim Jong-wook's house, where my family had taken refuge, was vacant and as silent as a grave. Realizing that all villagers had fled, I stood aghast, almost fainting. I looked around in a daze. Three men, who appeared to be North Korean soldiers, were standing guard on a small hill at the back of the village, and many others were moving southward along the Seoul-Suwon route across the rice field. I had entered an enemy-occupied zone!

Trembling with fear, I tried to escape. My old Ford had been left at Kim's home, but I could not find the key. My younger brother must have taken it with him when he was fleeing with my wife and three-year-old son. I broke open the dashboard, connected wires to start the motor, and frantically drove the car along a narrow lane. At a point about 300 yards from Kim's house, three North Korean soldiers suddenly emerged and ordered me to halt, blocking my way.

Apparently reassured that I was like a rat in a trap, they took their eyes off me for a moment to look around the neighborhood. Since any South Korean working for an American organization was to be shot to death, I immediately decided to throw away my wallet which contained my AP reporter's ID card, American greenbacks, U.S. postage stamps, and the emergency pass issued by Seoul Mayor Kim Tae-sun. I took a sink or swim risk. Watching for a chance while the North Koreans were looking away from me, I took out the wallet from an upper pocket and threw it into a bush by the car. Luckily the car window on the driver side had been open and no noise was heard thanks to the rainfall. My risky maneuver was not detected by the enemy soldiers!

Suddenly I noticed that I had carelessly left behind a very important thing, which would reveal my identity to the enemy soldiers if discovered by them. It was a briefcase containing copies of my reports filed for AP among others things. I had left it at the porch of Kim's house. Luckily it was not in the car when I was caught by the Communists, but the enemy soldiers would certainly find out who I was if they reached Kim's home. In order to escape from them without any moment's delay, I made up my mind to cheat them, acting as an ignorant, poor chauffeur because I knew that intellectuals and rich people were treated as enemies by the Communists.

Of the three enemy soldiers, the man with North Korean army captain's shoulder straps began to interrogate me. "Where are you heading?"

Since I knew that the Communists never allowed South Koreans to go southward, I said without hesitation, "I am going to Seoul."

"Not a single step southward is allowed. What is your job," he said.

"I am a chauffeur."

"Show me your hands."

I showed my hands with the fingers bent a little.

"How can a driver's hands be so neat? Don't tell a lie!" the captain raised his voice.

"Because I have been driving only private passenger cars, my hands are rather neat," I said. But he would not believe me and searched my pockets, only to find my South Korean driver's license and some South Korean won currency.

"Whose car is this?"

"I stole this. Because there was no key, the motor was started by hooked wires like this," I explained.

"Who can believe it?"

Taking advantage of the car's number plate still bearing "Nebraska" mark, I said calmly, "I stole the car in front of the deserted American Embassy. Please take a look at the license plate."

After seeing the "Nebraska" mark, without a word, he checked my clothes in the rear seat. Picking up my shirts and neckties, the captain said, *"jalsaratta, jalsarassoh* (well-off, well-off)"

"I stole them too. They were left behind by American Embassy staff when they fled before you comrades liberated Seoul."

The North Korean soldiers seemed to believe me after they saw the "made in U.S.A." labels on my neckties.

Narrowly Escape Death

The only means left for my survival was to escape from my captors without losing a second, because many things were left at Kim's home such as my pictures and foreign books besides the briefcase that would certainly disclose my identity.

I was horrified when the enemy soldiers got in my car and ordered me to drive. To stay with them any longer meant death for me, I thought. Taking advantage of the narrow, muddy road in the rain, I purposely drove the car into a roadside ditch.

"I am sorry. The road condition is so bad that I can hardly drive," I muttered, pretending to move the car out. "If any of you can drive, please try in my place," I said. Luckily there was none. They tried their best to pull or push the car, but I kept the gear in forward position, hitting the accelerator pedal stealthily so that the car went further into the ditch.

I got out of the car and told my Communist captors in a friendly voice, "I want to give this car to you, comrades. You can pull it out after the rain stops and use it for your 'liberation work.' Although it's an old car it still runs pretty well." Saying so, I took the bundle of my clothes out of the car. Trying to bear it on my back, I pleaded the captain, "Please help me." He grudgingly lifted it onto my back.

"You must never go southward, even one step! Be sure to go back to Seoul." he said sternly.

"Yes. I will surely go back to Seoul," I reassured him. With those words I started walking without haste until I reached a road bend, and then ran for my life making sure the enemy soldiers were out of my sight. Trotting along the footpath between rice paddies from where Shinwon-ri hamlet could not be seen, I reached a road leading to Suwon to the south. At this point, I attempted once again to go southward, but was warned by a nearby North Korean soldier, "You will be shot if you walk one more step southward."

Numerous South Korean refugees, mostly elderly men and women, were plodding along in ranks toward the north escorted by North Korean soldiers. The refugees believed the Communist propaganda that they would be given a sack of rice each if they went to Seoul. They did not seem to know that it was their march to hell.

Against my will, I got to the ferry on the southern bank of the Han River. Firmly determined to escape at any cost, I said to myself, "return to Communist-occupied Seoul means death."

Even when my turn to get on the ferry had come, I sneaked behind the line many times in a "delay tactic," watching for a chance to escape.

Suddenly a loud command was heard; a North Korean Army officer yelled, "Everybody must get on the ferry before dark. Hurry up! The ferry is for military use."

I was afraid that his order had been directed to me. So I went to him and said, "Thank you very much for your trouble. I, too, would like to go back to Seoul as soon as possible. But my pregnant wife (she was indeed pregnant) who departed together with me from the place of our refuge has not arrived here yet. Therefore I am anxiously waiting for her."

"What is your occupation?" he asked.

I said: "I am a chauffeur of a private passenger car. Being a poor man, I was living in a rented house in Seoul, but had to escape because I was scared when the house was bombed. Unless I return to Seoul together with my wife, I am afraid that we cannot but use the ferry many times trying to find each other."

"So what do you want to do?"

"I am certain that my wife is waiting for me at that village (pointing a nearby hamlet). She must have been late because of her physical condition approaching the month of childbirth. May I go to that village to bring her here?" My scheme was to get out of the sandbank where even an ant could be seen, and lie hidden somewhere in the village once I got there.

"Who in the world can guarantee that you will come back?" said the officer.

"Please go with me. I beg of you!" I promptly responded assuming that he would never do so.

He pondered and said, "Be sure to come back within 20 minutes."

I was glad I had passed a big hurdle. Remembering seeing a young man being shot to death when he was walking toward the village across the sandbank a while ago, I told him, "Thank you very much. Certainly I will come back. Please let your men know that you have given permission." He nodded.

I walked cautiously toward the village, trembling with fear that I might be shot from the back at any moment. The hamlet I so desperately wanted to reach was Jamsil-ri about 500 yards from the southern bank of the Han River.

Dusk was gathering after sunset. I wished darkness would come faster.

Getting in the village safely at last, I found a ramshackle farmhouse at the back of the road. I knocked at the tightly closed wooden gate to beg for a night's stay. A white-haired old women, over 70 years old, opened the gate.

"I am a South Korean refugee. Please let me stay here overnight. I pray to you," I appealed.

The seemingly good-natured old woman said, "It's all right for just one night," and showed me to a small *ondol* (heated floor) room.

"There was a fierce battle here yesterday. So, all my family have escaped. I am fearful too, but I stay here thinking that even the Communists will be tolerant to such an old woman like me," she said with an air of sympathy toward me. I was especially grateful to her for the meal of rice mixed with barley, *kimchi* (pickled vegetables), and *kochujang* (hot bean paste) she offered me so kindly.

Recaptured by Communist Troops

After one night's sound sleep at the farmhouse, my physical and mental fatigue of the past two days was soothed and I felt much refreshed. But I was at a loss on how to flee to Suwon from the enemy-occupied zone.

About 10 a.m., June 30, the roar of gunfire echoed over the hills for several minutes. I could not think of a battle with South Korean troops in the Communist-occupied area. But the old woman came and urged, "It is dangerous for a young man like you to stay here. Please run away."

"I am all right. You yourself had better go to a safe place as soon as possible," I told her. As the gunfire calmed down, I stepped out of the house. Then someone shouted, "It's curfew!" I hurried back to the house and noticed the old woman had disappeared. There was a black quilt hung like a curtain on the wall between the old woman's room and the kitchen. Somebody in the family must have been hidden behind it, I thought.

At 3 p.m., it appeared that full-scale combat had started as gunfire intensified along with the buzzing of aircraft. The whole area was in commotion. I punched a hole in the Korean-style paper window and peeped out. North Korean soldiers were busy transporting weapons and ammunition.

A team of enemy soldiers was violently kicking the locked wooden gate bellowing, "Open the gate!" As I remained silent, they broke into the small yard. I watched through a crack in the door. Five enemy soldiers put down a sack of rice on the ground, saying, "After a break here, we will go to Suwon today." My hair stood on end.

As they opened the door, the group's leader, an army lieutenant, ordered me, "Hands up," and took out whatever I had in my pockets. Then he began a severe interrogation.

"What is your job?"

"I am a driver."

"Why are you here all by yourself?"

"I took refuge here for a short while, but the whole family of this house disappeared this morning." Checking the identity of the picture on my driver's license, which he had taken out of my pocket, the lieutenant asserted, "You don't look like a driver." Then he asked a question I had feared the most.

"Where are you from?"

As a North Korean, who had escaped from the Communized North across the 38th Parallel, I was prone to use my native dialect. I knew that the Communists treated North Koreans who had fled to the south as their enemies. Judging from his accent, I could detect that he came from Hamkyongnamdo, the same province I had come from.

Fearing that my dialect might reveal my native place, I answered, "Although I was born in Hamkyongnamdo, I was brought up in Seoul since my parents had moved here when I was a little child."

"What kind of education did you get?"

"I could attend only a primary school because my parents were so poor."

"Don't tell me a lie," the Communist officer shouted. At this crucial moment, there was a bellow outside, "We're in a battle now. All troops must come out and fight!"

The enemy soldiers interrogating me had to go out at once with their rifles. I drew a long sigh of relief, thanking God for his Providence. I thought that all the soldiers had gone out, but groans of *"Aigubaeya, aigubaeya* (Oh, my aching stomach)" were heard from the yard. I peeped out and found one soldier was writhing in agony, his hands on his belly.

"I am not afraid of one sick person like him," I thought and turned my attention to the battle outside. Bullets penetrated the walls of the room. Air raids were going on. I lay on my face, covering my ears. Resigned to leave everything to fate, I could maintain my composure all the better. Dirt blown by the bullets penetrating the clay walls fell on my face which was covered with sweat, and my hands wiping it were covered with mud. Some bullets came within four inches of my head.

Rescued by South Korean Army Counterattack

At about 5 p.m., I heard voices urging, "Hurry up, hurry up." I looked out through a hole in the paper window. Enemy troops were trying to turn their ammunition carts north and running with wounded soldiers on their backs.

The enemy troops were retreating! I heaved a deep sigh of relief. But gunfire still roared. After the enemy troops had left, a voice from outside roared, "Anyone in the house come out at once, or be ready to die." I peeped out through a crevice at the window. There were South Korean soldiers in place of North Korean troops. I went out with a bundle of clothes on my back, holding up my South Korean driver's license with my picture in order to prove at one glance that I was a South Korean citizen.

A soldier shouted at the point of the bayonet, "If you are really a South Korean, show us *taegukki* (South Korean flag)." As I found that they were indeed South Korean soldiers, I instantly cried *mansei* (hurrah)! But, I did not have a South Korean flag; as I was in the Communist-occupied zone, I had abandoned even my AP reporter's ID card.

"I don't have it with me now. But I am a reporter of the Associated Press of America," I cried out.

"If he hasn't a *taegukki,* shoot him!" another soldier roared.

I roared back at the highest pitch, with glaring eyes: "Don't you know President Syngman Rhee's decree concerning prisoners-of-war? The Presidential decree says that our soldiers must capture alive even enemy troops in accord with the Geneva Convention, if they surrender. [In truth, Rhee had not issued such a decree; I coined the remark as a ploy to escape death.] How can you threaten to kill a South Korean civilian like me?" They walked away in silence.

But another group of South Korean soldiers came and acted the same way as the previous ones. I bellowed in wild rage, "To kill a person like me will inflict a big national loss. I am an American AP reporter. The fact that U.S. fighter planes are helping the South Korean Army now is due to reports from such world news agencies as AP, stressing the urgent need of American military assistance. You will find out what I am if you take me captive and escort me to your seniors in Suwon."

After saying this, I jumped on a nearby South Korean army truck. I thought it would be too dangerous for me to go to Suwon by myself at night. On the truck two North Korean prisoners-of-war were shivering in fear. I immediately began gathering information from them. The haggard captives, 19 and 20, testified that they belonged to the North Korean 4th Division which had marched into Seoul together with the Communist 3rd Division after capturing Uijongbu, and that they had been sent to the 38th Parallel under the pretense of a "military drill" one week before the June 25 attack.

The South Korean soldiers who witnessed my taking notes in English suddenly became polite and gave me a Japanese-style *nigiri* (rice ball) saying, "Sir, you must be hungry. Please take this." I devoured with thanks the large *nigiri* which was covered with dust as if powdered with soybean flour. The reason why the soldiers, who first had threatened to kill me and then called me "Sir," offered the rice ball, must have been that they realized I was really an American newsman.

The truck left for Suwon at about 9 p.m. Although much relieved by then, I was worried about my missing family. When the truck was passing Shinwon-ri, I saw the whole village burning. The soldiers escorting the two North Korean POWs said that their unit led by Colonel Lim Sun-ha had encamped in a valley near Shinwon-ri the previous night and thrown concentrated fire in the dead of night on the enemy troops who had gone on a spree far into the night to celebrate their capture of the village.

The army truck parked in front of a barracks in Suwon that night. There I was heartily welcomed by Colonel Lim Sun-ha and Chief Judge Advocate Sohn Sun-kyum. After friendly talks with them, I left for Taejon in a jeep provided by Colonel Lim, arriving there safely at midnight June 30, thus closing the drama of my nightmarish ordeals.

Colonel Lim's army unit that had recaptured Jamsil-ri was forced to retreat again by an enemy counterattack the following day. In retrospect, it seemed as if Colonel Lim's unit had recaptured Jamsil-ri only to rescue me! But I had lost touch with my family and was worrying about their safety.

U.S.-LED U.N. FORCES

Prompt American Assistance

The U.S. government promptly resolved to assist South Korea against the North Korean aggression by dispatching American troops to Korea. This quick U.S. action, motivated by its goal of checking Soviet hegemony in the Far East, was good luck for the Republic of Korea after it had been disheartened by the speech of U.S. Secretary of State Dean Acheson on January 12, 1950, drawing the U.S. defense line in the Far East from the Aleutian Islands to the Philippines, excluding Korea.

Behind the quick American resolution, there were the contributions of John Foster Dulles, a consultant to Secretary of State Dean Acheson, who had visited South Korea on June 18, one week before the outbreak of the war, and General MacArthur who had promised

President Syngman Rhee to do his best when he was roused by Rhee's phone call at 2:30 a.m., June 26 for immediate help.

When Dulles inspected the frontier at the 38th Parallel on June 19, South Korean 7th Division Commander Brigadier General Yoo Jae-hung requested that "America provide the Republic of Korea with more assistance to prevent Communist aggression." Dulles told reporters that he was much moved by General Yoo's appeal.

Hearing protests from Rhee that America was letting him down, Dulles promised the National Assembly the next morning: "You are not alone. You will never be alone as long as you continue to play worthily your part in the great design of human freedom."

Dulles, resting in Tokyo from his trip to South Korea, was chatting with General MacArthur at his office in the Daiichi Building on June 25. MacArthur, who had received the first report on the North Korean attack commented, "This is probably only a reconnaissance in force." But Dulles, who remembered what he had learned at the 38th Parallel and the ardent appeal from President Rhee, told MacArthur that the situation was "very grave." He wrote a message to Secretary of State Dean Acheson and Assistant Secretary of State Dean Rusk on his yellow drafting pad:

"To sit by while [South] Korea is overrun by unprovoked attack would start a disastrous chain of events leading most probably to world war." [1]

Meanwhile, General MacArthur, who realized the seriousness of the Korean situation after receiving an urgent phone call from President Rhee the following night, cabled to Washington calling for emergency help for the Republic of Korea as he had promised to Rhee.

On the morning of June 27, President Truman met 14 congressmen. Taking his seat next to Acheson, he asked the secretary of state to present a summary of the Korean crisis. Acheson explained that the military situation was desperate and that many nations were afraid that America might not take action to repel the aggressors. He pointed out that an unresisted aggression might lead to World War III. [2]

After listening to Acheson, Truman disclosed that he had already ordered the U.S. air and navy forces to assist the South Korean government troops. The President's decision received support from the legislature and the press.

Ambassador Muccio sent his aide Ernest Drumright to Taejon to meet President Rhee there and convey the report that President Truman had ordered the U.S. air Force and navy to help Korea below the 38th Parallel. Rhee received a similar message from MacArthur, telling the president, "Please be reassured."

Encouraged by the U.S. decision, Rhee told his people over the Taejon Radio, "Now that America has decided to fight for us by dispatching air and naval forces, please have a little more forbearance and be reassured that the enemy will be repelled." The people heard Rhee's voice for the first time since the outbreak of the war.

On the morning of June 27, four U.S. fighter planes, escorting transport planes evacuating American citizens, were attacked by North Korean YAKs. In the first aerial combat over the Korean sky, three enemy planes were shot down first and four more a few hours later.

On June 29, MacArthur, accompanied by 13 officers and 20 enlisted men, arrived at Suwon airstrip to inspect the war situation. Soon after his takeoff from Tokyo, MacArthur was ordered by the Joint Chiefs of Staff to command all U.S. forces in Korea. He immediately set up the Advance Command (ADCOM) at Suwon Agriculture College, assigning it to assist South Korean armed forces.

Brigadier General John R. Church, who had been sent as chief of the war situation survey team from MacArthur's headquarters, told South Korean Army Chief of Staff Chae Byong-duk to move into the same building and assemble all available troops to defend the Han River. Chae deployed about 1,000 officers and 8,000 men along the southern bank of the Han River.

South Korean troops who had trudged to the south of the Han River within one week after the fall of Seoul numbered 22,000. The 6th and 8th Divisions which had been fighting at the eastern and central fronts, broke out of the Uijongbu area where the Communist attacks were concentrated and reached south of the Han with their men and equipment almost intact. Thus, 54,000 men — 40,000 less than the number at the start of the war — were accounted for. KMAG estimated that 44,000 men were killed, captured or missing.

After his inspection tour of the Han River front, MacArthur concluded that air and naval support alone were insufficient to stop the onrushing enemy forces. He was determined to throw in American ground troops. Upon his return to Tokyo, MacArthur reported his findings to Washington, requesting full-scale support for South Korea.

President Truman, after discussions with the Defense Department on MacArthur's request, decided at midnight on June 30 to dispatch two U.S. infantry divisions stationed in Japan to Korea and intensify the naval blockade of North Korean waters. MacArthur, who had been approved use of ground troops, decided to send the 24th Division stationed in southern Japan. While the dispatch of ground forces was in progress, U.S. Air Force planes flying from Japan bases raided North Korean military facilities daily. Furthermore, U.S. warships engaged the North Korean naval forces, destroying many torpedo boats and other vessels transporting Communist troops to Chumunjin, a fishing port on the east coast.

The U.S. decision to participate in the war dealt a heavy blow to the Pyongyang regime and its guardian, the Soviet Union. They had thought that America would not fight in the remote Far East. Their erroneous view was due to the fact that (1) South Korea was placed outside of the U.S. defense line of the Aleutians-Japan-Okinawa-the Philippines and (2) the U.S. occupation forces stationed in the South since the end of World War II had been pulled out leaving only about 500 KMAG personnel.

U.N. Resolution

Receiving the news of the North Korean invasion by telephone from the U.S. State Department, Secretary-General of the United Nations Trygve Lie was stunned: "This is war against the United Nations!" At the request of the American government, Lie convened an emergency meeting of the Security Council at 2 a.m. June 25, New York time (3 a.m. June 26 in Korea). To the Norwegian statesman, the North Korean attack was "clear-cut aggression apparently well-calculated, meticulously planned, and with all the elements of surprise which reminded me of the Nazi invasion of Norway." [3]

Taking advantage of the Soviet's absence from the U.N., Lie and the Western powers passed a resolution stating that the armed assault upon the Republic of Korea constituted a breach of the peace. The resolution called for:

1. An immediate cessation of hostilities,

2. The authorities of North Korea to withdraw their forces back to the 38th Parallel, and

3. All member nations to render every assistance to the United Nations in the execution of this resolution and to refrain from giving assistance to the North Korean regime.

Voting for the resolution were Nationalist China, Cuba, Ecuador, Egypt, France, India, Norway, the United Kingdom, and the United States. At that time both Cuba and Egypt, untroubled by revolution, were in the Western bloc.

The Soviet Union was not in attendance. Since January 10, 1950, the Soviet delegate had been boycotting Council meetings over the issue of seating Communist China.

On the fourth day of the invasion, in a resolution momentous in the history of the world, the Council declared:

"[The Security Council] recommends that the members of the United Nations furnish such assistance to the Republic of Korea as may be necessary to repel the armed attack and restore international peace and security in the area."

For the first time, a world organization of states had taken up arms to oppose aggression and keep the peace. The Soviet Union was again absent, as it was on July 7 when the Council authorized a unified United Nations command for Korea and asked the United States to appoint a commander for it. In accord with this resolution, the U.S. government named General MacArthur as commander in chief of the United Nations Forces in Korea.

The United Nations was now at war against the Communist aggressors, committed to protecting the Republic of Korea which the U.N. had brought into being in August 1948, and already asking member nations to contribute arms, money or medical aid to the task.

U.S. Army Enters War

The men of the North Korean 3rd and 4th Divisions, upon completion of their occupation of Seoul, crossed the Han River, wading or swimming or paddling across in wooden boats, and captured the industrial suburb of Yongdungpo and Kimpo Airport on July 1.

Finally on July 3, T–34 enemy tanks began rumbling over a repaired railway bridge across the Han. The 4th Division, the 105th Armored Brigade, and the 107th Tank Regiment were rushing south through the course of Seoul-Yongdungpo-Suwon-Osan-Pyongtaek-Taegu-Pusan, topographically the best southward invasion route toward Pusan at the southern tip of the peninsula.

MacArthur, who had been authorized by President Truman to command all forces in Korea, designated the 24th Division stationed in Japan to go to Korea with Maj. Gen. William F. Dean as commander. The 1st Battalion, 21st Infantry Regiment, 24th Infantry Division, commanded by Lieutenant Colonel Charles Bradford Smith was ordered to proceed to Korea first. Smith was to lead the first American combat troops — 406 infantrymen and 134 artillerymen — into Korea as Task Force Smith.

On July 5, Task Force Smith opened the first U.S. battle against a North Korean tank unit at Osan, 7 miles south of Suwon. By about 7:30 a.m. Colonel Smith clearly saw through a telescope from Jukmiryong Ridge a tank column grinding toward his ridge. When the tanks were about one mile ahead, gunners of the 52nd Field Artillery Battalion loaded shells into the stubby 105 howitzers and set their sights. At the order of Lieutenant Colonel Miller O. Perry, commanding the 52nd Field, all guns belched flames in a barking chorus.

The enemy T–34 tanks advanced arrogantly, seeming unconcerned by the exploding shells about them.

The troops dug in along the ridge could count 33 tanks strung out on the road. At 700 yards, 75–mm recoiling rifles and 2.36 rocket launchers slammed into the tanks. But the tanks were still pouring down the hillside road, shells bouncing off their sides like rubber balls.

By about 9 a.m. on the rainy day, the North Korean tanks had passed over the Jukmiryong pass. Soon a column of the 16th and 18th regiments of the North Korean 4th Division, the conquerors of Seoul, closed in on the ridge. At 2:30 p.m. Smith gave the order to withdraw, and Task Force Smith, sandwiched between the enemy tank unit and infantry column, began to fall apart as a military unit.

The young Americans, who had lived an easy life in defeated Japan with little combat training, were no match for the enemy tanks pouring down the road where there was not a single antitank mine.

Approximately 150 men were killed, wounded or reported missing from Task Force Smith on that first day of American ground action in Korea. The efforts of the South Korean Capital Division and the 1st Division, which were defending the Pyongtaek-Ansong front to support Task Force Smith, also were in vain.

Pyongtaek Falls

Following up its victory at Jukmiryong Ridge, the North Korean main force struck south at a stretch, breaking through Pyongtaek on July 6.

Meanwhile, the men of the U.S. 24th Division who had landed in Pusan were shipped north by train and deployed north of Taejon. Major General William F. Dean commanding the division had arrived in Korea on July 3 and set up his headquarters at the South Korean Army Headquarters building in Taejon. Dean's 24th Division defending the Kum River-Taejon front and the South Korean troops defending the Bowun-Munkyong-Tanyang-Yongju front were the first joint operations between American and South Korean forces.

The South Korean Army which had been suffering successive defeats achieved the best triumph in the war by annihilating a North Korean regiment in the afternoon of July 6. The 2nd Battalion of the 7th Regiment under the 2nd Army commanded by Major General Kim Hong-il completely vanquished the North Korean 48th Regiment, 15th Division, led by Major General Park Sung-chol (later, vice president of the Pyongyang regime) while billeted in the Dongnak Primary School grounds in Munak-ni, Chungchong-pukdo.

In the surprise attack, 2,943 enemy troops were killed and 188 captured, with the seizure of 24 field guns, 31 mortars, 7 armored vehicles, 62 heavy and light machine guns, 65 trucks and 197 rifles.

One of the captives was a major, an ordnance staff officer of the ill-fated 48th Regiment. The man, whose name was withheld for security reasons, was questioned by newly appointed South Korean Army Chief of Staff Major General Chung Il-kwon:

"How did your regiment find the billeting place?"

"We were decoyed by the villagers."

"What do you mean?"

"When we reached the village we asked the villagers where the South Korean troops were. They said all of them had fled by cars the previous night."

"That's why you people took it easy. Is that right?"

The Communist major did not answer.

On July 7 Major General Dean, shocked by the collapse of the Pyongtaek-Ansong line, ordered Major John J. Dunn, operations officer of the 34th Infantry, to defend Chonan south of Pyongtaek at any cost.

Chonan was a transportation hub, from which good roads ran west and south. When Pyongtaek was abandoned, General Dean's left flank had been exposed and with the capture of Chonan, the North Koreans had entered into most of western and southern Korea. As Chonan fell to the enemy hands on July 8, Dean was forced now to try to defend along the Kum River, which was the first large river south of the Han. It was a natural defense line, a great watery moat encircling the important city of Taejon.

Taejon was the last militarily important center in South Korea, with the exception of Taegu and Pusan behind the Naktong River, far to the southwest. If Taejon fell, there was no real defense line short of the Naktong River. General Dean therefore was determined to make every effort for the defense of Taejon. Because Taejon constituted the most important transportation center leading to Pusan in the southern tip, he wanted to do his utmost to hold the Kum by delaying the enemy advance until the arrival of reinforcements from the Eighth Army under the command of Lieutenant General Walton H. Walker.

For that purpose he had deployed Colonel Dick Stephens' 21st Regiment at Chochiwon, a strategic point for the defense of the Kum which was targeted by the enemy. The North Korean 3rd and 4th Divisions had attempted to attack the Kum, but their advance was delayed by the massive air assaults of the U.S. Air Force, destroying 38 tanks and 100 trucks. Yet the 21st Regiment was forced to abandon Chochiwon, and crossed south of the Kum on July 12, taking up a new blocking position on the south shore.

The 24th Division was in poor shape. The 21st Regiment had come apart at Osan and Chochiwon; the 34th Regiment had been shattered successively at Pyongtaek and Chonan; the 19th Regiment had retreated south of the Kum. Not only were the regiments weak in men and equipment, they were exhausted and their morale was low. The 24th Division lost roughly 30 percent of its 12,200 men as well as enough gear to equip a full-strength division.

With that the 21st Regiment retreated across the Kum River and Chochiwon was lost, thus becoming the fourth straight victory of the onrushing North Korean 3rd and 4th divisions.

General MacArthur was compelled to send the 29th Regiment from Okinawa to Korea, as well as to instruct the Far East Air Force under Lieutenant General George Stratemeyer to use B–26 and B–29 bombers against the North Korean thrust down the central mountains.

Elements of the U.S. 25th Infantry Division had already begun to arrive in Korea as reinforcements in the collapsing central sector, while on the east the American Navy was placing more naval gunfire to assist the embattled South Korean divisions. On the east also, it had become increasingly important to hold the little fishing harbor of Pohang, about 60 miles northeast of Pusan. The U.S. 1st Cavalry Division was rushing to Pohang by sea.

The reality on July 13, the day of General Walker's arrival, was that a force of 76,000 men — 58,000 South Koreans and 18,000 Americans — had been thus far powerless to halt the North Korean rush. The battle situation as of that day was as follows:

On the far west, the North Korean 6th Division had fanned out below Pyongtaek and was battling a South Korean division and a force of police on a drive south aimed at Pusan's left flank. East of this, the North's 3rd and 4th Divisions continued to strike south along the road from Seoul through the U.S. 24th Division, and still farther east the Communist 2nd Division was advancing on Chongju against two battered South Korean divisions.

In the central mountains three enemy divisions were pushing back the remnants of two South Korean divisions. On the east coast the North Korean 5th Division was coming down the narrow road against a South Korean regiment.

Under these circumstances on July 13, Lieutenant General Walker's Eighth Army Headquarters moved from Japan to Taegu, setting up Eighth U.S. Army in Korea (EUSAK), and on July 17 both the South Korean Army and Eighth Army, as well as the United Nations troops which would subsequently be included in the latter, came under General Walker's command.

President Rhee summoned Defense Minister Shin Sung-mo and Army Chief of Staff Chung Il-kwon on July 9 to the residence of Kyongsang-pukdo Governor Cho Jae-chon, where he was staying temporarily, and told them about his decision to transfer command of the South Korean Army to U.N. command:

"I will revoke the transfer of the command of operations whenever deemed necessary. Keep this in your mind, and I hope you will overcome our national crisis in full cooperation with the American forces." Rhee reported the transfer in a letter to General MacArthur complying with an earlier agreement on the necessity of the unified command of the United Nations Forces.

On July 10, the Security Council of the United Nations directed the establishment of a unified Korean Command, and General MacArthur was officially named Commander in Chief for the U.N. Forces. On July 17, the blue-and-white U.N. flag was hoisted in a ceremony in Taegu. The flag had been brought to Taegu by a representative of U.N. Secretary-General Trygve Lie after its delivery to MacArthur in Tokyo by General L. Lawton Collins, U.S. Army chief of staff.

On July 18, General Walker flew into Taejon. He had been assembling a great deal of data on the Korean situation, and was becoming nervous over the 24th Division's frustrating situation.

During the night of July 19 the North Koreans, who had already crossed the Kum, moved their tanks up, and at 3 a.m. on July 20 they struck hard with infantry and armor, coming down both sides of the highway and quickly turning the American right flank. The 1st Battalion, 34th Regiment, was driven into the hills in disorder. On the west, the 2nd Battalion, 19th Regiment was also sent reeling back. At daybreak, the enemy T–34 tanks rolled into Taejon.

Dean awoke to heavy gunfire as the ragged defense line drawn around Taejon continued to shrink. He realized that his hope that help might arrive if he held two more days was fading.

Meanwhile, hundreds of North Korean soldiers, disguised in white Korean robes, infiltrated into the city. Once inside, they threw off their civilian attire and opened fire on American and South Korean troops. Soon snipers were everywhere.

By nightfall the city was completely encircled and much of it was in North Korean hands. General Dean had not left the city despite strong advice from his aides to leave. He had even attempted to destroy an enemy tank with a bazooka. When the long day drew to an end, Dean knew it was time to pull out of the city.

Dean's jeep dashed around stalled and flaming trucks, while the heat seared him and the men with him. The jeep however made the wrong turn and he was reported as missing for over one year.

Thus ended the 24th Division's 15-day ordeal that began when Task Force Smith went up Jukmiryong Ridge to intercept the enemy at Osan. During the following two days the shattered division regrouped at Yongdong, and on July 22 it turned its Yongdong positions over to the 1st Cavalry Division and went into reserve. At the same time, General Walker ordered Brigadier General John H. Church to assume command of the 24th Division in the absence of General Dean.

General Dean's Capture

Dean's whereabouts were unknown for more than one year and it was generally believed he might be dead. As a war correspondent of the Associated Press, I tried my best to find out the fate of the general. As a result, I learned from South Korean national police and Justice Ministry sources that Dean was betrayed by a pair of South Korean civilians who led him to a North Korean Communist trap.

On September 21, 1951, I wrote the following exclusive story:

> Major General William F. Dean, who had been reported as missing since last July, was led to a North Korean Communist trap by a pair of South Koreans while the general was straggling in the mountains near Chinan, 57 km (35 miles) south of Taejon, according to South Korean national police and justice ministry sources.
>
> The police said the two, identified as Han Doo-kyoo and Choe Chong-bong, had received a monetary award of 30,000 won ($5) each from the Reds for "enabling them to capture General Dean." But the two villagers insisted they had only intended to help the American general.
>
> The police said the two men were under house arrest until General Dean returns to find out whom they had really helped — General Dean or the Communists.
>
> Police records showed: On the afternoon of August 26, 1950, a hollow-cheeked American soldier was wearily dragging along a country road near Sedong, a Korean hamlet of mud huts in the vicinity of Chinan. The soldier, all exhausted from more than one month of hiding in the nearby mountains, met a white-clad farmer, Han Doo-kyoo. The American soldier asked the jittery villager for food. The Korean showed willingness to help the foreigner and told him to

follow. While they were walking toward Chinan, two officials of the Communist self-defense guard discovered them and took the unfortunate American to the Sangchun Communist police box. After spending one night in the police jail, the foreigner was moved to the Communist prison in Chonju.

After severe interrogations and cross-examinations through an interpreter, a former South Korean official, the American soldier was identified as Major General William F. Dean, commander of the U.S. 24th Division.

Lee Byung-ho, inspection chief and prosecutor of the Korean Ministry of Justice, told a dramatic story of how General Dean answered the interrogating Communists through an interpreter, Park Hwan-sang, a close friend of Lee. The Justice Ministry official himself was in the Communist prison where Dean was cross-examined in the same prison compound.

Lee, who had miraculously escaped a Communist massacre of 1,500 South Korean prisoners in Chonju prison in September 1950, told Associated Press the following story he had heard from the interpreter about Dean.

"General Dean spent only one night in prison before he was clearly identified. After the general told the Reds his name and rank, the Reds gave him humane treatment. They put him in a private quarters of the Communist prison commandant until taken to Seoul through Taejon several days later.

"Dean did not give any military information to the interrogating Reds, pointing out, 'All I need to tell you is my name and rank which you should report to the International Red Cross in Geneva.'"

My report on General Dean's capture was confirmed on December 23, 1951 when Wilfred Burchett, a Communist correspondent for the Paris paper *Ce Soir* working in North Korea, showed up in Panmujon and told U.N. war correspondents that he had interviewed General Dean two days earlier at an underground shelter of a North Korean prisoner-of-war camp.

According to Burchett, General Dean, while a fugitive behind Communist lines, had a revolver and 12 bullets. Eleven of those bullets were for the Reds. Dean was saving the last one for himself. Dean was finally taken captive because a Korean enticed him into a trap.

"I was absolutely determined never to become a prisoner of war," Dean told Burchett as they sat on the floor of a two-room underground shelter. Dean's hair was cut crew fashion, Burchett said, and he was wearing a pin striped civilian suit with the army shirt. He said, "Dean emphasized that he was receiving excellent treatment. He had written a letter of thanks to General Kim Il Sung." This remark of the Communist newsman was contrary to what Dean said in his memoirs written after his return to freedom on September 4, 1953 through Panmunjom.

I had an exclusive interview, on September 18, 1953, with the two South Korean civilians who had led General Dean to Communist captivity at the Central Police Station of Seoul where the two men were detained. As I had already reported their betrayal on September 21, 1951, the two were Han Doo-kyoo, 40, and Choe Chang-bang, 24, residents of Chinan, 35 miles south of Taejon.

Han said that he had accepted 30,000 won ($5) from the Reds for his part in the capture of Dean. He added that he returned the money to a Communist organization.

Han and Choe were arrested by South Korean national police two days after Dean was released. Police charged Han and Choe of leading Dean into an enemy trap after promising to help him return to allied lines.

Asked if he was the first Korean Dean met in the Chinan area, Han said "yes." "When was it?" I asked. Without hesitation Han said "August 25, 1950." Asked what the General said at that time, Han said, "I could not understand the few words he said."

Han claimed he had intended to lead Dean to a hotel. But, he said, a group of Communist home guards caught the General on the way.

Police said Choe had also accepted 30,000 won from the Reds, but he kept mum during the interview.

Dean's 'Judas' Says Reds Gave Him $5

2d 'Betrayer' Won't Talk

By BILL SHINN

SEOUL, Sept. 18 (AP). — A slightly built, 40-year-old South Korean said Friday he accepted $5 from the North Korean Communists in August, 1950, as payment for helping the Reds capture Maj. Gen. William F. Dean.

The Korean, Han Doo Kyoo, is one of two residents of Chinan, south of Taejon, held here on charges of betraying Dean.

HAN TOLD THE AP in an interview he accepted 30,000 won ($5) from the Reds for his part in the capture of Dean. He added that he "returned" the $5 to a Communist organization.

Dean, former commander of the U. S. 24th Division, was released two weeks ago at Panmunjom after more than three years as a captive. He has been under treatment at Tokyo Army Hospital for dysentery and is scheduled to depart for the United States Monday.

Han and Choe Chong Bong, 24, were arrested by South Korean National police two days after Dean was released.

* * *

I TALKED WITH them today outside the jail room of the Seoul

Shown after arrest in Seoul are South Koreans Han Doo Kyoo (left) and Choe Chong Bong, charged with leading Maj. Gen. William Dean into Red trap. Kyoo said he received $5 reward.

(AP RADIOphoto)

rean Dean met in the Chinan area, Han said, "yes."

"When was it?" I asked.

Without hesitation Han said "Aug. 25, 1950."

Asked what the General said at that time, Han said, "He did not say much. I could not under-

A newspaper clip of the author's exclusive interview on September 18, 1953, with the two South Korean civilians who led Major General William F. Dean, commander of the U.S. 24th Division, to Communist captivity after the fall of Taejon on July 20, 1950.

President Syngman Rhee presents General William F. Dean (center) the Order of Military Merit with Goldstar upon his return from a North Korean POW camp in September 1953, in Kyongmudae at a ceremony attended by U.N. commander General Mark Clark.

Dean wrote in his memoirs that while he was wandering for 36 days in the mountains, trying to elude capture, he was betrayed by a pair of South Korean civilians who led him to a North Korean Communist trap while pretending to guide him to safety.

While Dean was still missing, the American government awarded him the Medal of Honor in recognition of his devoted military services in Taejon. Upon his return to freedom in September 1953, Dean was conferred with the Order of Military Merit with Goldstar Taeguk by President Syngman Rhee. In a ceremony at Kyongmudae, which was attended by General Mark Clark, U.N. commander, Rhee said, "All Korean people join me in welcoming you home....We rejoice in your safe return. Thanks to such a great general as you, the American Army is reputed as the strongest in the world."

North Koreans Moving Toward Pusan

In 17 days of combat, the 24th Division had lost more than 30 percent of its personnel, including a high portion of senior officers. More than 2,400 men were reported as missing in action.

Other divisions from Japan, the 25th Infantry, the 1st Cavalry, and the 7th Infantry, displayed almost the same weakness of the 24th in action. Their men were not adequately equipped, trained, or mentally prepared for combat. By July 22, however, the North Korean Army and U.N. forces were almost on a par in men, with only a slight superiority on the North Korean side.

On this day, the 1st Cavalry (Infantry) Division entered combat at Yongdong east of Taejon, while the 25th Infantry Division moved into line in the Sangju area to the southeast.

Ten divisions of the North Korean Army, tightly deployed from the west coast to the east coast, were continuing their desperate advance toward Pusan. The 6th Division on the western front moved south through a west coast route avoiding the central course fighting. Their strategy was to attack Pusan at a stretch battling the scattered South Korean troops and police forces.

The 6th Division was threatening to break through the American lines, bypassing Chinju 50 miles west of Pusan and nearby Masan after seizing Kunsan, Mokpo and Yosu ports. Meanwhile the 4th

Division, which had occupied Taejon, assembled at Kochang passing Kunsan and Muju, thus preparing to strike the left flank of the American line to seize the main battle ground.

The mission of the Communist 5th Division was to march south on the east coast route. The 5th, whose passage was barred by the rugged Taebaek Mountains, kept on its independent combat, engaging with only a South Korean regimental force. But its advance was thwarted by the U.N. naval bombardment and land slides caused by heavy rainfalls. While the Americans were engaged in delaying action to stall the approach of enemy troops toward the Kum River, the South Korean 3rd Division with reinforcements recaptured Yongdok at the end of July.

However, the war front kept moving south. The Communist 6th Division in the western front advanced to Tongyung through Mokpo, Posong, and Yosu.

The two battalions of the U.S. 29th Infantry Regiment were ordered to proceed to Chinju to confront an enemy unit of the 6th Division headed by T-34 tanks. But the reinforcements were raw recruits newly arrived from Okinawa, where they had been briefly trained. Without time to zero in and testfire their weapons, they were expected to stop the onrushing enemy. On the night of July 25, their commander, Lieutenant Colonel Harold W. Mott, was ordered to occupy the town of Hadong with one of his two battalions.

The 3rd Battalion, 29th Infantry, went to Hadong guided by Major General Chae Byong-duk, who had been South Korean Army chief of staff during the Seoul disaster. Chae talked to the American officers about the deteriorating situation, and wanted to join the Americans with a few of his soldiers. The Americans agreed to let him serve as an assistant to Mott.

When Colonel Mott's unit entered combat to capture Hadong on July 26, Chae saw a group of soldiers approaching their defensive position on Hill 108. Many of these men seemed to be in American uniform, though some wore North Korean troops' mustard brown. Chae stepped forward and asked their identity. The group opened fire, and Chae was struck in the head and killed. Colonel Mott's 3rd Battalion had gone into a savage battle with some 757 men, and fell back to Chinju in disaster.

Leaving more than 300 dead behind, the remnants of the battalion reached Chinju. Many men retained only their boots and shorts by the time they reached safety.

Shortly afterward, the battalion was reorganized, and its companies sent to fill the gap in the 19th Infantry, 24th Division.

By July 31, the North Korean 6th Division occupied Chinju. Meanwhile, the Communist 4th Division moving down from Taejon to Kunsan cut inside the inner arc to capture Kochang 35 miles north of Chinju.

AP Correspondent Killed

On July 30, William R. Moore of the Associated Press was killed at Chinju-Masan front while helping a wounded American soldier. Of the 18 U.N. war correspondents who died during the Korean War, Moore's death was the most heart-rending to me; I became an AP correspondent thanks to Moore's recommendation to the AP head office in New York. When Moore was leaving for the southwest front from Taejon on June 20, I cautioned him, "Don't do anything too risky, Bill." That happened to be my last word to Bill Moore. He was a kind-hearted good journalist.

He had joined the AP in Denver in 1937 and served as an Army major in World War II. After Japan's defeat, his unit was sent to Korea for occupation duty.

In April 1948, Moore was assigned to Korea by the AP as its correspondent. He had returned to Seoul after a brief assignment to Hong Kong in June 1950. Within days after the North Korean invasion, Moore was covering the story and filing whenever possible from the temporary facilities that the U.S. Army set up along the route of retreat before the onrushing North Koreans. On July 30 he was at the Chinju battlefront and was seen with an American tank unit. The following day he was listed as "missing in action."

It was not until late October that Cpl. Carl M. Anderson reported how the AP war correspondent had died. Anderson had escaped from captivity during the U.N. drive into North Korea. Moore had accompanied his patrol, recalled Anderson. He explained: "We had come four miles toward Masan, out of Chinju, when we were stopped by a blown-up bridge. We could not get our tanks across. We had some wounded, including our lieutenant. But Bill Moore helped carry the litter holding the lieutenant. We made our way under the demolished bridge and stayed there....There were eight of us left, and Bill made nine, not counting three or four Koreans who jumped on the back of our tank. I don't know what became of the Koreans. Bill was killed between 2 p.m. and 4:30 p.m. by mortar, small arms and grenade fire. I saw his body lying in a pool of water. We found Koreans all right, but they were North Koreans, and they took us prisoner." [4]

Moore said in his last report from Chinju on July 26 that Communist ambush snipings had increased so much behind the U.N. line that "people cannot sleep at ease."

War Correspondents Rolling In

With the fall of Taejon on July 20, the South Korean government and U.S. and South Korean Army headquarters moved from Taejon to Taegu. War correspondents, who had been using a room at an old government building in Taejon, also moved to a primary school building in Taegu.

During the first two days of the North Korean invasion, the war situation was reported to the world by the few corespondents working for major news agencies such as the AP, UP, and INS (International News Service). On the evening of June 27, four American correspondents — Keyes Beech of *The Chicago Daily News,* Marguerite Higgins of *The New York Herald Tribune,* Burton Crane of *The New York Times,* and Frank Gibney of *TIME* — flew into Seoul from Tokyo on a courier plane.

In one memorable scene, the three male correspondents (Beech, Crane, and Gibney) got into one jeep, while Miss Higgins chose to ride with KMAG officers. After a short visit to the KMAG headquarters, they were fleeing smoldering Seoul across the Han bridge. When their jeep, driven by Crane, reached about midpoint of the bridge, the sky was suddenly illuminated by a huge flame and the bridge was blown up in front of the trio. Their jeep was thrown into the air. Gibney's glasses were shattered and Crane's face was bloodied. The three returned to Seoul and crossed the Han later by paddling a raft, and Higgins joined them finally in Suwon.

By early August, 270 correspondents from 19 countries were reporting the war. The front-line correspondents wrote the usual "I-was-there" copy. I especially remember the examples of Marguerite Higgins and Homer Bigart of *The New York Herald Tribune*. They often took chances at the front and competed with each other to get their by-line stories on the newspaper's front page. Higgins, an attractive, ambitious woman, once said that she did not want to marry "until I find a man who's as exciting as war."

DEFENSE OF PUSAN PERIMETER

"Stand or Die"

The war situation grew more aggravated with the frantic last-ditch drive of the North Korean forces toward Pusan, their ultimate goal. General Walker visited the 25th Division on July 26 and issued a warning order to its commanders: "There will be no more retreating, withdrawal, or readjustment of the lines, or anything else you want to call it." Correspondents had taken this as an order of "stand or die."

But on August 1, Walker commanded an orderly withdrawal across the Naktong to establish the last natural defense barrier to the port of Pusan. Walker had concluded that the U.N. forces under his command could only hold a line generally following the Naktong River from its mouth west of Pusan and stretching north to a point west of Andong, then turning east to Yongdok on the east coast. This line would eventually become famous as the Pusan Perimeter.

All U.S. and South Korean troops, except for a battalion of the U.S. 8th Cavalry remaining at Waegwan acting as a rear guard, streamed back across the Naktong by the evening of August 3. The battalion remaining on the west side of the river was preparing to come across so that the bridge could be dynamited.

But thousands of Korean refugees were pressing upon these men, clamoring to cross the bridge ahead of them. To make the problem worse, North Korean soldiers and agents disguised in civilian clothes with hidden weapons, tried to cross together with the civilian refugees. Warning cries that the bridge would be blown up did no good.

Now it was growing dark, and the enemy troops were closing. As the rear guard had crossed to the east side of the river, with the mass of Koreans close behind them, the bridge was blown up. Several hundred Koreans fell to the river with the crumbling bridge.

Unbroken Defense Line

Now that all forces had moved to the east of the Naktong, the U.N. forces could for the first time form an unbroken defense line. Behind the Naktong the U.N. forces held a rectangular terrain ranging 100 miles from north to south and 50 miles across. On the west was the Naktong barrier, and across the north rose high and rugged mountains, difficult for the enemy to penetrate.

By the time General Walker consolidated the Pusan Perimeter in early August, 70,000 South Korean troops had been killed, wounded, or were missing and American losses amounted to 6,000 men. The Koreans were widely acclaimed for their valiant fighting against the heavily armed and well-prepared enemy. Although the U.S. Army had initially estimated the enemy casualties at about 30,000, the actual figure was close to 60,000. And most of the slaughter was attributed to the desperate fighting of the South Koreans. On August 5, the enemy troops at the Naktong line were at half strength; the total combat strength of the reorganized eleven divisions, including raw recruits of South Korean inductees, were less than 70,000.

Meanwhile, by August 5 the U.N. forces — still exclusively Americans and South Koreans — stood at 141,000, of which some 47,000 were Americans. By August 19 there were 500 American tanks within the Perimeter, outnumbering the enemy armor by more than five to one.

On the other hand, the North Korean logistic problem was increasing. The enemy's long lines of supplies were attacked day and night by the planes of the U.S. 5th Air Force, by Navy and

Marine planes flying off the carriers, and by the guns of the U.S. and British warships patrolling the east coast.

The North Koreans forcibly conscripted South Korean youth to make up for the shortage of men. These untrained raw recruits were hardly soldiers, but they were under the command of sergeants and officers who were diehard veterans of the Communist Chinese 8th Route Army or the Soviet Army. Men who failed to obey were ruthlessly shot.

For the defense of the Pusan Perimeter, the U.N. command had South Korean 3rd, Capital, 8th, 6th, and 1st divisions along with the U.S. 1st Cavalry, 24th and 25th divisions plus the 5th Infantry Regiment from Hawaii. The reorganized five South Korean divisions were defending the northern half of the Pusan defense line between Waegwan, west of Taegu, and Yongdok on the east coast while the U.S. Eighth Army was charged with the defense of its southern half connecting Waegwan and Masan through Changyong.

The North Korean Army also reinforced its strength to eleven divisions and concentrated all forces on the Naktong line to achieve the final goal of driving "American imperialists and Syngman Rhee puppets" to the Korean Strait by August 15 as Kim Il Sung had exhorted. But the number of soldiers was no more important. While the enemy was faced with increasing logistic problem, the U.N. forces, now with numerical edge, held the other important advantage of having the interior line. The U.N. supply situation was now excellent, where it had once been miserable. Besides the steady reinforcements of fighting forces, military supplies continued to flow into Pusan across the Pacific. Japanese factories also started producing war supplies. (By playing the role of a military supply base, Japan, whose industrial production was just a fraction of pre-World War II levels, established a firm base for its rapid economic growth and ultimately became an economic superpower.)

Under these circumstances, General Walker, who now had an unbroken defense line, resolved to take offensive action for the first time. He ordered Major General William B. Kean, commander of the 25th Division, to form a task force to recapture Chinju. General Kean organized Task Force Kean with the 35th Regiment of his own 25th Division, the 5th Marine Regiment, and the 5th Regimental Combat Team (RCT). He sent his men southwest of Masan to strike the 6th North Korean Division, which had reorganized and was driving west again for a fresh assault on Masan.

The counterattack began on August 7. Led by the 5th Marine Regiment, Task Force Kean took the road from Chindong-ni to Chinju on the same day and drove rapidly into enemy territory. After a week of fierce combat, suffering the loss of most of an artillery battalion, Task Force Kean recaptured Chinju. But the violent, close-in battles over the Chinju Hill, called "Combat Hill," hit an impasse. Kean's unit was unable to capture the hill due to its ineffectual fighting and was forced to retreat.

On August 11, a North Korean regiment and two divisions nearly wrested the vital eastern corridor to Taegu out of U.N. control. Earlier, the enemy had forced the South Koreans out of Yongdok and then cut their 3rd Division off by roadblocks erected below Yongdok and above Pohang. They struck into Pusan on August 11. The U.S. Air Force squadron which had earlier evacuated Yongil returned to help the Americans and South Koreans back, thus South Korea's 3rd Division was taken out of the trap.

Now that the U.N. forces had a gapless defense line, the enemy could not employ encircling tactics by penetrating behind the U.N. units. Since the southern and eastern sides faced the sea and was defended by the American Navy, the enemy could no longer continue its swift and daring advance as before, and was forced to attempt frontal attacks only.

General Walker shifted combat units frequently in order to meet an emergency, and he himself, with a pistol on his side and a shotgun hung on his shoulder, was inspecting front-line troops at will on a jeep or in a light liaison aircraft.

Battle for the Naktong

In front of almost three-quarters of the Pusan Perimeter wound the Naktong River flowing south, averaging one-quarter mile in width and six feet in depth. Behind the river to the east, mountains rise to 2,500 feet and on its north, across the top of the Perimeter, they reach more than 3,000 feet.

There were four natural attack routes into the Perimeter. One was on the south through the port of Masan; another through the so-called Naktong Bulge to the important rail and road network at Miryang. A possible corridor of advance ran through the roads and rails to Taegu. Finally, on the far northeast, a valley ran down the seacoast through Kyongju.

In August, there were bitter battles almost all along the Perimeter. The most dangerous threats against the Perimeter developed when the North Koreans launched all-out attacks, typical of the whole bitter, desperate month. The point of attack was the Naktong Bulge or bend, where the river makes a big curve around an area about seven miles long, north-south, four miles wide, west-east. The Naktong Bulge is a mesa bound by the Naktong on three sides with three large lakes to the east, behind which there is the small town of Yongsan.

In the dead of night August 5, the 16th Regiment of the North Korean 4th Division crossed the ford of the Naktong led by red and yellow flares bursting over the river. About 800 Communist troops, many of them naked with their clothing bundled high on their heads, crossed the river swimming or on rafts. Upon reaching the east side of the river, they sneaked up to the U.N. defense strongholds and struck into the American units. Another crossing attempt above them was beaten back with heavy casualties by the 34th Infantry. The assaulted 24th Division, which had been at less than 40 percent efficiency in low morale, lost two hills near Yongsan in two days. From these hills, the strategic city of Miryang could be seen. If Miryang fell, the defense of Pusan Perimeter would be difficult.

Furthermore, the enemy brought heavy equipment across the river using an underwater bridge near the Naktong ferry and fired in salvo. The 24th and 2nd Divisions desperately resisted but the Naktong Bulge was on the verge of collapse. To overcome this critical situation, General Walker committed the 5,000 men of the 5th Marine Regiment whom General MacArthur had reserved for future amphibious operations.

After vicious battles for ten days, the North Korean 4th Division was cornered, losing an untold number of men of its three regiments with 1,500 men each. The enemy had forced the conscripted South Korean farmers to fight, but the untrained raw recruits were of no use. While many of them escaped at any chance, others were coerced to dig trenches or carry ammunition.

The U.N. forces, reinforced with the 5th Marine Regiment moved from Pusan, launched fierce attacks on the enemy. The North Korean 18th Regiment fled leaving more than 1,000 dead behind, and by afternoon, August 18, the 4th Division had retreated from the east side of the Naktong. Thus the first round of fighting at Naktong Bulge ended in victory for the U.N. forces.

The men of the North Korean 4th Division who had fled across the Naktong were less than 3,000 and the more than 1,200 corpses left behind were buried by the U.N. troops. If the 4th Division had been successful, Taegu would have been isolated, forcing the Pusan Perimeter to shrink to slaughter-pen proportions.

The 4th Division, which had taken Seoul with the 3rd, was the best in the North Korean Army. It was given the honorary title "the Seoul Division." Its commander, Major General Lee Kwon-mu, had marched with the Communist Chinese 8th Route Army and served as a lieutenant in the Soviet Army. By August, he had won North Korea's highest military honor: Order of the National Flag, First Class. After the August 18 defeat, Lee replenished the 4th Division, which was to attack from the west below Taegu while the over-whelming bulk of invading force struck from the north and north-west.

While the fighting for Naktong Bulge was threatening the existence of the Pusan Perimeter, the U.S. Eighth Army had serious troubles elsewhere. The southern front of the 1st Cavalry Division defending Taegu had leaks sprung by the enemy, and the eastern defense line of the South Korean divisions in the Kigye-Pohang area was near collapse. The enemy 12th Division driving down the east coast had crossed the rugged mountains and surrounded the South Korean 3rd Division, threatening the Yongil air base. Despite MacArthur's opposition, the U.S. 5th Air Force decided to abandon the air field and withdrew two F–51 squadrons to a Kyushu air base in Japan on August 11.

On August 16–17, the South Korean 3rd Division fought its way south under the cover of U.S. Air Force and Navy, and was able to halt the enemy advance which had briefly occupied Pohang-dong. Men of the Communist 12th Division could not but retreat north because they had left heavy equipment behind when they crossed the steep mountains and they were suffering from hunger.

Defending a line following the Naktong's east bank were the 1st Cavalry Division, the 27th Infantry and the South Korean 1st and 6th Divisions. Opposing them were the North Korean 1st, 3rd, 10th, 13th and 15th Divisions, with tanks of the 105th Armored Brigade.

On August 17, the 5th Regiment of the 1st Cavalry Division retook Hill 303 near Waegwan and found 26 American soldiers who had been captured and murdered by the enemy. These men of the Heavy Weapons Company lay shoulder to shoulder, their feet bloodied and bare, and their hands tied behind the back with ropes or telephone wire. They had been sprayed with burp-gun bullets.

As the battle increased in intensity, worse atrocities were discovered. Some had been burned and castrated before they were shot, and bodies were bound with barbed wire around the hand and mouth. Alarmed by the continued atrocities on war prisoners, General MacArthur broadcast an announcement on August 20, warning Kim Il Sung of criminal accountability for these acts.

While all this was going on, elements of two enemy divisions were being held off, only 10 miles north of Taegu by the South Korean 1st Division led by Brigadier General Paik Sun-yup. His right flank was connected with the U.S. 1st Cavalry division, but the enemy was trying to drive a wedge between them. By nightfall of August 17, an attack on the left flank of the 1st Cavalry Division at Hill 303, together with General Paik's 1st Division, made the Taegu defense critical.

As the U.S. 24th Division and the 27th Regiment of the 5th Division were fighting to stop the enemy advance along the Naktong valley corridor running from Sangju to Taegu, Paik's 1st Division occupied its surrounding ridge, facilitating the American artillery fire. At the same time, the U.S. Far East Air Force planes from Japanese bases continued massive air strikes to support U.N. ground actions and kept bombing North Korean military bases and facilities.

South Korean Victory at Tabu-dong

The South Koreans won a rare victory in furious battles waged at Tabu-dong near Taegu for 20 days from August 4. Brigadier General Paik Sun-yup's 1st Division and the U.S. 1st Cavalry Division were defending the 30 miles front between Waegwan and Nakjong-ni. The North Koreans had assembled 20,000 men of four divisions in front of the South Korean 1st Division targeting Tabu-dong. Paik's division had only a little more than 7,000 men, and the enemy was superior three to one in manpower and two to one in firepower. The Communists had aimed at this weak point of the South Koreans.

On August 4, the North Koreans crossed the shallow water of the Naktong together with armored troops and launched a fierce attack on the South Koreans. On the 5th, the South Korean division retreated from the east bank of the river to Tabu-dong 14 miles north of Taegu, which had natural defensive advantage with high mountains around the town. Commander Yu Jae-hung of the 2nd Corps to which the 1st Division belonged had agreed to the retreat. In the furious fights, the South Korean units even formed suicide corps, waging surprise attacks on enemy tanks. The crucial Tabu-dong battles ended on August 23 with the final victory of the South Korean 1st Division after bloody fighting for 20 days.

At the request of South Korean Army Chief of Staff Chung Il-kwon, General Walker had sent Colonel John "Mike" Michaelis' 27th Infantry Wolfhounds to support the hard-pressed 1st Division. On August 14, the Wolfhounds came to back up the South Koreans with two artillery companies and an M–26 tank company. In the fierce fighting for the Naktong valley of Tabu-dong, the Wolfhounds played a prominent role, destroying 14 enemy tanks and killing more than 1,000 North Korean troops. Tabu-dong on the Sangju-Taegu road had become the avenue for repeated North Korean night attacks, and it was named the "Bowling Alley" for the whanging of the red-hot 85–mm shells fired from the enemy's T–34 tanks.

During the 20-day bloody battle for Tabu-dong, total enemy casualties were estimated at 10,000. The South Korean loss was also enormous; about 600 men had been newly recruited every day to supplement the fighting men at the front. [5]

On August 30, General Paik Sun-yup placed Tagu-dong under the control of the U.S. 1st Cavalry Division, and moved his division to Shinyong.

Another South Korean Victory

The South Koreans won another big victory in the crucial fighting for Yongchon northwest of Taegu. In the midnight of September 4, the North Korean 15th and 6th Divisions led by T–34 tanks waged a fierce attack from Changyang immediately north of Yongchon. The South Koreans committed the 6th and 8th Divisions under the command of Brigadier General Yu Jae-hung's 2nd Army.

The enemy attack was designed to break through Yongchon and Taegu to march down and capture Pusan. General Walker had confided to South Korean Army Chief of Staff Chung Il-kwon that the American troops would be withdrawn from Korea if Yongchon fell. The defense of Yongchon was therefore a matter of life and death to the Republic of Korea.

Before the dawn of September 9, the 2nd Battalion of the 19th Regiment, South Korea's 6th Division, waged a surprise attack on the enemy's 15th Division under the support of M–26 Pershing tanks sent from the U.S. Eighth Army. The enemy artillery regiment marching down to Kyongju was crushed in a tunnel by the 2nd Battalion of the South Korean 8th Division. By September 13, the Communist 15th Division was completely destroyed and the men of the 8th Division were repulsed in all directions.

In the bloody fighting, 3,799 enemy troops were killed, 309 captured, and many T–34 tanks and other equipment including 83 vehicles were destroyed. The booty included 14 artillery guns and 2,327 firearms of various kinds. [7] While the fierce fighting was going on, President Syngman Rhee, accompanied by Defense Minister Shin Sung-mo and Home Minister Cho Byong-ok, visited a command post of the South Korean 8th Division on the banks of the Kumho River at the front, and encouraged division commander Lee Song-ka and his men.

Meanwhile, on the early morning of August 18, sudden bomb explosions roared seven times in succession within the city of Taegu, seizing its 700,000 residents with panic. Of the 700,000 Taegu population, 400,000 were refugees from the Seoul area, who had remembered the bitter experiences of their desperate flight. When they struggled to flee Taegu, "pacification teams" and hundreds of police lined up on the outskirts of the city to persuade the restless crowds to return home.

The bombs which blasted Taegu Railroad Station were 120–mm mortar shells fired from the Kumho riverside in the suburbs of the city by elements of the 14th Regiment of the North Korean 1st Division. One civilian was killed in the blast, seven wounded, and yard facilities were partially destroyed.

Meanwhile, General Walker told Ambassador Muccio that MacArthur was concerned about President Rhee's safety in case of a sudden enemy breakthrough. Muccio, accompanied by First Secretary Harold Noble, called on Rhee and advised the president to move to Pusan. Rhee had often refused to retreat again, saying that he would rather fight in the streets with his loyal men. But the ambassador solemnly told the president that Taegu could fall at any moment. Both MacArthur and Walker urged the president to go south immediately. Rhee finally decided to move and evacuated to Pusan with his Cabinet on August 18. War correspondents, including myself, also moved to Pusan on the same day.

The U.N. command succeeded in defending the Pusan Perimeter by desperate counterattacks of the ground, naval and air forces, and Kim Il Sung's call for the Communization of all Korea by August 15 had been wrecked. The North Korean Communists had left the corpses of their best men scattered along the Naktong River, and the survivors were rapidly bleeding themselves to death against the U.N. guns on the broiling hills and the fetid valleys.

Kim Il Sung had exhorted North Korean troops that "the war be carried out so that its final victory can be realized by August 15, fifth anniversary of the liberation of Korea." The troop exhortation was dated August 13 and found on the body of a captured North Korean colonel. While the crucial battle was going on in early September, Kim appeared at Kumchon and exhorted his division commanders to occupy Pusan by September 15. Admitting that his original plan to capture Pusan by August 15 had failed, Kim warned: "If you fail this time again, all commanders shall be dealt with as traitors." Kim had thrown his 15th and 8th divisions to the battle of Yongchon, which was thought as the last card to achieve his goal. But again he had failed.

By September 1, United Nations ground forces stood at 180,000, of which 91,500 were South Koreans. Thus the U.N. ground formations included five South Korean divisions, four U.S. Army infantry divisions approaching full strength, the British Brigade and Marine Brigade. To this were added 34,000 men of the U.S. Far East Air Force. Among those vital weapons brought to Korea were the medium Sherman and Pershing tanks and one battalion of the big Pattons.

The U.N. forces had been further strengthened since the end of August with the arrival of additional troops from Britain, Canada, Turkey, Australia, Thailand, the Philippines, France, and New Zealand.

The enemy strength was about 100,000 men. Less than 30 percent of the old Communist China veterans remained, and they were exhausted and hungry. Now only frequent summary executions and threat of death could hold the forcibly inducted South Koreans.

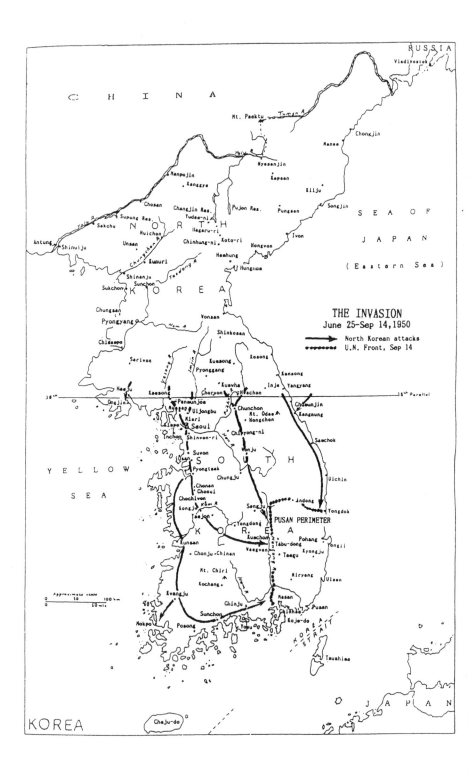

KOREA

CHAPTER THREE

U.N. COUNTEROFFENSIVE

INCHON LANDING

MacArthur's Gamble Succeeds

As early as the first week of the North Korean invasion, MacArthur had conceived an amphibious operation striking the enemy in the rear. It was then that he came to Korea to reconnoiter the Han River battlefront overlooking Seoul on July 29. He planned to use his preponderance of air and naval forces, plus the superb fighting ability of the U.S. Marines to go ashore against an enemy beach and destroy him by cutting his supply lines.

MacArthur instructed his chief of staff, Major General Edward Almond, to begin planning for an amphibious landing on the west coast of Korea. Almond set up Joint Strategic Plans and Operations Group to work out various strategies. Of a number of plans postulated by the Group, MacArthur favored an amphibious landing at the port of Inchon, coupled with a simultaneous breakout from the Pusan Perimeter by the Eighth Army.

MacArthur gave a secret instruction to South Korean Navy chief of staff Admiral Sohn Won-il to capture a few islands near Inchon prior to the D-Day, September 15, 1950. Sohn ordered Commander Lee Chang-hee to seize Dokchok-do Island off Inchon. After his occupation of Dockchok-do, Lee's landing force raided Yonghung-do Island and killed 40 and captured 100 North Koreans. Yonghung-do, located at the mouth of the Flying Fish Channel, which would be the route of MacArthur's landing fleet, was an important strategic position.

Admiral Sohn also assigned a spy mission to his intelligence chief, Lieutenant Commander Ham Myong-soo. Ham formed a 17-man espionage team, which infiltrated into Inchon and spied on the

113

strength of North Korea's Inchon garrison, its supply situation and mining in Inchon Harbor as well as topography of the landing site and the structural features of its seawalls. Han's clandestine team had found that Inchon was lightly defended.

MacArthur chose Inchon as a landing site because it was the second best port of Korea, South Korean Intelligence reported it lightly defended, and it was only 18 miles from Seoul, the nerve center of the North Korean invaders. The landing operation was designed to cut the North Korean supply lines and the landing force of the 10th Corps, which would be commanded by Almond, and Walker's Eighth Army driving northward would strike the enemy.

But Inchon posed enormous difficulties. Between Inchon and the open sea were expanses of mud flats, crossed by tortuous channels. The tides at Inchon were the second highest in the world with an average 29 feet rise and fall of the sea. Landing craft could approach the harbor only during certain hours of the day. In the middle of September, the landing forces would have to land against the 16-foot high seawalls surrounding the city with only two hours of remaining daylight.

Therefore, strong oppositions were raised by the Navy and Marine Corps and the Joint Chiefs of Staff. General J. Lawton Collins, army chief of staff, told MacArthur that it would be safer to land at Kunsan about 100 miles south of Inchon, a port with fewer natural obstacles. But MacArthur explained that the port of Kunsan would not achieve his goal because it was not far enough in the enemy's rear, and therefore would not cut enemy supply lines.

MacArthur, who had already decided on the Inchon landing operation by July 20, was adamant. He was confident that an Inchon landing was the only way to end the war quickly and that its chance of success was excellent. In Washington, he received solid support from Secretary of Defense Louis Johnson, who also wanted the war over as quickly as possible.

Finally, on August 29, the Joint Chiefs of Staff allowed MacArthur the green light: "We approve your plan and President has been so informed."

MacArthur moved ahead with his planning for Inchon and set September 15 as D-Day. He ordered his confidant Major General Almond to command the hastily activated 10th Corps comprising the

7th Infantry Division, 1st Marine Division, and Fleet Marine Force. General Walker shipped some 7,000 Koreans over from Pusan as KATUSA (Korean Augmentation to the U.S. Army) for the 7th Division. The young Koreans were all civilians, rounded up from the streets and refugee camps in Pusan, who would be on fatigue duty.

Meanwhile, a total of 641 young South Korean residents in Japan had volunteered to go to the front of their motherland with the American forces. They were divided into six groups in the order of their applications and the first two groups took part in the Inchon landing operation and the remainder were shipped to Inchon later.

On September 11, General Almond's 10th Corps set sail for Inchon, the 1st Division from Kobe and the 7th Infantry Division from Yokohama. They met the 17th Infantry Regiment at sea the following day. At about midnight September 13, MacArthur secretly boarded his flagship, *Mount McKinley* anchored in Sasebo, Kyusu. Throughout that night and the following day, the flagship and 13 other vessels — four cruisers, six destroyers and three rocket vessels — of the Joint Task Force commanded by Rear Admiral John Higgins were sailing for Inchon along with the 3rd Battalion, Fifth Marines, under Lieutenant Colonel Rober Taplett.

The landing fleet comprised a total of 261 vessels; 226 American vessels, 15 Korean, 12 British, 3 Canadian, 2 Australian, 2 New Zealand, and 1 French. As many as 75,000 persons participated in the landing operation. [1]

At 2:30 a.m., September 15, the long column of the gunfire ships worked their way north through Flying Fish Channel (Obi Suro). As they were approaching Palmi-do, Lieutenant Eugene F. Clark, who had been on the island on a scouting mission under MacArthur's order, lighted the lighthouse to guide the warships.

At 6:30 a.m., under an overcast sky, the 3rd Battalion, 5th Marines, followed heavy naval gunfire and air preparation onto the beaches of Wolmi-do. Three LSV's landed M–26 Pershing tanks on the northwestern shore (Green Beach), and the marines swept rapidly inland.

It took the Marines one hour and twenty-five minutes to overrun and secure the rocky, caverned island. Standing just west of Inchon, connected by a narrow causeway, Wolmi-do rose 495 feet above water and was the highest point of land in the Inchon area. The little pyramid of land was the important target of the landing operation. The 5th Marine veterans killed or captured 400 North Koreans of the 226th Independent Marine Brigade on Wolmi-do. Seventeen U.S. Marines were wounded. At 2:30 p.m., four cruisers and six destroyers belched a curtain of fire and steel over Inchon from their assigned positions. Fighter planes flying from carriers bombed the enemy military facilities avoiding residential areas and municipal centers.

By 4:25 p.m., the navy and air attacks ceased and three rocket vessels, entering the harbor, poured a rain of shells on Red and Blue Beaches.

At 5:53, landing craft of the 5th Marines grated against the seawall at Red Beach just north of Wolmi-do causeway, and Marines rushed into the city of a quarter-million people after piling over the wall on scaling ladders or crawling through holes blown in the barrier by navy gunfire.

The North Koreans doggedly resisted in hand-to-hand fighting, but within minutes U.N. troops were in Inchon streets. Twenty-five minutes after touching shore, the Marine flare ascended into the sky, signaling the capture of Cemetery Hill. Thus Red Beach fell completely by 7 p.m.

At almost the same time that the 5th Marine Regiment went ashore, the 1st Marines struck toward Blue Beach south of the causeway. After climbing the high seawall, the 1st Regiment moved north around the outskirts of the city to cut the Seoul-Inchon highway, blocking the enemy's retreat route.

Once Inchon had been encircled at 1:30 a.m., September 16, and initial objectives achieved, South Korean special Marines entered the city for mop-up operations. The city's 250,000 residents were stricken with panic and untold number of families fled.

The 2,000 troops of the North Korean garrison at Inchon were annihilated. The U.N. forces had lost only 20 killed, 174 wounded, and one missing.

Now General Almond's 10th Corps held a secure beachhead only 18 miles from Seoul, thanks to the Navy and the 1st Marine Division. On September 16, the 5th and 1st Marine Regiments recaptured Kimpo Airfield and by nightfall of the 18th, U.S. and South Korean Marines reached the southern shore of the Han River. Meanwhile, the North Korean 18th Division, bound for the Naktong front, turned north and engaged the 1st Marines, and the enemy's 70th Regiment hurried into Seoul from Suwon. The newly activated 25th Brigade, rushed from Chorwon, and the 87th Regiment under the 9th Division — a total of 20,000 troops — were defending the Seoul area.

Seoul Recaptured

On the early morning of September 20, elements of U.S. 5th and South Korean Marines crossed the Han and advanced to Seoul on the west through Susaek the next day. To their right, and south, the 1st Marines recaptured Yongdungpo on September 22 and reached the Mapo-ku area in Seoul on the 23rd.

For four days from September 22, the Marines and infantry locked the stubbornly resisting North Koreans in close combat over Yonhi Hill (Hill 66) along the western approaches to Seoul. The ridge, extending from behind Yonsei University to the shore of the Han, was the enemy defense line in Seoul. The low hills and caves of the area gave the enemy a good arc for defense, and they had committed the 25th Brigade which had just arrived from Chorwon.

American and South Korean Marines engaged in heavy fighting along the ridge lines until noon of September 25. The enemy doggedly resisted, but then panicked and ran away from the hill, leaving 1,200 dead behind. The South Koreans also lost 500 men, and 36 American Marines were killed.

With the loss of Hill 66, most of the enemy defense lines had collapsed. But fierce street battles inside Seoul were still going on. On September 25, the U.S. 7th Division seized Namsan (South Mountain). Just before midnight, General Almond announced the recapture of Seoul because he wanted to send the message exactly three months from the date of the North Korean aggression. But it was a little premature. Less than half of Seoul was in U.N. hands, and while certain enemy troops were evacuating, others stayed behind in last-ditch resistance.

While furious fighting was still going on from street to street, MacArthur issued United Nations Command Communique No. 9, on September 26 stating that Seoul was recaptured. For two more days American and Korean troops were mopping up the enemy.

United Press war correspondent, Rutherford Poats, depicted what he had seen during the fight for Seoul as follows:

> I followed the First Marines through the smoldering rubble of central Seoul the day after its premature "liberation." The last desperate Communist counterattack had been hurled back during an eerie 2 a.m. battle of tanks firing at point blank range, American artillery crashing less than a city block ahead of Marine lines, the echoed and re-echoed rattle of machine guns — all against the background of flaming buildings and darting shadows.
>
> Now it was almost quiet. The angry chatter of a machine gun up ahead now and then punctuated the long pause between mortar and artillery strikes. But on this street corner was condensed the full horror of war, stripped of the vital challenge and excitement which make it bearable to the men who must fight wars.
>
> Telephone and power lines festooned the streets or hung from shattered poles which resembled grotesque Christmas trees. Bluish smoke curled from the corner of a clapboard shack — the only building even partially spared destruction along the left side of the street. A young woman poked among a pile of roof tiles and charred timbers for her possessions, or perhaps for her child. A lump of flesh and bones in a mustard-colored Communist uniform sprawled across the curb up ahead, and the white-robed body of an old man lay on a rice-straw mat nearer the street corner. Marine ammunition and mess trucks churned the plaster and adobe rubble into dust as they shuttled back and forth from the front, six blocks north. Southbound ambulance jeeps, almost always fully loaded

with four stretcher cases on their racks, told the story of the pre-dawn battle.

A tiny figure wrapped in a Marine's wool shirt stumbled down the street. Her face, arms, and legs were burned and almost eaten away by the fragments of an American white phosphorous artillery shell. She was blind, but somehow alive. She was about the size of my little girl. Three other Korean children, luckier than she, watched as the child reached the curbing, stumbled, and twice failed to climb up on the sidewalk. The kids laughed. [2]

It was 6:10 a.m. of September 27 when the North Koreans had completely disappeared from Seoul. By September 28, Seoul had truly fallen, and the South Korean flag, Taeguk-ki, was hoisted at Government Building.

MacArthur and Rhee at Dramatic Ceremony

When MacArthur arrived at Kimpo Airfield from Tokyo on September 28, parts of Seoul were still burning. But a multitude of Koreans lined up on road sides and cheered as President Rhee and MacArthur drove to the National Assembly Hall. The legislative chamber had escaped destruction with only a broken skylight. Rhee and MacArthur entered the hall, which was packed with selected high-ranking American and Korean officials, General Walker and other military officers, and members of the United Nations Commission.

MacArthur spoke in his usual sonorous and dramatic style:

Mr. President: By the grace of a merciful Providence our forces fighting under the standard of that greatest hope and inspiration of mankind, the United Nations, have liberated this ancient capital of Korea. It has been freed from despotism of Communist rule and its citizens once more have the opportunity for that

immutable concept of life which holds invincibly to the
primacy of individual liberty and personal dignity....

MacArthur then asked the assembly to recite the Lord's prayer
with him, after which he turned to Rhee and said: "In behalf of the
United Nations Command I am happy to restore to you, Mr.
President, the seat of your government so that you may fulfill your
constitutional responsibilities." While MacArthur cited the Lord's
prayer, glass from the battle-shattered skylight tinkled down.
MacArthur paid no attention.

The aged president rose to speak, but for a few moments he
could not speak, overcome by emotion. He seized MacArthur's
hand, and said, tears filling his eyes, "We admire you. We love you
as the savior of our race. How can I ever explain to you my own
undying gratitude and that of the Korean people?"

The ceremony was over and MacArthur returned to Tokyo. He
received plaudits from President Truman, the Joint Chiefs of Staff,
and from all the non-Communist world. Truman cabled: "Few
operations in military history can match either the delaying action
where you traded space for time in which to build up your forces or
the brilliant maneuver which has now resulted in the liberation of
Seoul."

In order to perpetuate the gratitude and admiration of the Korean
people toward MacArthur, the Republic of Korea government
erected his statue in Inchon. The lofty bronze statue stands on the
hill of Liberty Park overlooking the Inchon Harbor where he had
succeeded in the historic U.N. landing operation on September 15,
1950.

Scoop on Inchon Landing

At 1:50 p.m. on September 15, I flashed the news bulletin of the
successful Inchon landing, reporting, "United Nations forces landed
on Wolmi-do Island of Inchon at about 6:30 this morning. In less
than an hour American flag was hoisted on the island's highest
hill...." I dispatched the scoop story via AP's Tokyo Bureau from

Pusan after obtaining authoritative confirmations at South Korean Navy headquarters as well as army intelligence.

However, General (ret.) Chung Il-kwon, then South Korean Army chief of staff, erroneously wrote in his memoirs *Chunjaeng-gwa Hyujon (War and Truce)* that "Shinn's AP dispatch from Taegu on September 13 said United Nations forces would launch landing operation at Inchon on September 15. The entire landing forces are now sailing for Inchon under the direct command of General MacArthur. I break into a cold sweat at the mere thought of what would have happened if the Inchon landing operation had failed because of such an advance report." [3]

Because of General Chung's name value, such an incorrect account in his book has been widely quoted in history books in Korea and elsewhere in the world. Stating that AP had filed an "advance report" on the crucial Inchon landing operation, which would determine the fate of the U.N. forces, might be interpreted as if AP had committed an act of providing the Communist enemy with the operational secret of the U.N. forces, thus bringing disgrace not only on the good name of myself as a war correspondent but on the Associated Press as a world news agency.

To straighten out the matter, I need to explain here how I had broken the success story of the historic landing at Inchon that turned the tide of the Korean War.

I had learned of the amphibious landing plans from correspondent colleagues in Tokyo and U.S. Marines in Pusan while they were awaiting orders to sail for Inchon. In fact there was little secrecy in allied press circles about plans for the landing, which was known at the Foreign Correspondents' Club in Tokyo as "Operation Common Knowledge."

As a war correspondent, I was well aware of the strict military code that advance reporting of military operational plans constitutes an act of "aiding the enemy" subject to court-martial. Therefore I had been waiting until the landing operation had taken place.

Unlike a large number of correspondents, including AP colleagues, who had sailed to Inchon harbor with MacArthur's landing armada, I had to cover the landing operation from Pusan because there was no way for me to go on land to Inchon far behind the enemy-occupied territory. But I was as eager as all other correspondents to be at the outcome of the crucial military venture.

From the early morning of D-Day, September 15, I strived to collect all available information on what was going on in Inchon from my sources at U.S. and South Korean navy intelligence as well as American Red Cross field officers who had access to the battle zone.

As a result, I found out that the 3rd Battalion of the U.S. 5th Marine Regiment had landed on Wolmi-do of Inchon at about 6:30 a.m. and secured the island. After double and triple checks for accuracy, I ran to the South Korean Navy headquarters on Pier No. 1 for final confirmation. Commander Lee Yong-woon, navy operations chief (later, navy chief of staff), was at his office.

"Congratulations!" I told Lee.

"On what?"

"The success of Inchon landing."

"How could you find that out?"

Judging from his immediate reaction and facial expression of surprise, I felt certain that the landing had been carried out successfully. I told him, "To save time, I will tell you first whatever I know about the landing. If you find anything wrong while I explain, please point it out for me." I cited all I had found out without a hitch.

After careful listening, he nodded his confirmation, without saying a word. Because of the important nature of the report, I wanted to attribute the news source to a qualified South Korean army authority instead of "reliable sources." I thought army chief of staff Major General Chung Il-kwon, who had been very friendly with me, would be the best suited person for that matter. So I visited South Korean Army public information officer, Captain Kim Kun-bae, who was General Chung's confidant and also a good friend of mine, at his office in Nampo-dong in downtown Pusan. I wanted to get Captain Kim's approval so I could dispatch the news as an announcement of General Chung.

Because I had assumed that heroic-minded MacArthur must have given a gag order to the South Korean government and army pending his own announcement, I stressed the following points to Captain Kim:

(1) Military secrets of the landing operation had been lifted at the time of the U.N. attack on Woldmi-do. Therefore there was no need to delay the release of such good news any longer because of MacArthur's gag order; (2) now that the United Nations forces had successfully landed on Wolmi-do in Inchon, South Korean authorities should feel obliged to release the news for the 16 nations fighting in Korea as well as the Korean people as soon as possible; (3) the war was being fought in Korea and the Korean people were suffering the most, and there was such an outstanding general as General Chung Il-kwon; (4) it is therefore more significant to make the announcement in General Chung's name. Should the United Nations Command put pressure on General Chung after his announcement, the Associated Press would be responsible.

Apparently moved by the remark that "AP would be responsible," Captain Kim said he would discuss the matter with his superior and let me know. Sensing that he would allow me to dispatch my report as General Chung's announcement, I had left my errand-boy at Captain Kim's office to get his answer and run to Pier No. 1 where I would be waiting for him. I told him to send me a hand signal of "V" while running if the answer was "yes."

As the boy was running with a "V" signal, I dashed to the office of South Korean Navy Chief of Staff Admiral Sohn Won-il to use U.S. Army phone there. But I was dumbfounded to find the door was locked. Sohn had gone to Inchon harbor to participate in the landing operation. Luckily, the next room was the office of Commander Lee Yong-woon, navy operations chief, whom I had visited earlier to get my story confirmed. I burst into the room and found a large transom on the wall between the two adjacent rooms. I still do not know how I had reached the transom, at least 12 feet above the floor, and managed to enter Admiral Sohn's office. I was beside myself for the purpose of using the U.S. Army telephone to send my urgent report as fast as I could.

Commander Lee's staff, well aware of my close friendship with Admiral Sohn, put up with my foolhardy act, apparently because they had heard my earlier conversation with their boss, Lee.

I picked up the handset of the military phone in Admiral Sohn's office and called AP's Tokyo bureau through a "Pusan Toll" operator. John Randolph answered the phone, joking, "Bill, are you still alive?" I cried, "I've got an urgent story. Hurry up," and dictated the report on the success of Inchon landing.

Soon after my report had reached Tokyo, MacArthur's headquarters requested the AP office to withhold my report until official release on the grounds that my dispatch was "premature." Accuracy of the report was not questioned. AP immediately rejected the demand pointing out that speedy, accurate reporting was a newsman's duty.

On the following day, September 16, I was denied further use of the military telephone that I regularly used between Korea and Tokyo for the reason that I was not accredited to the Far East command. The Associated Press lodged a strong protest with the U.S. Department of Defense, and the ban was lifted in two days.

The following is an AP dispatch from Tokyo on the telephone ban:

> Tokyo, Sept. 16 — (AP) — Bill Shinn, Associated Press correspondent, who was first with the news of the Inchon landing, today was denied permission by the Army to use the military telephone connecting Korea and Tokyo. He had been using the military telephone regularly.
>
> Maj. Buel A. Williamson, a public information officer in General MacArthur's headquarters here, said Shinn, a native of Korea, was not an accredited correspondent in the Far East command.
>
> Williamson said, however, that Shinn would be permitted to continue to work for the Associated Press in Korea and his dispatches could be telephoned to Tokyo by other Associated Press men on the scene.
>
> Shinn was the only correspondent for a world news agency present in Pusan yesterday when Maj. Gen. Chung Il Kwon announced to South Korean reporters that United States marines and South Koreans landed near Inchon. Within 20 minutes, Shinn had the only telephone to Tokyo he could use and was dictating the dispatch to Associated Press headquarters there.

The First Casualty, From the Crimea to Vietnam: The War Correspondent as Hero, Propagandist, and Myth Maker (by Phillip Knightley, Harcout Brace Jovanovich, New York and London, 1975) also says, "Bill Shinn, a young Korean-born Associated Press reporter... who had beat the army's own release by nine hours, was denied any further use of the military phone between Korea and Tokyo." [4]

General Chung's False Account

Contrary to those facts, Chung's memoirs had given utterly unfounded accounts about my Inchon beat alleging that I dispatched the story to AP from Taegu on September 13, two days before D-Day, after hearing about the secret landing plans from "Major" Kim Kun-bae in Taegu. The memoirs said, "Shinn had a party with Major Kim Kun-bae who had attended General Walker's meeting... and the two old friends exchanged drinking cups into the night.... Kim got drunk and told Shinn all about Inchon landing operation." The hard fact was that on September 13 both Kim Kun-bae and I were working in Pusan, he as a captain (not major) in charge of the army information office and I as an AP correspondent busy preparing for the newsbreak of the upcoming Inchon landing.

How General Chung had made such a serious mistake in his memoirs remains as a mystery to me. My only guess is that Captain Kim Kun-bae who had allowed me to attribute my Inchon landing report to General Chung's announcement might have made false reports to the general in order to elude a possible reprimand. Chung said in the memoirs that he had received a complaint from General Walker about the announcement, but that "there was no complaint from Tokyo."

In retrospect, the Inchon beat was the most rewarding experience in my long journalistic career. It was the first gratifying news of the Korean War — especially for those 16 nations which had sent troops for the United Nations police action in Korea — that turned their minds from frustration to hope.

The 3rd Battalion, 5th Regiment, 1st Marine Division, succeed in the brilliant amphibious landing on Wolmi-do Island in Inchon Harbor on the early morning of September 15, 1950.

General MacArthur and staff watch the naval and aerial bombardment of Inchon from the flag bridge of the *U.S.S. McKinley*.

A. P. Writer Denied Use Of Army Phone

TOKYO, Sept. 16. — (AP) — Bill Shinn, Associated Press correspondent, who was first with the news of the Inchon landing, today was denied permission by the Army to use the military telephone connecting Korea and Tokyo. He had been using the military telephone regularly.

Maj. Buel A. Williamson, a public information officer in General MacArthur's headquarters here, said Shinn, a native of Korea, was not an accredited correspondent in the Far East command.

A. P. wirephoto
BILL SHINN

Williamson said, however, that Shinn would be permitted to con-

North Korean troops surrender to the U.S. Marines on Wolmi-do Island on September 15, 1950.

A clip of an AP dispatch from Tokyo on the Far East Command's orders to bar the author's use of the military telephone. The ban was lifted in two days.

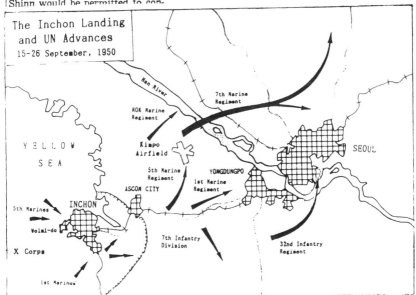

The Inchon Landing and UN Advances
15-26 September, 1950

Han River

7th Marine Regiment

ROK Marine Regiment

YELLOW SEA

Kimpo Airfield

SEOUL

5th Marine Regiment

YONGDUNGPO

ASCOM CITY

1st Marine Regiment

5th Marines

INCHON

Wolmi-do

X Corps

7th Infantry Division

32nd Infantry Regiment

1st Marines

Pleased by the scoop, the Associated Press granted me a special bonus, and I was called "Scoop Shinn" by some of my colleagues and American press officers.

Lost Family Found in Seoul

Upon arrival in Seoul from Pusan On September 30, I joined a group of war correspondents billeted at a house in the American Embassy compound, where I met AP correspondent O.H.P. King who had arrived there two days earlier from Tokyo. The minute he saw me, King excitedly searched his pocket, saying, "Bill, I've got a good news for you. This is it! Read it!" He showed me a copy of his report he had just filed.

I hugged him and jumped for joy, because I had a hunch that I could find my lost family. King's dispatch said he had learned that a woman resembling my wife was walking with a small boy toward the West Gate area in Seoul.

Since my wife's parents were living in Yongchon-dong, Sodaemun-ku (West Gate), and my son was three and a half years old, I had one hope of finding them. I drove a U.S. Army jeep at full speed to Yungchun-dong ignoring the curfew in the dark.

The moment I stepped into the yard of the house of Kim Ke-whan, my father-in-law, I called out for my son, "Johnny!"

"Yes. Is it Papa?" It was my wife's choked voice. She and her parents, who had been eating in dim candlelight, were overjoyed to see me alive. But, my little Johnny seemed unmoved.

Thus I was happily reunited with my wife and son after three months. I had lost contact with them on the night of June 29 during an enemy attack on the village of Shinwon-ri, where they had found refuge after crossing the Han bridge with me shortly before it was blown up.

I wrote about my strong sense of gratitude for our happy reunion in my dispatch to the Associated Press. It was widely reported with our reunion picture taken by AP Photographer George Sweers. The following old newspaper clip brings back my memories of 45 years past:

SEOUL, Oct. 1 (AP) — I shall never forget the dramatic moment when Correspondent O.H.P. King gave me the news about my family.

I found my pregnant wife, Sally, and my three-and-a-half-year old son, Johnny, alive among the numerous dead in the wrecked city of Seoul.

Our reunion joy can hardly be expressed, so great is our excitement, happiness and thanks.

When I returned to liberated Seoul from Pusan I went to a house in the American Embassy compound. My former home was one of the first houses in Seoul to be hit by Red shells on June 27.

I was washing up when Mr. King shouted to me. He began hurriedly searching his pockets. With trembling hands, he gave me a type-written sheet. He stared at me and I at him.

It was a story he had filed that day that he had learned my family was safe in a suburb. It also said that my 1929 Ford, in which I had traveled from Lincoln, Neb., to Chicago, Washington, New York, Indianapolis, St. Louis, Seattle, San Francisco and other major cities in America, was in usable condition if repaired.

I could hardly believe it. I asked Mr. King again and again if it were true. Again he assured me.

Then I forgot the hunger and fatigue I had been feeling after the three-day journey from Pusan.

Ignoring the curfew, I drove in the dark to find Sally and Johnny. Among the burned and destroyed homes, I found the small, straw-thatched house. Sally and Johnny were there eating supper with Sally's father and mother. They could hardly recognize me in the candlelight.

Only after I called "Sally" did my wife scream, "Bill?" In the dark room I could see Sally's eyes flooded with tears. Johnny was unmoved, as if I were an unwelcome guest.

I myself did not know what to begin to say. After a few minutes we started saying: "God saved us."

Sally fought through fear, threats, disappointment, worries, hunger and cold. However, she said, "all these unpleasant things now are gone. My heart is filled with hopes for rebuilding our homes as we will rebuild our country."

There is nothing left, but we are happy and thankful. We are praying that many other families reported missing may reunite as ours.

I am convinced that the sincere and grateful prayers of my good friends, both at home and abroad, have been answered by God. I happily recall a most heart-warming letter from Mrs. Sherman Hultquist, Oakland, Neb., whom I call "my American mother," because of her motherly love toward me while studying in the States.

She wrote, "If hoping and praying will bring Sally and Johnny back, I know you will find them because all your Nebraska friends are with you."

I also appreciate letters sent by the Rev. John Shell, York, Neb., and other friends in the States.

Three months ago I was here in the Seoul AP office. I was filled with fear and sorrow. Now, thanks to God, to the ROK [South Korean] and U.N. troops, and to my friends, I am back in the same office, fortunately undestroyed, with joy, courage, hope and thanks.

The changes of failure to success, lost to found, destruction to construction — these were brought to us by the war.

The bitterness helped us to better appreciate the sweet things when they came.

All the losses of properties and sacrifices will be more than paid for by the birth of a unified, independent and democratic Korea.

U.S. Marines dashing into Inchon city scaling a 16-foot-high seawall.

The author rejoices at a reunion with his family who had been lost in the enemy-occupied zone.

Indescribable sufferings

Sally had written down her sufferings with little Johnny in her diary:

> On the night of June 29, fierce fighting continued near Shinwon-ri and North Korean soldiers were approaching the village. We fled the village together with Kim Jong-wook's family to his brother's home deep in a steep mountain in Kwangju-kun (county). Farmers in the out-of-the-way hamlet were so poor that we barely staved off hunger by barter of personal effects for food. Because it was too much of a burden on the part of the poor family of Mr. Kim's brother, I decided to go to my parents' home in Seoul.
>
> Your younger brother, Wha-kyoon, who had been living a fugitive life in Seoul, eluding Communist search for young South Koreans to induct into the North Korean Army, was informed of my whereabouts by Mr. Kim's relatives. He kindly came to the remote village to take me to Seoul. I was about to collapse many times while trudging along the rugged mountain trails with Johnny. As a pregnant woman, I barely held out from hunger and fatigue thanks to the few vitamin pills on hand.
>
> On our way, we came across Communist soldiers. They ordered Wha-kyoon to show them his hands. I trembled with fear when they yelled at him, "Your hands are clean enough. You are not a laborer," and threatened to take him away. With bare life, we managed to arrive in Seoul in three days.
>
> For the first few days we stayed at our home in Shinsol-dong, where we had moved to on the day when the war broke out. But we became thoroughly disgusted with the Communists who knocked at the door before dawn everyday, shouting, "All young men in the house must come out," searching each room.

So I and Johnny went to my parents' home at Yongchon in the western district of Seoul. The Shinsol-dong house, standing on a hill, seemed to have been more conspicuous to the Communists.

Tribulation persisted even after I moved to Yong-chon-dong. Unable to buy food, we sustained life by eating dumplings in soy soup each day. While furious battles continued, we lived in an air-raid shelter built by the Japanese on the hillside of a rocky mountain during World War II. More than 20 persons used the shelter, about the size of 20 square feet with a small public toilet outside. I had to bring meals from my parents' home 100 yards down at the foot of the mountain. Being in the last month of pregnancy, I had to carry diapers and swaddling clothes for the baby.

The most terrifying was the United Nations air-raids during the furious street fights for the recapture of Seoul. While bringing meals from my parents' home, I saw gruesome corpses scattered around, and many old women dying from bomb shrapnel. Although their targets were the Communist troops, I felt sorry that the bombs dropped by American Air Force planes hit many South Korean civilians.

Despite all the hardships I and little Johnny had, my waking and sleeping thoughts were about you because I had no way of knowing your whereabouts since you had gone to Suwon from Shinwon-ri on the early morning of June 29.

Enduring hunger, fatigue, threats, and anguish until the last month of her pregnancy, and caring for little son Johnny, Sally gave a safe birth to another son on October 30, 1950. I attributed this fortune to God's great Providence and thanked Him. Rejoicing over my wife's easy delivery, my AP colleagues proposed to name the newborn baby. But I named him "Shinn Se-whan," who is now a naturalized citizen of the United States and a businessman.

Communist Brutality

During their occupation of South Korean cities and towns, the North Korean Army and Communist agents had wreaked frightful brutality on thousands of innocent South Koreans. They executed or kidnapped to the North the families of South Korean policemen, soldiers, government employees, members of the National Assembly and other prominent persons. Those who had worked at American organizations as well as foreign missionaries and correspondents were also arrested and taken to Pyongyang.

Furthermore, the Communists searched for young South Koreans to induct into the North Korean Army. Many young people, as in the case of my younger brother Wha-kyoon, had to live under the floors or in the attics of the houses of their relatives or close friends to keep themselves out of sight of the Communists. Anyone found hiding was mercilessly executed.

Among those arrested and taken to Pyongyang were French and British diplomats and Catholic fathers and sisters from Belgium and five other nations who had not left Seoul before the Communist occupation believing that they would be safe because they were foreigners. French news agency AFP's correspondent Morris Changteloup, a friend of mine, was also captured at the Chosun Hotel on July 8, 1950. After spending three years in prisoner-of-war camps in North Korea, he returned to Paris in May 1953 via Russia and East Europe.

On July 11, the Apostolic Delegate, Father Patrick Byrne and his 82-year-old secretary, Bishop Paul Villemot, were arrested in Seoul along with 13 fathers and seven sisters from France, Belgium, Ireland, Australia, the United States, and West Germany. They were tried by "People's Court" before crowds sympathetic to Kim Il Sung. Then they were taken to Pyongyang on a freight train on July 21 and jailed. Bishop Byrne, who had been seriously ill, died on November 25, 1950.

Upon their seizure of Taejon on July 20, the North Koreans rounded up hundreds of citizens and tied their hands with wire before shooting them to death in groups and stuffing their bodies into mass graves dug in the outskirts of the city.

The first official photograph of a murdered American soldier found on the South Korean front. The picture was taken by Captain Lim In-sik, South Korean army photographer, and made available to the author for the AP on July 11, 1950.

Bodies of some 400 South Korean civilians are left in and around burial trenches in a Taejoin prison yard by North Koreans who bound them and executed them.

On July 11, I obtained the first official photograph of a murdered American soldier found face down, his hands tied behind his back, near Chonui, midway between Pyongtaek and Taejon. The picture was taken by Captain Lim In-sik of the South Korean Army signal photographic unit and made available to AP for my report. Later Lim told me that Mrs. Lora Sims of 506 Division Street, Indianapolis, Indiana, who had seen the dead body's picture in *The Indianapolis News*, wrote him: "...This picture taken by you looks so much like my son that it makes me cry.... His name is Pfc. Ernest E. Sims, RA 13267450, 34th Infantry Regiment, 24th Division..."

When the U.S. forces recaptured Taejon in the wake of Inchon landing, thousands of corpses, including those of 40 American prisoners, were discovered in wells and trenches. A large number of other victims of the Communist massacre were found in Mokpo, Kongju, Hamyang and other areas the enemy had advanced.

On September 28, a battalion of the U.S. 19th Regiment, 24th Division, found 400 corpses of South Korean policemen and civilians in two open trenches in the Taejon Prison premises. Numerous other bodies were crammed into wells in the same prison compound.

Execution of Communist Sympathizers

During their three months occupation of South Korea, the North Korean invaders massacred 165,000 South Korean civilians and abducted 122,000 others to the North. In Seoul alone, 9,500 innocent citizens were slaughtered. [5]

Learning what the Communists had done in their captured cities and towns, the South Korean Army showed no mercy to Communists or their sympathizers, and South Korean officials were determined to uproot the Communist underground in South Korea. Anyone who had acted as a Communist agent persecuting innocent citizens was court-martialed and executed as a "war criminal."

On November 5, 1950, I witnessed a mass execution scene and reported as follows:

SEOUL, Nov, 5, (AP) — The ROK [South Korean] Army today executed sixteen men and four women as "war criminals" on a hill four miles (6.5 km) west of Seoul. They had been sentenced to death by a court-martial on charges of benefiting the enemy and violating the ROK security law.

When the "war criminals," guarded by six military policemen, were ordered to get on a truck at West Gate Prison, an elderly man pleaded, "I have left my blanket in the cell. I am afraid it may be lost." Apparently the prisoners were not aware where they were heading for.

The truck stopped at the foot of a hill in a short while. As they were told to walk up the hill, it struck them all that they were facing death. On the hill, a large gaping pit — 8 feet long, 6 feet wide, and six feet deep — dug by ROK MPs, was waiting for the ill-fated men and women.

Both hands tied in the back and face down, the condemned criminals dragged their heavy feet at the gunpoint of MPs. As they trudged along the withered hillside path, some of them began to wail. Others were protesting that they had been falsely charged.

A white-clad woman, about 30, spoke to me shedding bitter tears of anguish: "Sir, I realize that all is over now. There is no hope before me anymore. But for mercy's sake, please give my best love to my three small children. They are an eight year old daughter, a six year old son and a six month old son. They are left with my sister..."

A black-clad middle-aged man walking beside, showing no remorse or grief, told her coldly, "Hey, it's no use to say such a thing now. It's too late."

MP Captain Kim told me that she had been the head of a Communist organization called "women's re-education committee," and urged its members to sew undergarments for the North Korean soldiers.

The twenty convicts, aged 18 to 48, were ordered to crouch in the pit. At that time, the mother of three children made a pathetic appeal to the people around: "I have been a bad woman. I wish my children to be well. So please be merciful to them!"

"If anyone else wants to leave a word, you may do so," Captain Kim said. A 40-year-old man said, "I have helped twelve family members of the ROK Army and police to escape from Communist captors." Another middle-aged man implored, "Please give me just one more day so I can prove I am innocent." Others were saying something in such screeching wails that I could not understand what they were saying.

An eighteen-year-old girl, the youngest of the group, knelt calmly with eyes closed and prayed in composed voice, "Our Lord in Heaven, please take me under your protection!" She had been convicted of serving the North Korean Army as a volunteer and throwing a hand grenade at American soldiers when the United Nations forces advanced to Seoul on September 23.

The six-man firing squad held light machine guns at the ready, awaiting an order to fire. Witnessing the scene were judge advocate Captain Choo, army surgeon Lieutenant Sohn and myself.

The sky was blue and clear and all was quiet on the hill. Suddenly the sound of gunfire rumbled. The convicts were shot in the head or back and fell down one upon another, gushing pools of fresh blood. Two women died in the first shots. The MPs fired revolvers at those who were writhing before their last breath. After confirming that everybody was dead, the white-helmeted MPs heaped earth over the corpses.

The "war criminals" executed today were classified by occupations as follows:

One telephone operator, one maidservant, two students, one farmer, two day laborers, four merchants, one accountant, one public official, one carpenter, one banker, one blacksmith, one actor, one printer, and two jobless.

A few days after I had filed the above report, soldiers of the British 29th Brigade sighted another execution carried out on the same hill. Peter Webb of the United Press wrote at British brigade headquarters: "White-helmeted military police — their nationality is not known — with orders to keep U.N. troops at a distance, stood guard today while a South Korean firing squad executed another batch of prisoners on Seoul's 'Execution Hill,' according to eyewitnesses."

THE ROLLBACK OPERATION

U.N. Forces Break out of Pusan Perimeter

In the wake of the Inchon landing, United Nations forces broke out of the Pusan Perimeter on September 16 and began striking north. The U.S. 38th Infantry Regiment, 2nd Division, crossed the Naktong River on September 28, attacking the disorganized North Koreans by surprise. The advance company took more than a hundred prisoners, including a major and eight other officers. They also captured more than a hundred tons of ammunition and arms.

Meanwhile, north of the Naktong Bulge, the 5th Regimental Combat Team, 1st Cavalry Division, recaptured crucial Hill 268 on September 18, and the town of Waegwan was flanked. Leaving more than 250 dead on the terrain between the hill and the Naktong, the North Korean 3rd Division fled to the north. In five days of savage fighting, the enemy defense line in front of Taegu collapsed, and the U.S. 24th Division secured a strongpoint for crossing the Naktong.

The North Korean High Command could not ignore the U.N. Inchon landing any longer as the U.S. forces had already crossed the Naktong. The news was out, spreading chaos and panic among the North Korean troops around the Pusan Perimeter. The enemy 6th and 7th Divisions in the far south began a fast retreat during the night of September 18–19.

On the east coast, the South Korean 3rd Division recaptured Pohang, and repulsed the Communist 5th Division northward. The South Koreans now could advance in the rugged mountains just west of the coast.

On September 19, the 12th Regiment of the South Korean 1st Division commanded by General Paik Sun-yup discovered a gap between the lines of the North Korean 1st and 13th Divisions and penetrated into the enemy's rear. The North Koreans, who were desperately resisting on the ridges around Taegu, hurriedly retreated to Sangju.

On September 20, the 24th Infantry Division crossed the Naktong on the left of the 1st Cavalry Division. Combined with the breakthrough of General Paik's 1st Division on the Cavalry Division's right, the U.N. forces overwhelmed the retreating enemy. An American battalion captured as many as 1,700 enemy troops overnight while multitude of others surrendered to other U.N. units.

North Korean 13th Division, which had retreated from the ridges near Taegu, was on the verge of collapse. Before dawn on September 21, its chief of staff, Senior Colonel (equivalent to brigadier general) Lee Hak-ku, had slipped away from his unit and awakened two men of the 8th Cavalry Regiment sleeping in a foxhole in Tabu-dong near Taegu and wanted to surrender.

When taken to a rear command post, the thirty-year-old Communist officer readily gave full information on the chaotic state of his division, revealing: (1) they held no front line, (2) the regiments had lost communication with their division headquarters, (3) the division, 75 percent of whose members were forcibly inducted South Koreans, was down to 1,500 men, (4) men were fleeing because of a lack of food supply, (5) there were no tanks, and only a few self-propelled guns and mortars, and (6) of their 300 trucks, only 30 could run.

Although Lee talked at length about the crushing blow to his division, he did not give the full story of why he had surrendered.

Tabu-dong, where Lee had surrendered, was a beautiful town surrounded by verdant mountains. But it became the furious battle ground of powerful armies, and its burned houses and desolate fields were full of corpses. The town met misfortune because it was the natural gateway to Taegu 14 miles to south, a strategic point on the way to Pusan.

The North Korean Army had tried to seize Tabu-dong first for the purpose of taking Taegu, seat of the provisional government of South Korea. The Communist forces began an all-out attack on Tabu-dong on August 4, sending tanks along sandy roads, but American artillery fire supporting the South Korean 1st Division crushed the tanks one after another. American soldiers who had heard the shells from enemy tanks and saw the balls of fire hurtling down the road through the night dubbed the Tabu-dong valley the "Bowling Alley." By September 23 when the fierce fighting ended in victory for the 1st Division, Tabu-dong had been turned into a wasteland. The battle of the Bowling Alley was over and Taegu was saved.

By late September, it was North Koreans instead of Americans who straggled through the hills, broken, demoralized, shoeless, and hungry.

On September 25, the 38th U.S. Infantry Regiment of the 2nd Division moved northwest toward Kochang. It broke through the thin defensive crust of the North Korean 2nd Division and was in the enemy artillery areas, over-running guns, vehicles, and heavy equipment. The 38th Infantry killed more than 200 enemy soldiers, captured 450 more. The commanding general of the enemy division and the remnants of his men melted into the hills, where they became guerrillas.

The American troops, well supplied with vehicles, were advancing faster than the enemy could flee. General Walker had ordered the divisions to forget about their flanks, to press ahead against a beaten enemy.

Meanwhile, units of the 1st Cavalry Division sweeping north and the 7th Infantry Division moving southward from Inchon carried out a pincer attack against the enemy after meeting at Osan, where the American forces had fought their first battle in the Korean War.

Marching North of the 38th Parallel

Trapped between the anvil of the X Corps on the north, and the hammer of the Eighth Army smashing upward from the south, no more than 25,000 survivors of the North Koreans were able to retreat north of the 38th Parallel. American field commanders now could feel easy, and their soldiers relished the chance of attacking the routed enemy instead of being chased and killed by them as before. The American government had regained confidence after the initial reverses.

It was inevitable that the United States should take the position that the North Korean Communist state must now be destroyed for its lawlessness and that all Korea should be united under the government of the Republic of Korea.

The desire to unite the two halves of Korea under Syngman Rhee was deemed unquestionably proper, and in the best interests of the United Nations — if the U.N. had the power to accomplish it.

On September 27, 1950, the Joint Chiefs of Staff instructed General MacArthur as follows:

1. His primary objective was to be the destruction of all North Korean military forces.

2. His secondary mission was the unification of Korea under Syngman Rhee, if possible.

3. He was to determine whether Soviet or Chinese intervention appeared likely, and to report such threat if it developed. [6]

Following the directive, two days later General George C. Marshall, the new secretary of defense, sent General MacArthur a personal letter saying that MacArthur was free both tactically and strategically to proceed across the 38th Parallel and that President Truman concurred. [7]

Whatever the ploy and counterploy of the great powers, it was considered to be in the vital interest of the Republic of Korea to expand to the Yalu River to reunify the country. President Rhee, who had devoted his life to Korean independence, could never accept anything less.

On September 29, President Rhee summoned Army Chief of Staff Chung Il-kwon to Kyongmudae, the presidential mansion, in Pusan.

"Can you order the Korean Army to march north beyond the 38th Parallel?"

Chung pointed out that the operational authority to do so was in the hands of the commander of the United Nations forces.

"Aren't you the chief of staff of the Korean Army? Whose order will you obey, the U.N. commander or the president?"

"Your Excellency, of course I will obey you."

On the morning of September 30, Chung met Brigadier General Kim Paek-il, commander of the 1st Corps, at his headquarters on the northeast front. They decided to let the 3rd Division, led by Brigadier General Lee Jong-chan, march north across the 38th Parallel, and one battalion of its 23rd Regiment was ordered to the demarcation line at 11:30 p.m., October 1. The South Koreans crossed the artificial barrier triumphantly.

On October 1, MacArthur broadcast an ultimatum to Kim Il Sung demanding unconditional surrender of the North Korean forces, stating: "The early and total defeat and complete destruction of your armed forces and war-making potential is now inevitable." But Kim did not respond.

On October 7, the United Nations General Assembly adopted a resolution, approving U.N. military action north of the 38th Parallel for unification of all Korea. The resolution, submitted by the British delegate with American backing was overwhelmingly approved by 47 nations. Five Communist bloc nations voted against it and seven members abstained. The Joint Chiefs of Staff sent a copy of the U.N. resolution to MacArthur, who took it as a mandate for his conquest of North Korea.

On the same day, U.S. and British troops smashed across the Parallel through Kaesong in the west, while the South Koreans marched northward to the east. On the night of October 10, the South Korean 3rd and Capitol Divisions secured the important port city of Wonsan about 100 miles north.

President Syngman Rhee had told the South Koreans, "We have to advance as far as the Manchurian border until not a single enemy soldier is left in our country."

The 7th and 8th Divisions of the South Korean 2nd Corps began striking up the center of the peninsula toward the Iron Triangle, an important communication and supply center encompassing Chorwon, Kumwha and Pyongyang. Its capture on October 13, along with the fall of Wonsan, augured well for the U.N. counter-invasion.

On the western front, the U.S. 1st Cavalry Division and the British 27th Brigade, South Korean 1st Division, and U.S. 24th Division rushed north one after another. As the U.S. Cavalry Division and the South Korean 1st Division were competing to enter the North Korean capital city of Pyongyang first, General Walker reaffirmed his confidence.

Under these circumstances, MacArthur urged Kim Il Sung again to surrender, but again Kim made no reply. Kim had already been informed of the Communist Chinese Central Committee decision to dispatch a "volunteer army" to North Korea.

Kim Il Sung, who had moved his capital to the vicinity of the Yalu, broadcast to his army on October 14 proclaiming, "Do not retreat one step further. Now we have no space in which to fall back." He declared that traitors and agitators were to be shot on the spot, regardless of rank, and a new "surveillance army unit" of politically reliable veterans was to be formed.

When President Truman learned that two U.S. fighter planes had attacked a Soviet airfield near Vladivostok 62 miles above the North Korean border on October 8, he decided to hear MacArthur's view on the possibility of Chinese or Soviet intervention. The two met on Wake Island, midway between Honolulu and Tokyo, on October 15. Among those accompanying the President were General Omar Bradley, the army chief of staff; Army Secretary Frank Pace; Admiral Arthur W. Radford, commander for the Pacific Fleet; and Secretary of State Dean Rusk. MacArthur brought along John J. Muccio, ambassador to Korea.

After discussing the rehabilitation and reunification of the two Koreas, Truman asked what were the chances for Chinese or Soviet interference. MacArthur confidently replied:

Very little. Had they interfered in the first or second months it would have been decisive. We are no longer fearful of their intervention. We no longer stand hat in hand. The Chinese have 300,000 men in Manchuria. Of these probably not more than 100,000 to 125,000 are distributed along the Yalu River. Only 50,000 to 60,000 could be gotten across the Yalu River. They have no air force. Now that we have bases for our air force in Korea, if the Chinese tried to get down to Pyongyang there would be the greatest slaughter. [8]

MacArthur expressed concern that the Soviets might provide air support to Chinese ground troops, but he said it would not be effective.

At the end the two discussed President Syngman Rhee. MacArthur criticized a U.N. General Assembly draft resolution that equated the South Koreans with the North Koreans in terms of a postwar settlement. The resolution ignored the elections the South Koreans held in 1948 and called for a new vote in both parts of the country. "It would be bad to turn out of office a government which had stood up so well and taken such a beating, and to treat them just like the North Koreans," MacArthur said. Truman agreed. "This cannot be done and must not be done....We must make it plain that we are supporting the Rhee government and propaganda can go to hell." [9]

While Truman and MacArthur conferred at Wake on October 15, four Chinese Communist armies, 120,000 strong, were already inside North Korea. They would be followed in just a few days by two more armies, so that by the end of October 180,000 Communist Chinese forces had crossed the Yalu River. By the middle of November 1950, approximately 180,000 Chinese troops waited in front of the Eighth Army, while 120,000 lurked in the mountains surrounding the Changjin Reservoir on X Corps's flank. Yet American intelligence did not know they were there.

On October 14, when Kim Il Sung exhorted his troops to "fight to the last," U.N. forces had already broken through the Pyongyang defense line. American intelligence estimated enemy troops deployed for the defense of the North Korean capital city at less than 8,000.

South Korean 3rd Division soldiers marching north show U.N. forces a road sign reading, "YOU ARE CROSSING THE 38th PARALLEL."

U.N. troops take over Kim II Sung's office in the capitol building after capturing Pyongyang on October 19, 1950.

The final attack on Pyongyang was launched on October 19 spearheaded by the U.S. 1st Cavalry Division which broke through the peripheral defense line while the South Korean 1st Division rolled into the city crushing the enemy troops with tanks. Because there was not much street fighting, the city could escape such big destruction as was inflicted on Seoul at the time of the North Korean occupation. Perhaps for this reason the citizens welcomed the U.N. troops more heartily, waving hand-made U.N. flags.

President Rhee Enters Pyongyang

Exultant President Syngman Rhee flew to Pyongyang across the 38th Parallel on October 30. I accompanied him as the only reporter to cover his historic trip to the fallen North Korean capital. Defense Minister Shin Sung-mo, presidential secretary Kim Kwang-sop, and chief bodyguard Kim Chang-hung were in the suite of the presidential party, escorted by a squadron of South Korean Air Force planes.

When crossing the 38th Parallel, I was reminiscing on my flight from Communized North Korea across the artificial line at the risk of my life in early September 1945. Now that the Communist invaders were being defeated, I was imbued with new hope for the future of my country and myself.

Upon arrival at the conquered North Korean capital, Rhee was greeted by an exultant crowd of some 50,000 Pyongyang citizens at the City Hall plaza waving South Korean flags, crying, "Mansei" (Long live) for the white-haired South Korean president. He was waving his hat, with joyous tears in his eyes, to the cheering throng.

Rhee told them in an emotion-filled speech:

> As the same lineage of Tangoon [mythical founder of
> the Korean nation twenty-four centuries before
> Christ], we must unify our nation and preserve free-
> dom and peace for ever in this beautiful land of ours
> by repelling the Communists. Now is the time for us to
> be united in one mind....As a homogeneous race for
> more than four thousand years, we are the people
> sharing the lot of life or death by helping each other

even in dire poverty or hardship. You, the citizens of Pyongyang who have assembled here today, should stand in the way of our march to the Yalu.

Many citizens were moved to tears over the return of the life-long unification champion. President Rhee walked into the crowd and hugged elderly citizens, causing security concern among his bodyguards.

While the welcoming ceremony was going on, I hurriedly looked around part of the captured capital. I marveled at the trappings of the houses of Russian officials around the Soviet embassy. There were large stores of vine, vodka, caviar and large pictures, posters and busts of Joseph Stalin.

I also took a look in Kim Il Sung's office. It could be approached through four antechambers, each with a portrait of Stalin, and the inner sanctum was rich with gorgeous rugs of intricate patterns and expensive furniture. There was Kim's enormous mahogany desk with a huge portrait of Stalin hung on the wall behind it.

Accompanying the presidential party, I went to see the ancient pavilion "Pubyongnu" on the hill by the Taedong River. On the way, we saw the corpses of two American soldiers under a large rock on the riverside. Both were lying face down with their hands tied behind them. Aged about 22 or 23, the two wore civilian pants and GI shirts of the U.S. Army. They appeared to be American prisoners-of-war killed by North Korean troops during their flight from Pyongyang before the onrushing U.N. forces.

As the president wished to extend his North Korean tour to Hamhung in the northeastern district, seized by the South Korean Capital Division on October 17, his plane landed at Chujimyon airstrip near Hamhung at dusk. I was thrilled at the thought of visiting Hamhung, where I had attended a Christian mission school.

To my great regret, however, the South Korean Army officer who greeted the presidential party at the airstrip strongly advised the president to cancel his visit to Hamhung and return to Seoul on grounds that it would be extremely dangerous at night in that still insecure zone. So the presidential party could not but comply with the officer's earnest plea. (President Rhee visited Hamhung later, on November 22.)

Cheering Pyongyang citizens pack Pyongyang City Hall Plaza to greet President Syngman Rhee on October 30, 1950.

While flying back to Seoul, I asked President Rhee, "How do you feel today?"

Without a sign of fatigue, the aged Rhee said:

> I have never been happier than today. When I ordered our people to fight against the Communist aggressors, I envisioned our victory. Today I realize that our victory is being achieved. Not an inch of our territory should be in Communist hands. Not a single person should live a life of slavery under Communist rule. Now people in Pyongyang, too, have come to lead a free life. All this has become possible thanks to divine protection. I am deeply grateful to the United Nations which protects us from the Communist aggressors as well as American forces and our officers and men so gallantly fighting under the command of General MacArthur.

Optimism Shattered

Meanwhile, three divisions — the 6th, 7th, and 8th divisions — of the South Korean II Corps, high in morale with the capture of Pyongyang, were mopping up enemy troops in the mountains of central Korea, about 30 miles north of the 38th Parallel.

The U.S. Eighth Army, with I Corps in the vanguard, was advancing to the Chongchon River, midway between Pyongyang and the Yalu. Military leaders believed that seizure of the Chongchon banks was the war's last objective.

The 187th Airborne Regiment, which had earlier landed in Korea but had been kept in reserve, dropped 3,000 paratroops at Sukchon and Sunchon, about 28 miles north of Pyongyang, on October 20 in an effort to trap North Korean officials and troops escaping from the conquered capital city of Pyongyang. But most of the enemy troops and government leaders had already passed the drop site.

But its 3rd battalion and the 27th British Brigade's Australian battalion, converging on the road north of Pyongyang, crushed a

2,500-man North Korean regiment, the last enemy force to leave the capital.

As October waned, cold winds of the approaching winter were blowing into the mountains of North Korea. The winds were surprisingly chilly, but not many of the U.N. and South Korean troops steadily advancing northward complained because they expected to be home by Christmas as General MacArthur had predicted.

Families halfway across the globe felt relieved, too, in the belief that the war was practically over. The New York Times reported on October 29: "Except for unexpected developments along the frontiers of the peninsula, we can now be easy in our minds as to the military outcome."

The "unexpected developments" mentioned here referred to the possibility of intervention by Communist China.

However, this optimism was shattered when the widespread Chinese intervention became apparent. The first blow came on October 25, when the first Communist Chinese soldier was taken prisoner by an American tank battalion which was supporting the 15th Regiment of the South Korean 1st Division near Unsan 15 miles northwest of the Chongchon River. Twelve Chinese became prisoners of war in the ensuing battles. Up to November 24, almost one hundred Chinese troops were captured.

There was a great deal of confusion about the POWs and the way in which they were captured, indicative of a certain confusion among the enemy. American intelligence began assuming that the North Korean Army had been reinforced with certain small groups of Chinese from Manchuria. By the middle of October, the U.N. forces in North Korea stood very close to total victory. The North Koreans had deteriorated into remnants. The South Koreans had seized the important port of Wonsan on the east coast, and most of the vital areas of North Korea had been overrun. The U.N. Command therefore had paid little attention to the ominous Chinese intervention.

However, General Walker had been worried about the future of X Corps advancing on the east coast under the direct command of MacArthur's headquarters in Tokyo. He felt that it should cease to report separately to MacArthur's headquarters and come under his command for better coordination.

Instead of merging X Corps with the Eighth Army, MacArthur had decided to deploy it on the east coast of Korea, and keep it subordinate, not to General Walker, but to himself in Tokyo. The X Corps was moving overland, marching toward the far reaches of the north, where the Yalu and Tumen Rivers roared through gloomy gorges, and where Korea touched Manchuria and Siberia.

MacArthur felt he could coordinate the advance of each column, the Eighth Army in the west and X Corps in the east, better from Tokyo than could Walker from Korea. MacArthur's reasoning was based on the Korean terrain.

As a native of the northeastern region of Korea, I am familiar with topographical features there. Above the Seoul-Wonsan corridor, there is only one good lateral route of communication running across Korea — the Pyongyang-Wonsan road and rail line. North of this, the Nanglim Mountains rise to dizzying heights. Running north and south, they cross the land with rugged crests and vast, dark gorges, forming a trackless waste across which even Koreans cannot go. Until the valley of the Yalu River or the Tumen River is reached, there is no lateral road connecting east and west.

Because of the horrendous mountains in east central Korea, contact between the two advancing U.N. commands was difficult. As the U.N. forces advanced toward the Yalu-Tumen Rivers, this mountainous gap spread as wide as 60 miles in places. Nothing like a contiguous line or solid front could be maintained.

MacArthur had told Eighth Army Commander Walker and X Corps Commander Almond to press up to the Yalu. This instruction was in violation of a September 27 directive from the Joint Chiefs of Staff to permit only South Korean troops to operate near the Manchurian border — a restriction which the Truman Administration had imposed in a hopeful effort to keep Communist China from being antagonized by the drive north.

MacArthur replied that the South Koreans alone could not handle the situation. In response to MacArthur's directive, Walker ordered his commanders to let their columns speed ahead, without bothering to coordinate with the advance of the units on their flanks. Despite difficult logistic problems due to geographical conditions, the Eighth Army crossed the Chongchon on October 24.

CHINESE INTERVENTION

Chaos on Two Fronts

By the middle of November 1950, the Communist Chinese had succeeded in sending 30 full divisions into Korea: 18 divisions or 180,000 men of the XIII Army Group in the west and center opposing the U.S. Eighth Army and the South Korean forces, and 12 divisions or 120,000 men of the IX Army Group facing the U.S. X Corps in the east. It was incredible that American intelligence never accepted the fact that the Communist Chinese Forces (CCF) were in Korea in force during October-November 1950. No concrete evidence that the Chinese were in Korea could be put forth. Americans believed it impossible that an army of significant size could cross the Yalu and deploy in Korea without observation by their air forces. American aircraft flew daily over North Korea, and no Chinese forces were sighted.

In late October, the South Korean 1st Division was advancing as the right flank of U.S. I Corps when it met a surprising show of enemy resistance near Unsan. The U.S. 1st Cavalry Division, in reserve at Pyongyang, was brought up to take over the attack from the South Koreans.

East of Unsan, the South Korean division broke. On November 1, the Chinese sprang a carefully prepared trap against the 3rd Battalion, U.S. 8th Cavalry Regiment. The battalion was surrounded, and a roadblock thrown up in the rear. The Chinese Communists, fighting hand-to-hand, swarmed over the battalion's command post. The 8th Cavalry lost more than 600 men. On the Cavalry's right, South Korean II Corps losses were also heavy.

General Walker ordered the 1st Cavalry Division to pull back to the Chongchon and consolidate there. East of Unsan, the enemy had struck against the II Corps at the same time they had hit the South Korean 1st Division, and within a few days the assault shattered the entire corps, leaving the Eighth Army's right flank completely exposed.

The 7th Regiment of the South Korean II Corps' 6th Division had reached the banks of the Yalu north of Unsan. That regiment was cut off and destroyed with a loss of more than five hundred men. But some of its soldiers who survived and made their way back carried a bottle of Yalu water for President Syngman Rhee.

Only in the far northeast corner of Korea did the advance of the U.S. X Corps push forward during November. Here there were no Chinese, and the South Korean elements of the 7th Division marched against failing North Korean Army resistance to the Yalu.

The swift drive of the South Korean 3rd and Capital Divisions up the east coast, and the uneventful landings of the U.S. 1st Marine Division at Wonsan and the 7th Division at Iwon had secured that much of the coastal area for the X Corps. The terrain in this eastern part of North Korea dictated three general avenues of pursuit for X Corps: one along the coastal road toward the extreme northeast corner of the peninsula; a corridor to the west, running almost due north from Iwon; and southwest of that, an inland road from the Hamhung area through the Changjin Reservoir.

Winter came early, in the second week of November, with sub-zero winds howling down from Siberia. Moving over ill-defined roads, climbing thousands of feet into high hills, the U.S. 1st Marine Division was strung out in a long and vulnerable column.

The 1st Marine Division had already been in battle with the Communist Chinese 124th Division. On November 2, the 7th Marines collided with the Chinese at Sudong along the road to Changjin Reservoir, at virtually the same site of the South Korean 3rd Division's late October defeat. The Marines drove the Chinese Communists back and advanced steadily up to the high Koto-ri plateau, about 50 miles northwest of Hungnam. From captured prisoners, they learned of large enemy forces being deployed around Changjin Reservoir.

Meanwhile, the X Corps continued its northward drive. The most satisfying of all these was the U.S. 7th Division's advance along the road from Iwon. It encountered only light opposition, and on November 21, the lead battalion of the division's 17th Regiment moved into Hyesanjin, on the banks of the Yalu. In his message of congratulations MacArthur said the 7th Division had "hit the jackpot."

Major General Oliver P. Smith, the 1st Marine Division commander, who did not share the general's optimism for the task ahead, deliberately slowed his advance, securing his supply lines as he went, building a base with an airstrip in Hagaru for future operations.

On November 15, the Marine Division's mission changed. Instead of striking north from the reservoir, they were directed to proceed westward first to cut the road and rail line coming down from the Yalu town of Manpojin. MacArthur now realized that the Eighth Army's advance in the west had become difficult. This late show of caution on MacArthur's part did not mean his new offensive plan had changed.

Eighth Army Withdrawal

When General Walker's Eighth Army pushed off on its offensive on November 24, I Corps' 24th Division and South Korean 1st Division were on its left flank and on the right was South Korean II Corps. In the center of the Eighth Army line was IX Corps, divided by the Chongchon River. In reserve were the U.S. 1st Cavalry Division, two British brigades, and the newly arrived Turkish Brigade.

The offensive went well for the first day, but beginning early the next morning, the Chinese forces launched a counteroffensive which changed the course of war. The Chinese pushed along the entire Eighth Army front, striking the U.S. 24th Division which had advanced north of the Chongchon, and forcing the South Korean II Corps to retreat. Then they broke through the exposed right flank of the Eighth Army attacking the 2nd Division in the rear and encircling the Eighth Army. The Turkish Brigade, British Brigade, and the U.S. 1st Cavalry Division resisted, but they were overwhelmed by the enemy's strength.

As the Chinese launched an all-out attack along the entire Eighth Army line forcing the United Nations forces to pull back to the Chongchon River, General Walker decided to withdraw the Eighth

Army to Pyongyang. He could use U.S. Air Force and naval vessels off the coast to check the enemy advance during the retreat across the river, with the U.S. 2nd Division covering the withdrawal on the ground, holding above Kunu-ri.

South of the broad, shallow Chongchon, some 30 miles northwestward from the Yellow Sea, the forlorn village of Kunu-ri sat across the junction of the north-south road from Sunchon and the lateral road running from Huichon to a connection with the main coastal highway at Shinanju.

To the east, or right, of Kunu-ri the mountains rose, high and terrifying in a foggy sky, becoming virtually impenetrable at Huichon. And to the east, along the road, on both sides of the river, spread the 2nd Infantry Division, from Kunu-ri to Kujang-dong. On their right were deployed the two divisions, the 6th and 8th of the South Korean II Corps. West of them, a rifle regiment of the U.S. 25th Division held the line on a front generally facing northwest toward Huichon and the forbidding mountains.

On November 28, the U.S. 2nd Division was falling back toward Kunu-ri. While the 38th Regiment was being pushed back on the right and south, the 9th, across the Chongchon, was also being forced backward. Strung out along the river and road, the division was nearly taken by a double envelopment of the Chinese.

To the north and east, the U.S 25th Division, also bloodied, though not to the extent of the 2nd, was falling back toward the Kunu-ri junction.

On December 1, the 2nd Division began to pull back to Sunchon. Midway along the road, it was assaulted by a Chinese ambush at a narrow pass between two cliffs.

Some infantry groups attacked the Chinese positions, and air strikes kept pounding away at them. Eventually, in the early dawn hours of the next morning, with a British force holding open the bottom of the pass, the last of the 2nd Division cleared the pass. The British had lost 3,000 of the 7,000 men who had started out on the retreat from Kunu-ri.

The Chinese did not pursue the Eighth Army back to Pyongyang. Walker's motorized troops easily outraced them under air cover. Estimated enemy casualties in the first two weeks of December were 33,000.

Top American commanders pose with President Syngman Rhee in Pusan in 1951. Left to right: Lt. Gen. John B. Coulter, Eighth Army deputy commander; Lt. Gen. James A. Van Fleet, Eighth Army commander; President Rhee; Gen. Mathew B. Ridgway, United Nations commander; John J. Muccio, U.S. ambassador to South Korea.

Kim Il Sung (right) poses with Peng Teh-huai, commander of the Communist Chinese Forces.

Refugees from Pyongyang crawl over the twisted steel girders of the Taedong River bridge as the Eighth Army withdraws from Pyongyang city on January 5, 1951. This picture, taken by AP photographer Max Desfor, won a Pulitzer Prize.

For a while Walker hoped to form a U.N. line from Pyongyang east to Wonsan. But the Chinese forces captured Songchon, on the lateral road between those two cities. So, on December 5 the Eighth Army abandoned Pyongyang, burning all the supplies it could not take with it, and blowing up everything of military value. The army crossed the Taedong River and headed south, to form a line around the 38th Parallel.

In the outskirts of the abandoned North Korean capital, ammunition depots were blown up and flames from fuel oil storages were scorching the sky. Innumerable refugees climbed over the demolished Taedong Railway Bridge in a desperate attempt to cross the river. An and number of them fell and drowned. AP photographer Max Desfor shot the tragic scene, and won a Pulitzer Prize.

Although the Eighth Army was saved after its skillful withdrawal, MacArthur had lost the left arm of his massive operation in the west. The U.S. 1st Marine Division's push westward from the Changjin Reservoir (74 miles in circumference) area across the Nanglim Mountain range also ran into a wall of Chinese human wave attacks, thus losing the right arm of his ambitious maneuver in the east.

Bloody Retreat from Changjin

Far to the east, Major General Oliver P. Smith's 1st Marine Division had begun to march through a much longer ambush of no less than seven enemy divisions in the cruel and unrelenting cold. On the Kaema plateau to which the 1st Marines had come in late November, the temperature was consistently at –5° F to –20° F or –25° F during the night and only infrequently above 32° F during the day.

North from the port of Hungnam on the cold, gray waters of the Sea of Japan (Eastern Sea), a narrow, dirt and gravel road snaked into the hills. For some 43 miles — the distance from Hungnam to Chinhung-ni — the road contained two lanes and moved across reasonably rolling ground.

But at Chinhung-ni, where my family had lived, the road rose 2,500 feet into cold, thin mountain air. The road crept ribbon-like into the soaring mountains, a yawning abyss on one side and a precipice on the other.

The U.S. Marines climbed and climbed, struggling upward to the Kaema plateau, on which sat the single, forlorn village of Koto-ri. From Koto-ri the road crept through 5,300-foot high hills to the city of Hagaru, straggling near the southern tip.of the 30 miles long Changjin Reservoir.

Hagaru, where I had attended a primary school, was an important center before the war, located in a bleak bowl of frozen earth some three miles across. Here the road forked.

One fork, the right hand, passed north and east into equally desolate terrain. The other skirted the reservoir and turned west; it climbed the 4,000-foot-high peaks of Toktong Pass, and after 14 miles through gorges it led into a broad valley ringed by five great ridges.

Here, in this valley, sat the lowly village of Yudamni, 3,500 feet above sea level, hardly sheltered from the bitter winds and snows of Siberia by its 5,300 feet high ring of peaks. Here, and along the whole length of the road from Hungnam, the land is barren and bleak in winter.

It was in this winter of 1950 that the men of the 1st Marine Division had been marching north toward the light blue sheet of ice that was Changjin Reservoir while the Communist Chinese IX Army Corps came stealing down the east side of the gap dividing the United Nations Forces, thus ensnaring the 105,000 U.S. and South Korean troops.

As the 5th and 7th Marine Regiments stepped off for their drive west from Yudam-ni near Hagaru with the bitter winter wind lashing at them across the reservoir, the Chinese struck. In all, seven divisions of the Communist Chinese IX Army Corps had been sent into northeast Korea with the specific mission of destroying the Marine division.

On the night of November 27, Chinese forces attacked with savage force. The 79th and 89th Divisions hurled their assault battalions against the Yudam-ni ridge, where seesaw fighting raged until dawn, while the 59th marched south to cut the road between Yudam-ni and Hagaru.

On the following night, two more Chinese divisions attacked Hagaru and came within an eyelash of capturing it, with its important air strip, and the following night elements of two more struck at Koto-ri. A Task Force of British Marines lost two-thirds of its 1,000 men fighting its way north from Koto-ri to Hagaru to help the Americans keep the vital air strip. During these three days the Chinese blocked the road at points along the 34 miles from Yudam-ni, 14 miles north of Hagaru.

In the first few days of December the predicament of the 1st Marine Division seemed hopeless. The Chinese had already flanked the Marines on the west to a depth of 35 miles and had fragmented them by seizing the road linking the four strongholds from Yudam-ni at the reservoir south to Hagaru to Koto-ri to Chinhung-ni.

By the afternoon of December 4, the marines of Yudam-ni had successfully gained Hagaru, having suffered 1,500 casualties — a third of them were from frostbite. General Smith, meanwhile, had arranged to fly out his casualties, as well as to fly in reinforcements.

On December 6, as the men of the 5th Marines began pulling down from the Hagaru hills, the last of the U.S. transports flew the final 4,312 casualties out of the trap. By the night of December 7, the column from Hagaru had fought its way into Koto-ri, and there were now 14,000 men under General Smith's command, of whom a little less than 12,000 were Marines. It cost the column twenty-two hours of agony to cover the nine miles from Hagaru to Koto-ri. On arrival there were 600 more wounded. At Koto-ri, these wounded were flown out, and the dead were buried in shallow graves cut out of the frozen ground by bulldozers.

And so the 1st Marine Division and its attached soldiers broke out of the Chinese trap, suffering about 7,500 casualties, half of them from frostbite, while inflicting, with air support, an estimated 37,000 casualties on the enemy.

The entire U.S. X Corps drive throughout northeast Korea had collapsed with the Chinese attack on the U.S. 1st Marine Division. The two South Korean divisions of the I Corps — the Capital Division and the 3rd Division — were pulled back all the way to Hungnam. The U.S. 7th Division, too, was able to make its way back to Hungnam without serious trouble.

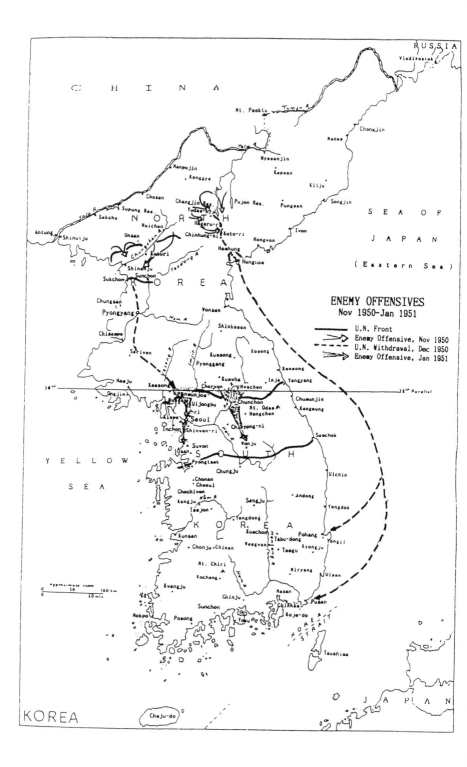

The 5th Marines pulling back from the Hagaru hills on December 6, 1950.

The Marines descend the steep Whangchoryong pass from Koto-ri on December 10, 1950.

U.S. and South Korean navy landing craft remove 100,000 suffering refugees, most of whom expected to be killed by the Communists if they stayed behind, from Hungnam on December 24, 1950.

In a perimeter around the beachhead, the U.S. 3rd Infantry Division kept the port of Hungnam open while behind it the U.S. Navy had executed the greatest evacuation in its history: 105,000 men of X Corps in all, and 91,000 [North] Korean refugees. As many as 5,000 refugees crowded into each LST. One hundred nine ships, making 193 trips, carried this human cargo away from Hungnam, along with 17,500 vehicles and 350,000 tons of equipment. It was all done in ten days. [10]

Hungnam was blown up, and the port city set afire. Even the docks were destroyed. On Christmas Eve, with the coastline a mass of flame and billowing dark smoke, the convoys took to sea, leaving the shore to the enemy.

A close friend of mine since high school days in Hamhung, Dr. Hyun Bong-hak, was given credit for the evacuation of the multitude of North Korean refugees. Hyun, who was civil affairs advisor to General Almond, had been begging the general to save the thousands of North Koreans who had been cooperating with the U.N. forces. When Hyun, now professor of pathology at Thomas Jefferson University in Philadelphia, learned from Almond's deputy chief staff Colonel Edward Forney how many fellow Koreans had been taken out of Hungnam, he could not find words of thanks. Hyun wrote later: "When Colonel Forney told me that 100,000 Koreans had been taken out of Hungnam, I tried to thank him, but was unable to speak. The X Corps had helped more people than I would ever have thought possible."

Reminiscences of Changjin

The U.S. 1st Marine Division and attached army troops had fought against the Chinese human sea assaults while the bitter Siberian winds came whistling down desolate mountain peaks, freezing the rivers, choking the gorges with snow and glazing the rocks with ice. Some had to fight from behind the heaps of dead and frozen bodies. Changjin ("Chosin" in Japanese), therefore, was dubbed "Frozen Chosin" by the U.N. troops.

Had the battles been fought in summer, when the highest temperature was 80° F to 82° F with alpine plants blooming on the hills, the war situation might have been much different — without the miserable frostbite casualties of so many United Nations troops. I am especially sorrowful that Changjin, my birthplace, was the site of such a disastrous battle site for the U.N. forces.

I was born in the remote village of Shinha-ri, near Hagaru-ri, on the 3,960-foot-high Kaema plateau, and attended Hagaru Primary School, graduating with honors in 1932. I gave up going to a higher school because my parents were so poor, and was employed by Hagaru Savings and Loan Association as an office boy. I was living in lodgings since childhood because my parents lived 18 miles away from Hagaru-ri.

Besides the regular office work, I performed hard chores for the family of the Association's president, Kim Sung-guk, who lived in the same premises. The work included such jobs as fetching water from a nearby well and chopping firewood for Kim's family bath. It was especially severe in winter when the average temperature stood at –5° F.

Aspiring to go to a higher school, I saved half of my meager monthly pay of 15 yen for two years. In February 1934, I visited my father for the first time after he had moved to Chinhung-ni at the foot of Whangchoryong Pass (3,960 ft) adjoining Changjin-kun on Kaema plateau in the north. I begged him to let me apply for an entrance examination at Yongsaeng High School, a Presbyterian mission, in Hamhung, 10 miles northwest of Hungnam. But my poverty-stricken father flatly said, "No."

Despite father's objection, I applied for admission using his seal "Shinn Ye-kyong," a chop that I had secretly engraved by myself. After passing the entrance examination in the following month, I confessed, with deep apology, to father what I had done against his will. He was furious.

During the first year at Yongsaeing, school expenses were covered with the money I had saved at the Savings Association. From the second year I was exempted from tuition each school-year as an honor student and earned board working as a private tutor.

Reminiscing on the scenes of the mountains and rivers of Changjin, so indelibly etched on my heart in boyhood, I now pray: May the U.N. heroes fallen in the tragic battles in Changjin rest in peace!

RIDGWAY IN ACTION

General Walker Killed in Accident

Hordes of Communist Chinese forces, assembled at the Yong-chon-Kumwha-Hwachon line in the central front, broke through the 38th Parallel on December 24, and swarmed into the South Korean side. On the previous day, Lieutenant General Walton Walker, riding in his jeep, was killed in a highway accident. He had been riding along a narrow, icy road to visit a unit in the Uijongbu area 14 miles north of Seoul to present a Silver Star to his son, Lieutenant Sam Walker. A weapons-carrier truck of the South Korean 6th Division coming south suddenly pulled out of line in an attempt to pass and collided with the general's jeep. He was killed almost immediately. (The weapons carrier driver was arrested.)

Within a few hours of notification of the Eighth Army commander's death, the Joint Chiefs of Staff appointed Lieutenant General Mathew B. Ridgway, who had commanded the 82nd Airborne Division during World War II, to take Walker's place.

Walker had done his best, against great odds, in the Korean War. He fought in a way completely new to his experience. His blunt, bulldog outspokenness and stubbornness had much to do with the successful defense of the Pusan Perimeter.

Ridgway, a well-built, bald soldier with the look of an eagle about his strong-nosed face, was the kind of leader the Eighth Army needed. He had an excellent World War II combat record and a reputation for being a general who understands the shifts and turns of international politics. Meeting President Syngman Rhee for the first time upon his arrival in Korea on December 26, Ridgway said: "I am glad to be here. And I've come to stay."

The following three days Ridgway spent traveling the front, hoping to find a reason to attack. What he found instead was an Army braced in fear along its line north of Seoul, waiting for the new Chinese assault which was expected any time. Ridgway wrote later: "I must say, in all frankness, that the spirit of the Eighth Army as I found it on my arrival there gave me deep concern. There was a definite air of nervousness, of gloomy foreboding, of uncertainty, a spirit of apprehension as to what the future held..." [11]

To restore the Army's lost confidence, Ridgway posted the following statement for his troops:

> ...To me the issues are clear...The real issues are whether the power of Western civilization, as God has permitted it to flower in our own beloved lands, shall defy and defeat Communism; whether the rule of men who shoot their prisoners, enslave their citizens and deride the dignity of man, shall displace the rule of those to whom the individual and his individual rights are sacred; whether we are to survive with God's hand to guide and lead us, or to perish in the dead existence of a Godless world. If these be true, and to me they are, beyond any possibility of challenge, then this has long since ceased to be a fight for freedom for our Korean allies alone and for their national survival. It has become, and it continues to be, a fight for our own freedom, for our own survival, in an honorable independent national existence...These are the main things for which we fight. Never have men of any military command had a greater challenge than we, or finer opportunity to show ourselves and our people at their best — and thus to do honor to the profession of arms, and to those brave men who bred us. [12]

The U.S. Eighth Army, meanwhile, had taken on a truly international character as it now had 365,000 men under its command from 16 foreign nations — the United States, Great Britain, Australia, Canada, New Zealand, Colombia, South Africa, France, Greece, the Netherlands, the Philippines, Thailand, Turkey, Belgium, Ethiopia, and Luxembourg. Besides the troops rallying under the U.N. flag, there were hospital units from Sweden, Norway, and Italy, a hospital ship from Denmark, and a field ambulance from India. The U.S. Army fed the various nationalities — modifying its ration setup to accommodate the demands of a multinational diet.

The Eighth Army's combat formations were disposed on a line beginning in the flats of the Han River delta south of the 38th Parallel and running northeast along the Imjin River before bending eastward through high mountains to the Sea of Japan (Eastern Sea). The I Corps under Major General Frank Milburn was on the left or west of this line, then Major General John Coulter's IX Corps in the center, with the mountainous right held by the South Korean I, II and III Corps. The X Corps, which had withdrawn from Hungnam and landed its troops and equipment at Pohang and Pusan, had begun reorganizing in Pusan.

Opposing this force were an estimated 485,000 enemy troops. The battle formations consisted of 21 divisions from Communist China's Fourth Field Army and 12 divisions of the North Korean Army.

At the dawn of January 1, 1951, elements of seven Communist Chinese Armies and two North Korean corps struck southward toward Seoul and the rail center of Wonju 50 miles to the southeast. The I Corps and IX Corps received the brunt of the enemy's blow. Thousands of Chinese, sweeping over snowy hills and frozen paddies, were killed during their first fierce onslaught.

By mid-morning the enemy had driven deep into the U.N. lines and had broken the South Korean 1st and 7th Divisions.

Strategic Pullback

General Ridgway knew that Seoul was untenable. If he withdrew to positions farther south, he thought he could take advantage of the enemy's forced halt for reinforcements when it came, and seize the initiative. Withdrawal also would make capital of the Chinese inability to sustain a lengthy advance.

The Chinese guns, ammunition, and supplies had to be brought down from the Yalu under constant U.N. air attack, over poor roads, and on a limited amount of transport. The Chinese enemy had manpower, including thousands of Korean laborers, and could live on very little, but there was a limit to the operations of an army that has to bear its ammunition hundreds of miles over mountains, principally by muscle power.

Thus the new exodus out of the capital city of Seoul began on January 4, 1951. And into the night the South Korean government, which had returned from Pusan on October 27 the previous year, and the steady columns of soldiers, foreigners, and hundreds of thousands of refugees fled across the frozen Han River in –5° F weather. Women with tiny babies in their arms and men bearing their old, sick, crippled parents and children on their backs were fleeing helter-skelter southward. Many were pulling two-wheeled carts and ox-carts loaded with their meager household effects.

Because they could walk over the thickly frozen ice, there was no such confusion as seen in the previous evacuation in June 1950, when hundreds of citizens fell from the blown-up Han River bridge and were drowned. Recalling the unutterable Communist persecution, those who had failed to flee before the enemy seizure of the capital last time were racing southward lest they fail this time again.

Foreign correspondents also left the "Naija Apartments" — their office and billets — to go south. I, too, went to Taegu together with Seoul Mayor Kim Tae-sun in his car. It was very fortunate that my younger brother's three-year-old daughter, Chong-suk, who had been missing since two days before, was found in front of the Seoul railway station on the critical day of evacuation. Hal Boyle, AP columnist, flew to Taegu with the little girl and delivered her to her parents.

The Chinese forces had begun entering Seoul, and to the U.S. 25th Division and the British 29th Brigade fell the assignment of holding them off while the rest of the Eighth Army gained the south bank of the Han. Nearly 500,000 gallons of fuel and 23,000 gallons of napalm stored at Kimpo Airfield were destroyed and other installations were burned by the U.S. Fifth Air Force.

The South Koreans in the right and center also fell back, and the entire United Nations command took up a position beginning with Pyongtaek on the west, stretching northeast to Wonju in the center, and from there due east to Samchok on the east coast. Intermediate positions were taken at Suwon to cover the withdrawal of great stocks of supplies.

Ridgway brought his command down to a new defense line, running from Pyongtaek on the west coast — whose loss the preceding summer had opened all of southwest Korea to the enemy

— across the peninsula through Wonju to Samchok on the east coast. Failing to trap the U.S. I and IX Corps in the west, the Chinese and North Korean forces had shifted their strongest blows to the center and the east. These came against the U.S. 2nd Division and the South Koreans, and were assisted by the North Korean II Corps, which had infiltrated the eastern mountains during December. Their target was Wonju, the central bastion of Ridgway's new line. Here the 2nd Division, reinforced with the French and Dutch battalions, fought a gallant battle which took revenge for its beating suffered in December running the gauntlet below the Chongchon River.

In the Wonju action, the 2nd's soldiers held off the enemy in battles fought during fierce snowstorms with the temperature at –5° F. On January 10, with the collapse of the South Korean divisions on the 2nd's right, Wonju was abandoned. The Chinese rushed into the city, and were subjected to saturation bombardment by American B–29s and lighter aircraft. On the same day, Ridgway ordered the U.S. 1st Marine Division to move to the front from Masan against the thousands of enemy soldiers who had poured through the gap on the 2nd Division's right and infiltrated to the rear of the South Korean III Corps.

Counteroffensive Launched

Meanwhile, in the west, Ridgway gained the pause he was hoping for. Patrols moving deep into the north had virtually lost contact with the enemy. To reestablish it, and also to take some of the pressure away from X Corps, he sent a reconnaissance in force forward from the I Corps sector on January 15. The 27th Infantry Task Force, the Wolfhounds, moving up toward Seoul and passing through a frozen and desolated countryside, encountered no serious enemy resistance. Even as the Wolfhounds were moving out, the threat in the center was easing, and X Corps troops were able to stabilize on a line south of Wonju.

It was in this suddenly encouraging situation that the Joint Chiefs of Staff members, General J. Lawton Collins of the Army and General Hoyt Vandenberg of the Air Force, were sent to Korea by

President Truman to find out what the situation really was. They were heartened by what they found. There was no talk of evacuation. Instead, Collins told reporters at Ridgway's headquarters in Taegu: "As of now, we are going to stay and fight."

Wolfhound, and another reconnaissance which followed soon after by IX Corps, found that the enemy held no strong positions near the United Nations lines in the west. To exploit this situation by seeking out the enemy all the way to the Han River, Ridgway launched Operation Thunderbolt, a campaign involving both corps, each utilizing one division and one South Korean regiment.

The attack was ordered forward the following day, January 25, 1951. Seven columns struck north from the two-corps western front, moving warily, relying heavily on air support, methodically destroying enemy pockets while maintaining an unbroken front across the hills.

Meanwhile, the left flank was guaranteed against amphibious surprise by U.S. warships patrolling the west coast. Gradually, Ridgway fed more power into the advance, putting the U.S. 3rd Infantry Division into line on January 27, sending armored spearheads probing boldly toward Seoul, massing artillery and striking the enemy with aerial bombs and napalm.

In the west, the advance units approached Inchon and Kimpo Airfield to the west of Seoul. On February 9, enemy resistance collapsed there, Inchon and Kimpo were taken without a shot the next day, and U.S. soldiers once more looked across the frozen Han into the blackened desolation that was the city of Seoul.

Seoul was still heavily defended, but Ridgway was in no particular hurry. He wanted to bring up the center of his line. X Corps had reclaimed Wonju after patrols found it deserted. And when it also took Hoensong, the next town on the road north, Ridgway told X Corps and South Korean III Corps to coordinate an envelopment of Hongchon, which would bring them abreast and even a little above the two corps on the west. The attack code-named "Roundup," however, encountered a massive enemy counterattack. With the sounds of bugles and whistles which had rung through the frozen November nights, Chinese and North Korean forces struck the South Koreans spreading X Corps' advance in a massive counterattack, and sent them streaming southward.

Chipyong-ni Victory Turns the Tide

On the night of February 11, the Communist Chinese Forces struck south again, this time against the X Corps, which now contained the 23rd Infantry Regiment of the U.S. 2nd Division and the French Battalion. The enemy wanted Chipyong-ni 19 miles northwest of Wonju, for it was the key which could unlock the Eighth Army's entire defense line.

To the northwest of Chipyong-ni, the 23rd dug in across a section of frozen rice paddies, and on the other sides of the valley the line lay across a series of low hills. Here the 23rd, including a French battalion, supported by the 37th Field Artillery of the 5th Cavalry Regiment and Air Force, was fighting against the massive Chinese assault.

The front lines on either side of Chipyong-ni shrank, and Colonel Paul Freeman, commander of the 23rd, his patrols reporting Chinese all sides of him, conferred with X Corps commander General Almond on February 13. Freeman wanted to pull back 15 miles to prevent encirclement; the 2nd Division commander had already approved.

Almond agreed, and submitted the request to Ridgway.

Ridgway's comment was simple: "No."

The word went north to Freeman, who immediately strengthened his perimeter and called his various subordinate commanders in. He advised them, "We're going to stay here and fight it out."

Soon after dark, there was skirmishing, and a few violent close-in brushes on the south of the perimeter, where the 2nd Battalion of the 23rd Infantry, the French Battalion, and a Battery from the 503rd, a ranger company, defended.

Then, two hours past midnight, the Chinese blew bugles and whistles and ran forward toward the lines of the French Battalion which contained many gallant Algerians. As the first platoon of the Chinese troops rushed them, a Frenchman cranked a hand siren, setting up an ungodly screech. A single squad fixed bayonets, grabbed hand grenades, and when the enemy was twenty yards away, came out of their holes and charged. The Chinese, with four times as many men, stopped, turned, and fled into the night.

With light, the Chinese Communists withdrew to the circling hills, and the defenders had a breathing spell. The Air Force came over to scorch the hills with rockets and napalm, and cargo planes made two-dozen ammunition drops. On the night of February 14, the battle took the form it would follow for the next few months; the Chinese throwing in men in vain.

All day during February 15, the Chinese fought stubbornly against air and tank-supported infantry attack, while American artillery pounded them. All day the best they could do was to hold the single hill they had taken at such cost, and with dusk their spirit broke. Those Chinese who could still walk faded into the hills.

After dark, a soft snow fell, covering thousands of Chinese corpses lying in a ring about Chinpyong-ni.

At Chinpyong-ni on February 15, 1951, a massive Chinese offensive had been blunted. On this date the Chinese suffered their first tactical defeat at U.N. hands. They would try again, and again, but now a new pattern had been set.

As the Chinese forces were crushed at Chipyong-ni, the hills yielded plenty of grim evidence that the sustained shelling and aerial bombardment which had preceded the U.N. ground attack had had its effect: they were strewn with the bodies of so many enemy dead that the U.S. Eighth Army used the carnage as a psychological weapon; U.N. planes spilled leaflets reading "Count your bodies!"

A U.S. Army record described their plight:

> When the Chinese Communists attacked in November, they had been fresh, confident and unhurt. By the time their mid-February attack died down, they had been weakened by U.N. air and ground action, and had suffered cold, hunger and disease. The cold, in particular, had affected the Chinese much more than the U.N. forces for most of them were inadequately clothed. Moreover, they did not have, by Western standards, proper medical facilities. As few towns were left standing, they could not find buildings to protect them from the freezing weather. When they did, U.N. aircraft wiped out the buildings with the enemy soldiers. Frostbite and trenchfoot were taking their toll

U.S. Marines look at the more than 400 bodies left behind by the retreating Communist troops who had waged a spring offensive on the central front in early January 1951.

within enemy ranks, and, if prisoners of war were to be believed, they were plagued by typhus, that age-old scourge of armies. Fighting 260 miles south of the Manchurian border, the Chinese found the situation quite different from that in November when they had bases to their immediate rear.[13]

Seoul Retaken for the Last Time

By February 19, 1951, Ridgway moved the U.N. defense line north by pursuing a limited but rapid offensive maneuver. He launched the new Operation Killer for the IX and X Corps to beat the enemy as hard as possible. He also assigned the 1st Marine Division, which had been mopping up Communist guerrillas in the Taegu area, to the IX Corps for the Killer operation. Operation Killer, however, had not lived up to its name, and Ridgway extended his January-February offensive with a new attack called Operation Ripper.

Operation Ripper began on March 7 and was successful from the beginning. Substantial gains were made all along the front of the U.S. IX and X Corps, except at a point 15 miles east of Seoul. Here the soldiers of the 25th Division crossed the Han River in rubber assault boats. By March 10, however, enemy opposition to the Han bridgehead had collapsed, and it became apparent that the Communists were failing back all along the west-central front.

The initial key action was the 25th Division's. When enemy resistance collapsed, and Ripper had a foothold on the enemy's side of the Han, the South Korean 1st Division sent patrols cautiously across the river to probe into the southern outskirts of Seoul and found it virtually deserted. On March 15 U.N. forces moved in, and for the fourth — and last — time, Seoul changed hands, although this time, there was very little to change.

There was no ceremony this time to equal the first liberation of the capital. MacArthur did not come over for the occasion. He had been in Korea a week earlier when Operation Ripper started.

Meanwhile Operation Ripper was pressed forward on all fronts. To the east, four South Korean regiments had at last polished off the

North Korean guerrillas who had been a problem since the breakout
of the Pusan Perimeter in September 1950. Then Ripper was
enlarged to include an I Corps advance; the 187th Airborne
Regiment parachuted into Munsan, 20 miles northwest of Seoul, and
an armored task force pushed forward to link up with it. By the end
of March, IX and X Corps had reached their Ripper objectives, and
the U.N. Command stood poised again at the 38th Parallel.

MacArthur Relieved

By March 1951, the Chinese Communist Forces had been halted,
hurt, and forced back. But this time there was no exultation in
Washington, no confidence in cheap victory. With each of its allies
screaming for an end to the war, now deeply aware of the dangers
involved in humbling Communist China, Washington was willing to
negotiate.

President Truman, who had also been finicky about Soviet
intervention, planned to deliver a resolution which would indicate a
willingness to negotiate with the Communists before any U.N.
advance with major forces north of the 38th Parallel. On March 20
Truman, Dean Acheson, George Marshall, and the Joint Chiefs
discussed the matter, and informed MacArthur:

> The State Department planning a Presidential an-
> nouncement shortly that with clearing of bulk of South
> Korea of aggressors, the United Nations now prepar-
> ing to discuss conditions of settlement in Korea.
> United Nations feeling exists that further diplomatic
> efforts toward settlement should be made before any
> advance with major forces north of the 38th Parallel.
> Time will be required to determine diplomatic reac-
> tions and permit new negotiations that may develop...
> Your recommendation desired. [14]

MacArthur sent a message back that no further restrictions
should be placed on his command, since those already in force — no

bombing of Manchurian bases or diversions against the Chinese Mainland — precluded the possibility of clearing North Korea.

On March 24, without advance notice to Washington, MacArthur issued his own communique from Tokyo. Although it acknowledged that "the fundamental questions continue to be political in nature and must find their answer in the diplomatic sphere," the statement concluded:

"...I stand ready at any time to confer in the field with the commander-in-chief of the enemy forces in the earnest effort to find any military means whereby realization of the political objectives of the United Nations in Korea, to which no nation may justly take exceptions, might be accomplished without further bloodshed."[15]

To Truman, the MacArthur communique was an open defiance of his orders as president and as commander in chief under the Constitution; MacArthur had delivered Communist China an ultimatum.

On December 6, 1950, when the U.N. had begun to grow restive, Truman had sent a directive to MacArthur, instructing that all public statements be cleared through Washington.

It was on April 5, 1951, that Truman resolved to relieve MacArthur of his command. On that date Representative Joseph Martin, Republican House leader, read a personal letter from MacArthur, implying that the general agreed with Martin's proposal that Nationalist Chinese forces on Formosa be used in an invasion of Mainland China.

To President Truman, MacArthur's letter to Martin was clear evidence of the general's insubordination. On the afternoon of April 9, the President signed an order relieving MacArthur of all his several commands, and replacing him with General Mathew B. Ridgway. Secretary of State Dean Acheson sent the orders through Ambassador John Muccio in Korea, with instructions that Secretary of Army Frank Pace, then in Korea, was to proceed immediately to Tokyo, to deliver them in person. Pace could not be reached; he was up near the Eighth Army front.

At 1 a.m. on April 11, Truman's press secretary gave a group of sleepy-eyed reporters a presidential release:

> With deep regret, I have concluded that General of the
> Army Douglas MacArthur is unable to give his whole-
> hearted support to the policies of the United States
> Government and of the United Nations in matters
> pertaining his official duties....I have, therefore,
> relieved General MacArthur of his commands and
> have designated Lieutenant General Mathew B.
> Ridgway as his successor. [16]

General MacArthur took the news, which came to him as a slap in the face, while entertaining luncheon guests with his wife. The general continued the luncheon as if nothing had happened. When Ridgway and Pace reported to him at his office in Tokyo the next afternoon, they too found the general was quiet, composed, helpful and friendly.

South Korean Army Chief of Staff Chung Il-kwon, who was also shocked at the news, immediately reported to President Rhee. "Truman has killed our hopes," Rhee exclaimed, shedding tears. Rhee was losing hope for Korean reunification.

On April 11, a violent storm broke over much of the front in Korea. It snowed, hailed in some sections, and a howling wind blew, leveling tents and stinging the eyes of the soldiers who now heard the news of the historic dismissal.

MacArthur, an erect, brilliant, but old man, returned across the lonely Pacific almost alone on April 15. And the storm broke across America, violent, emotional and as indecisive as the one that had whipped the Korean front. Where MacArthur went, millions cheered him, and many protested that his relief meant a victory for the Communists.

It was on April 19 that General of the Army Douglas MacArthur had his greatest moment. He entered the House of Representatives to thunderous applause. Addressing a joint session of Congress, General MacArthur stated his case. In part, he said:

> ...I address you with neither rancor nor bitterness, in
> the fading twilight of life, with but one purpose in
> mind: to serve my country....

It has been said, in effect, that I am a war monger. Nothing could be further from the truth....But once war is forced upon us, there is no other alternative than to apply every available means to bring it to a swift end. War's very object is victory, not prolonged indecision....In war, indeed, there can be no substitute for victory....Why, my soldiers asked me, surrender military advantage to an enemy in the field? I could not answer....I am closing my fifty-two years of military service. When I joined the Army, even before the turn of the century, it was the fulfillment of all my boyish hopes and dreams. The world has turned over many times since I took the oath on the Plain at West Point, and the hopes and dreams have all since vanished. But I still remember the refrain of one of the most popular barracks ballads of that day, which proclaimed most proudly that old soldiers never die; they just fade away. And like the old soldier of that ballad, I now close my military career and just fade away, an old soldier who tried to do his duty as God gave him the light to see that duty. Good-bye.

Van Fleet Takes Eighth Army Command

The Eighth Army command in Korea passed from General Ridgway to Lieutenant General James A. Van Fleet on April 14, after which Ridgway assumed General MacArthur's duties in Tokyo.

Van Fleet had been a division commander and then a corps commander in Europe in World War II, and after the war he had served as the U.S. military adviser to the Greek Army while it fought, successfully, to defeat an insurgency by Communist guerrillas.

By early April 1951, the U.N. forces, now half a million strong, had crossed the 38th Parallel in most places. The Communist Chinese forces, bleeding badly from multiple wounds inflicted by

U.N. air, sea, and ground action, were hurrying more and more troops into North Korea.

In the meantime, the Eighth Army kept making limited attacks, until in the third week of April its forces were 10 miles above the 38th Parallel everywhere except at Kaesong. In the center of the line, U.N. forces were striking toward the Chorwon-Kumwha-Pyongyang complex, an important communication and supply area called the Iron Triangle.

Now spring had come to Korea, with spring rains, and the countryside was briefly beautiful with grass and flowers. But the skulls of men killed during the winter snows, loosened by the thaw, rolled down the hills to rest among the azalea and forsythia just bursting into bloom.

The U.S. 3rd Infantry Division struck toward Chorwon, up the road running from Seoul, and on April 21 was some ten miles north of the Imjin River. On its right, U.S. IX Corps, consisting of the 1st Marine Division and the South Korean 6th Division, prepared to attack along the line running from Kumwha to the Hwachon Reservoir. On the 3rd Division's left stood the British 29th Brigade, with a frontline strength of 4,000, and the South Korean 1st Division.

The Communist Chinese forces first cracked Van Fleet's line with a massive assault against the weakest part of the IX Corps sector — the South Korean 6th Division. That unit went reeling back, leaving a gap between the 24th Division and the 1st Marine Division. Both these divisions now were subjected to intense battles. But the enemy's chief concern was to exploit the gap between them. Troops poured through despite the efforts of task forces from the U.S. 1st Cavalry Division and the British 29th Brigade which were rushed in to stop them, and cut the road leading northwest from Seoul. And IX Corps, four days after the enemy offensive began, was forced to pull back all the way to the Hongchon River, just below the highway.

On April 22, an estimated half of the 700,000 Communist Chinese and North Korean forces were committed in a three-pronged assault. The first thrust, a secondary one, came in the center striking the British 29th Brigade with six divisions, more than 50,000 men. The next day the Chinese, their horns and bugles raucous in the clear cool night, came across the Imjin River in wide, massive waves, but the British Brigade, attacking in incredible force, stood fast. By dawn the South Korean 1st Division, on their left, had been forced back, and by mid-morning the Chinese crawled over the flinty hills on the Gloucestershire Regiment's flank and rear. The 29th Brigade fired until almost every round of British ammunition in Korea had been exhausted, and at times they fired into Chinese riflemen less than 300 yards away. The American air force tried to drop supplies to them, but the battle was so close around the beleaguered hills that the air drops often landed in the wrong place. But all the air power that could be thrown into the battle swarmed down from the sky, rocketing, blasting, searing the Chinese-dotted hills with napalm.

To the right of the British Brigade, U.S. I Corps was being pounded. The Puerto Rican 65th Infantry, reinforced by a Filipino battalion, was in bad shape. So were the Turks to their right, thus endangering the U.S. 25th Division farther east.

The U.S. 3rd Division, which had fallen back south of the Imjin now and which was not yet under heavy pressure, abandoning its own probe toward Chorwon, tried to break through with tanks and infantry. On the hill the 29th Brigade held fast. By dusk, a gap of seven miles had been opened between them and the other units of the 29th Brigade.

All night of April 24, the Brigade fought off the Chinese, now coming at their hill in desperation. The Brigade was spoiling the Chinese "first step, fifth offensive," at its very start. Campaign historians attribute losses of 10,000 killed and wounded to the Chinese, against 1,000 29th Brigade casualties in the battle, around a quarter of the British frontline strength. [17]

Once again the poorly supported Communist Chinese Forces had demonstrated their inability to sustain an offensive for more than a few days. The Communist attackers did not hold the cards. They possessed ample mortars, which they used to great effect, but had no air or artillery firepower.

One of the British Brigade's units, the 1st Battalion, Gloucestershire Regiment, performed what Van Fleet called later "the most outstanding example of unit bravery in modern warfare" by hanging on for three days astride the road to Seoul, even after it was surrounded and its position hopeless. Few of its men survived, but the delay in the enemy's drive was of incalculable importance.

New Defense Line

While the British 29th Brigade stood on the Imjin front, Van Fleet hastened to create a reserve position north of Seoul, where the Eighth Army had no difficulty holding the Communists, the momentum of their offensive spent. Yet, the Chinese continued to reinforce. On May 15, they launched a new assault with twenty-one Chinese and nine North Korean divisions. Once again the South Korean III Corps collapsed. The South Korean 5th and 7th divisions gave way, but on the right, the South Korean I Corps held its ground. Despite sustaining some 900 casualties, the U.S. 2nd Division also stood firm.

The 38th Field Artillery Battalion alone fired thousands of 105-mm shells on the night of May 16, wreaking a terrific toll on the attackers. The U.S. 3rd Division and the 187th Airborne Regimental Combat Team (RCT) plugged the gap on the right of the 2nd Division opened by the South Korean collapse. By May 20, the Chinese offensive was spent, at an estimated cost of 90,000 casualties.

For all practical purposes, the Eighth Army was back on the Kansas Line — the strong defensive position north of the 38th Parallel by June 1. During early June, the Iron Triangle in the west-center was brought under concerted attack by Americans, Filipinos, South Koreans and Turks, and its Chorwon-Kumwha base fell on June 10.

In the center-east, meanwhile, the 1st Marine Division and the South Korean 7th and 5th Divisions had fought into the Punchbowl, a circular depression in the mountains at the eastern rim of the Kansas Line. With its capture on June 16, Van Fleet now held a line beginning west of Munsan-ni 10 miles below the Parallel, running 40 miles northeast to the Chorwon-Kumwha base of the Iron Triangle, then running on a southeast gradient to the Punchbowl and the east coast.

The Communists were ready for the destruction of United Nations forces by mid-June of 1951, but they failed. The April and May offensives had subjected the Communist Army to a frightful pounding and the May assault had clearly revealed its inability to support large bodies of men moving against modern firepower. North Korea was a shambles, its railroads ruined, its communications crippled, and its industry close to nonexistence.

At the end of May 1951, the Chinese Communist Forces had proved they could not prevail in open warfare in the more maneuverable ground of southern and central Korea. But the U.N. Command had been ordered not to push and pursue them back into the horrendous terrain girding the Yalu. Unless Manchuria could be interdicted, the Chinese would fight here from a base of strength, while the U.N. would again be restricted and far from its sources of supply.

General Van Fleet's plan to strike farther north was shelved, chiefly because the notion of complete victory was by then already in disfavor. In mid-June, Washington had at last spelled out its policy of limited war. The Eighth Army's victories had already renewed hopes of obtaining a satisfactory cease-fire somewhere along the 38th Parallel. So, the Joint Chiefs of Staff ordered Van Fleet not to proceed beyond the general vicinity of his Kansas Line, though Ridgway had granted him permission to conduct local advances to seize better ground. [18]

Washington Seeks Truce

By now, Washington was seeking any means out of the Korean conflict that might be achieved without surrender, and with honor.

On June 1, U.N. Secretary-General Trygve Lie, understanding completely the views of the Truman Administration, mentioned that the time seemed right for stopping the bloodshed, since on this date the Chinese and North Koreans had been driven back across their line of departure. If a cease-fire could be obtained along the 38th Parallel, Lie said, the Security Council resolutions of June 25 and 27, and July 7, 1950, could be considered carried out. On June 7, U.S. Secretary of State Dean Acheson told a Senate committee that any reliable armistice based on the 38th Parallel would be acceptable to the United States.

On June 23, almost one year from the hour that the North Korean Army attacked across the 38th Parallel, Jakob A. Malik, Soviet delegate to the United Nations, made a speech on the U.N. radio, denouncing the U.S. armed intervention in Korea. Then, running overtime, he said:

"The Soviet peoples further believe that the most acute problem of the present day — the problem of the armed conflict in Korea — could also be settled. This would require the readiness of the parties to enter on the path of peaceful settlement of the Korean question. The Soviet peoples believe that a first step discussions should be started between the belligerents for a cease-fire and an armistice providing for the mutual withdrawal of forces from the 38th Parallel." [19]

On June 30, acting on orders from Washington, Ridgway broadcast the following message to the Commander in Chief of the Communist forces:

> As Commander in Chief of the United Nations Command I have been instructed to communicate to you the following:
>
> I am informed that you may wish a meeting to discuss an armistice providing for the cessation of hostilities and all acts of armed forces in Korea, with adequate guarantees for the maintenance of such armistice.
>
> Upon the receipt of word from you that such a meeting is desired I shall be prepared to name my representative. I propose that such a meeting could take place aboard a Danish hospital ship in Wonsan Harbor. [20]

Kim Il Sung, supreme commander of the North Korean Army, and Peng Teh-huai, commander of the Communist Chinese forces, radioed on July 1, 1951, agreeing to a meeting, but not on the Danish ship as Ridgway proposed, but at Kaesong in Communist territory just south of the 38th Parallel. It came to be known that the

Communists proposed nothing, not even truce sites, without an eye to their own advantage. But Ridgway accepted Kaesong and proposed that three liaison officers from each side meet there to prepare details of the meeting. The Communists agreed and set the date for July 10.

And here, a certain amount of amity between the United States and the Republic of Korea was lost. With divergent aims, neither Washington nor Seoul now fully trusted the other. South Korea saw no honor in the proposed cease-fire, which left its people ravaged and still divided. A settlement along the 38th Parallel, for all the American and U.N. protestations of continuance of the goal of uniting Korea by peaceful means, meant the continued and perhaps long separation of Korea into two blocs.

The South Korean government spokesman, Ryee Chol-won (Clarence Ryee), said in a statement, that no peace terms will be accepted by the Korean people until "south and north are completely united."

The Republic of Korea had gone into the war with its whole heart; it had been devastated, and one in twenty of its people killed or injured. Millions of homeless and orphans wandered through its ruins. To end the war after such wholesale sacrifice with nothing but the unsettled status was more than aging President Rhee or the Koreans could bear.

Rhee issued a statement on June 30, 1951 which stated that the Republic of Korea's conditions for peace were: the Chinese forces must withdraw north of the Yalu; all North Korean Communists must be disarmed; Soviet and Chinese arms assistance to the North must end, under a U.N. guarantee; full South Korean participation in any settlement; and no settlement conflicting with the sovereignty or territorial integrity of the Republic of Korea.

From this time on, Rhee never materially changed his demands, and he was to experience a continually worsening press in both Europe and America. Rhee, threatening again and again to block an armistice, became more and more a stubborn leader of South Korea.

CHAPTER FOUR

ARMISTICE TALKS

TWO YEARS OF HAGGLING

Communist Tricks at Kaesong

Despite Rhee's protests, the truce talks began at Kaesong. On July 10, Vice Admiral C. Turner Joy, commander of the U.S. Naval Forces, Far East, led the U.N. delegation to the conference site, a teahouse called *Naebongjang*. He was followed by Major General Laurence Craigie, vice commander of the U.S. Far East Air Force; Major General Henry Hodes, deputy chief of staff of the Eighth Army; Rear Admiral Aleigh Burke, deputy chief of staff of the Far East Naval Forces; and Major General Paik Sun-yup, whose distinguished record with the South Korean 1st Division had already brought him quick promotion.

The Communist delegation included Lieutenant General Nam Il, Major General Chang Pyong-san and Major General Lee Sang-cho of the North Korean Army, and Major General Hsieh Fang and Major General Tung Hum of the Communist Chinese Forces, or "Chinese People's Volunteers" as they continued to call themselves. The 38-year-old Nam Il, the product of the strictest Russian tutelage like his friend and mentor, Kim Il Sung, was the chief delegate and Hsieh Fang was the chief spokesman for the group.

From the selection of the site at Kaesong — in Communist hands, yet still below the 38th Parallel, one of the few spots in Korea where this condition obtained — the forcing of U.N. negotiators to enter Communist territory displaying white flags, as if they were coming to surrender, to the seating of Admiral Joy in a chair substantially lower than Nam Il's, the Communists showed that nothing was too small to be overlooked for their advantage.

189

They also took pictures inside the conference room of a large North Korean flag towering over a much smaller United Nations pennant. Even with their own newsmen present, the Communists refused to admit U.N. reporters into the area. Admiral Joy called the talks off and they remained canceled for three days until the Communist negotiators gave in.

The Communists intended merely to transfer the war from the battlefield, where they were losing, to the conference table, where they might yet win something. In the midst of fleeting optimism for an early conclusion of the war, no one, including Washington, dared guess that it would take 159 plenary sessions and more than two years of haggling to end the killing.

On the afternoon of July 15, the teahouse conference resumed. Joy opened the meeting by outlining Ridgway's proposal for neutralizing the Kaesong area, five miles in radius, with only a minimum of armed personnel for military police duty, to which Nam Il agreed.

On July 16, General Ridgway met with President Syngman Rhee at Eighth Army headquarters to outline the basic concept for creating a demilitarized zone, which had been agreed by both sides to include in the agenda. Rhee heatedly argued that the U.N. forces should push on to the Yalu to realize Korean reunification. Ridgway politely told the restive Rhee that there was not going to be another major offensive.

The next morning, Rhee sent a personal letter to Ridgway:

> The substance of the position of my government is that we cannot maintain our nation in half our country. A divided Korea is a ruined Korea, unstable economically, politically, and militarily....In every Korean heart and in every Korean mind the fact is clear that our nation would be plunged into irrevocable disaster by any acceptance of a continued dividing-line....It is the Communist Empire which is rotten with internal weakness. Negotiations continued with this conviction should lead to success. In this spirit there is no need to settle short of the goal of reunification and free election.

South Korean Army representative Major General Paik Sun-yup said in an interview:

"Eighth Army Commander Van Fleet first suggested that I would be Republic of Korea Army representative, and then our army chief of staff Lee Jong-chan officially appointed me. On July 8, two days before the start of the truce talks, I met President Rhee in Pusan. The President told me, 'The American side wants to go ahead with armistice talks. Our nation believes that a truce without realizing our national reunification makes no sense. If the armistice talks are carried out, our land will remain divided. But as a gesture of cooperation with the United Nations Command, I want you to do what you can.' President Rhee, as a veteran statesman who had devoted his career to the cause of national independence, was against the truce talks from the very beginning."

On July 17, the Communists wanted to include on the agenda the restoration of the political boundary of the 38th Parallel, and removal of all foreign troops from Korea. Nam Il maintained, "We cannot consider the 38th Parallel as an imaginary line. It is the principle that the question of the cease-fire must be concluded also on the 38th Parallel line. Therefore this must also be on the agenda."

Joy stressed again that the establishment of a truce line be discussed first, and then its location and limits could be debated. After pressing their arguments for several days, the Communists suddenly agreed to keep the subject of demarcation line "general" on the agenda. They warned however they would definitely take up the matter again when the time came.

Meantime, the U.N. also conceded two points it had wanted to include: the visit of Red Cross representatives to prisoner-of-war camps prior to deliberations on POW release, and the composition of inspection teams to supervise the military activities on both sides during the truce period.

On July 26, when the negotiators began deliberating the fixing of the demarcation line, Nam Il insisted again that the 38th Parallel must be the dividing line between the two forces. The U.N. position was that the 38th Parallel was a political issue outside the scope of the truce talks.

Joy pointed out that the line along which the fighting would stop would have to be defensible and therefore located geographically in

U.S. army vehicles move toward the truce talk site at Kaesong, a teahouse called Naebongjang.

Chief delegates of the Kaesong truce talks, Lieutenant General Nam Il of the North Korean Army (left) and U.S. Vice Admiral C. Turner Joy, arrive at the conference site on July 10, 1951.

relation to the existing military situation. Nam Il blasted the U.N. proposal as "illogical, absurd, and arrogant."

The Communists, having been beaten on the field, now sought to win back lost ground at the conference table. Their proposal of a cease-fire along the 38th Parallel would guarantee them against a U.N. offensive while the truce talks continued. Any ground gained in such attacks would, of course, have to be surrendered when the armistice was signed.

While the truce debate grew acrimonious and with President Rhee still seething in the middle of August 1951, President Truman sent a message to President Rhee, telling the Korean people: "We shall not fail you nor forsake you." His message was read to 1,000 Korean political leaders gathered in Pusan on August 15 to celebrate the third birthday of the Republic of Korea and the sixth anniversary of the end of Japanese colonial rule.

President Rhee, National Assembly Speaker Shin Ik-hi, U.S. Ambassador John J. Muccio, and Sen. Pote Sarason of the U.N. Rehabilitation Commission spoke to the large anniversary gathering.

Truman's message read:

> On this third anniversary of the proclamation of the Republic of Korea, the people of the United States join me in conveying to your excellency and to the courageous people of Korea hearty greetings and sincere good wishes for a secure future.
>
> Though the battle is joined, the conflict is not yet won. The enemy is powerful and again is capable of launching further aggressive attacks. But whatever the future holds in store, we are resolved to fight for freedom and are determined to preserve the principles of justice, tolerance and humanity for which we have fought so valiantly throughout our history.
>
> We shall not fail you nor forsake you.
>
> With God's help and strength that comes from that knowledge that what we fight for is right, we shall ultimately be victorious.

President Rhee told his people in a prepared address: "Liberty is worth saving — even at the risk of our lives. We must stand together to protect democracy or we shall all become victims of Communism....We are caught in a gigantic global struggle between Communism and democracy. Coexistence of these two ideologies is impossible. Either one or the other must go. This is the great and tragic historical fact which our generation must face and understand."

About two weeks before the Truman message reached Rhee, Muccio was so concerned about Rhee's bitter reaction to the truce talks that he cabled Secretary of State Dean Acheson: "President Rhee, on blindly emotional ground, is attempting to sabotage armistice."

Meantime, at Kaesong charges of violation of the conference zone's neutrality intensified the tension of the atmosphere. On August 10, a company of armed Communist soldiers approached the building in which the U.N. delegation was meeting. The Communists produced the body of a guard they alleged had been killed by a U.N. raid into the zone; they invited the U.N. delegation to attend a memorial service in his honor.

Finally on August 23 the Communists accused the U.N. of dropping a napalm bomb in the conference area the previous night. A U.N. investigation team found the incident to be fraudulent, and Ridgway rejected the charges as "false... preposterous, and... obviously manufactured for your own questionable purposes." The Communists thereupon broke off the meetings.

When the Communists suspended the truce negotiations, the Eighth Army began to apply military pressure once more. Van Fleet renewed his offensive to drive the enemy back from the Hwachon Reservoir area, which was Seoul's source of water and electricity. On August 31, the U.S. 1st Marine Division began attacking the northern rim of the Punchbowl, and two days later, the U.S. 2nd Infantry Division on the Marine's left or west advanced north against Bloody Heartbreak Ridge above the Iron Triangle. Fierce fighting developed in both sectors, but American infantrymen drove out the Chinese forces. Meanwhile, the South Korean I Corps moved up the coast toward Kosong, an advance of about ten miles. In the west and west-center, five divisions — the 1st British Commonwealth, the South Korean 1st Division and the U.S. 1st Cavalry, 3rd and 25th Infantry — struck north along a 40-mile front from Kaesong to Chorwon, advancing the front, jumping farther north. By the second week in October, the Communists, having been beaten once more, were ready to take up again the talk of peace.

Conference Site Shifted to Panmunjom

Ridgway had become increasingly convinced that he had made a mistake in agreeing to hold the truce talks in Kaesong controlled by the Communists, for they had been consistently able to manipulate circumstances there for their own propaganda benefits.

So Ridgway set down a condition for the resumption of the talks: shift the conference site from Kaesong to Panmunjom, midway between the front lines of the opposing forces, with both sides responsible for its protection.

The Communists came back to the talks on October 25 with no further demands to make regarding the 38th Parallel. The firmness of the U.N. stand and the strength of its forces had convinced them that they could not resist any longer.

After almost a month of fruitless haggling and jockeying, Washington came up with a formula which the U.N. negotiators presented on November 17, 1951. It proposed that the present line of contact become the demarcation line if a general truce agreement were reached within thirty days.

The Communists accepted at once. Ridgway and Joy were convinced that Truman and the Joint Chiefs had made a serious mistake by diminishing military pressure and giving in to the Communists.

To implement the 30-day truce agreement, there was still the task of tracing the line of contact on a map. Each point on the line was disputed until finally one side or the other conceded the position. But by November 27 the line finally was drawn on paper, and the 30-day trial period, which became known as the "Little Truce," began.

The Communists used the 30-day de facto truce period to begin building the defense line across Korea which would have almost the same effect as a cease-fire. Battles would still be fought, but no significant ground would change hands.

Debate at Panmunjom now was conducted on two items concurrently: "concrete arrangements for the realization of a cease-fire and armistice in Korea, including the composition, authority and functions of a supervisory organ for carrying out the terms... and arrangements relating to prisoners of war." The U.N. took the stand that no prisoner from either side should be forced to return to his own country against his expressed wishes. The Communists insisted that all prisoners, willing or not, should be repatriated.

On April 28, Admiral Joy, acting on instructions from the Truman Administration which wanted desperately to see the Korean problem settled, presented what he called the U.N.'s "final offer." It capitulated completely on the U.N. proposition to ban the construction of airfields after the truce. But, it asked in return for this acquiescence a Communist concession on the matter of voluntary repatriation of prisoners.

However, by this time the prisoner-of-war issue was tied in with the hottest propaganda weapon the Communists had. They rejected the U.N. offer, and for the final bizarre year of the war the gate which could lead to peace or renewal of conflict hinged on the intricate issue of prisoners.

Colonel Hanley's Atrocity Report

From the middle of 1951, acrimonious charges and counter-charges on the prisoner-of-war issue polluted the atmosphere in Panmunjom. It worsened in the wake of a statement made by Colonel James M. Hanley, Eighth Army's chief judge advocate general, that the Communists had killed at least 5,750 United Nations soldiers in atrocities since the start of the war.

I interviewed Colonel Hanley in Pusan on November 14 and American newspapers carried my report with such banners as: "U.S. REVEALS REDS KILLED 5500 GI CAPTIVES IN KOREA," or "REDS BUTCHERED MORE AMERICANS THAN FELL IN 1766." The following is from an old clip of *Los Angeles Evening*

Herald Express headlined "REDS MURDER 5500 YANK WAR PRISONERS:"

Pusan, Korea Nov. 14 — (AP) — The head of the U.S. Eighth Army's legal section today said the Communists have killed at least 5,750 United Nations solders — about 5,500 of them Americans — and some 250,000 Korean civilians in atrocities since the start of the war.

Col. James M. Hanley of Seattle, Eighth Army judge advocate general, said in a statement that 200 captured U.S. Marines were killed in a single day — last December 10 — near Shinhung in northeast Korea.

Shinhung is about 20 miles north of Hungnam. Last December, remnants of the U.S. 1st Marine Division and the U.S. 7th Infantry Division were pulling back toward Hungnam port in a bitter retreat.

Hanley said the Marines were killed on order of the commander of the Twenty-third Regiment, Eighty-first Division.

He said 17 Turkish war prisoners were slain by Chinese Communists on May 15, 1951, near Yanggu and 12 others on April 10 near Yongchon.

Hanley said the count of military prisoners slain did not include South Korean troops. He gave no estimate of these, but indicated the number was about twice that of other United Nations soldiers killed by Red captors.

Civilian men, women and children were slaughtered, Hanley said, without trial or even a formal death sentence. He said 700 civilians were driven into the horizontal shaft of a gold mine near Haeju, 80 miles southeast of the North Korean capital of Pyongyang, on September 26, 1950, bound and gagged and dropped down a vertical shaft. They were left to die, he said.

Four hundred more were given the same treatment
on October 9, 1950, Hanley said. Three days earlier,
he said, still another 40 were bound, gagged and
buried alive in three big holes at Haeju airport.

Hanley said his statement had "nothing to do with
the cease-fire negotiations" at Panmunjom.

He accused the Communists of making a sham of
the Geneva Convention on treatment of prisoners of
war. The United Nations, he said, cared for the Communists it captured "in complete accordance with the
Geneva agreement."

"None of the Communist war prisoners have been
killed by us," he added.

Hanley made the revelation without the knowledge of Ridgway.
Colonel George Patrick Welch, public information officer for
Ridgway's headquarters in Tokyo, was ordered to Korea to talk with
Colonel Hanley. Welch also talked with Colonel Kenneth L. Booth,
U.S. Eighth Army public information officer.

Colonel Hanley said that in September he submitted a memoran-
dum to the office of the Judge Advocate General at general headquarters in Tokyo asking authority to tell the story. At that time,
Hanley was leaving Korea for a trip to Washington. He said that on
his return he was notified the story could be released. He said he
assumed the approval came through normal channels.

After hearing reports from Welch on his findings in Korea,
Ridgway made a formal statement to the press:

It may perhaps be well to note with deep reverence
that in His inscrutable way God chose to bring home
to our people and to the conscience of the world the
moral principles of the leaders of the forces against
which we fight in Korea....It may well be that in no
other way could all lingering doubts be dispelled from
the minds of our people as to the methods which the
leaders of Communism are willing to use, and actually
do use, in their efforts to destroy free peoples and the
principles for which they stand. [1]

Ridgway emphasized that publication of the Hanley report "had of course no connection whatever with the current armistice negotiations."

Meanwhile, the U.S. Defense Department announced that a total of 6,113 American prisoners of war had died in Korea.

A few days later, U.N. war correspondents at Panmunjom asked Wilfred Burchett, a Pyongyang-based Australian correspondent for the left-wing Paris newspaper *Ce Soir,* to comment on the Hanley statement. Burchett asserted that it was a provocation and a lie. He claimed that he had visited POW camps in North Korea and found the Americans in good shape.

Bob Eunson, AP Tokyo Bureau chief, told Burchett: "If you say our prisoners are alive and well, then I believe you. But we have a veteran photographer, Pappy Noel, who was taken prisoner. Why not let us send a camera and film up the road to Pappy? Let him take pictures of the prisoners. We'll publish them in the hometown papers and people will start screaming to get them home again." Burchett replied: "Why not, if the AP wants to risk a camera." [2]

As Hanley's revelation of the Communist brutality was widely reported, the Communists considered it a good propaganda chance for them to show that Major General Dean, the highest ranking U.N. prisoner of war, was in good health.

Contrary to what Burchett had reported, Dean wrote about the Communist ill-treatment in his memoirs after his return to freedom on September 4, 1953 in accord with the prisoner-of-war exchange agreement of June 8.

Dean revealed that he was confined for the past year in a cave 40 miles north of Manpo near the Yalu River and was not allowed to stand except when he went to the toilet.

Burchett returned to Panmunjom on December 24 and told U.N. correspondents his version of the details of his interview with Dean, which were widely reported on the following day. But no mention was made about the fact that Dean had been so badly treated by the Communist captors.

Burchett said that he interviewed Dean in a prisoner of war camp in North Korea on December 21. The Communist newsman claimed that Dean emphasized that he was receiving "excellent treatment," adding that Dean had written a letter of thanks to Kim Il Sung.

Burchett quoted Dean as saying: "My food has been better than that of my guards. I have eggs and butter although I never have made a personal request for special food. Now that I have my health back, the eggs should go to the sick and wounded."

Burchett had turned over the negatives of Dean's pictures to UP and the photos showing him playing Korean chess with his guards, shadow-boxing, doing exercises, and strolling in a forest appeared in newspapers, including the U.S. Army paper *Stars and Stripes.* Ridgway was so disturbed to see the double-page spread of Dean's made-up pictures that he fired the editor of the paper.

KOJE-DO POW CAMPS

Communist Riots

Koje-do rises green and lovely from the sea in the Korean Strait a few miles off the southern tip of the Korean peninsula, about twenty miles southwest of Pusan. It is a land of lush hills, clear streams, and delicately tinted paddies, and a fishing center teemed with thousands of fishing boats. Early in the Korean War the island became a reception center for approximately one million refugees who had been driven to Pusan by the Communist invasion. Then in early 1951, the United Nations Command decided to use the island as a base for prisoners of war.

By mid-1951, U.S. military police had constructed four vast barbed-wire enclosures, each in turn split into eight compounds into which were crammed some 130,000 North Korean and 20,000 Communist Chinese prisoners.

Debate on exchange of prisoners formally commenced on December 11, 1951. At that time, the U.N. casualties stood at 305,000 dead, wounded, missing or captured, of which 192,000 were South Koreans, 104,000 Americans and 9,000 other U.N. troops.

Pressed for a list of U.N. prisoners, the Communists on December 18 reported holding a total of 11,559 U.N. prisoners of war: 7,142 South Koreans, 3,198 Americans, and 1,219 other U.N.

troops. The U.N. negotiators thought these figures incredible; the first months of war the Communist radio had reported some 65,000 captives. The U.N. list on the other hand contained 132,474 names: 95,531 North Koreans, 20,700 Chinese, and 16,243 former South Korean troops who had been captured and pressed into the Communist army.

On February 17, 1952, the Communists agreed to the screening of prisoners, perhaps because by this time their agents ruled many of the massive prison compounds on Koje Island and seemingly could control the results by continuing the brutal and murderous intimidation which had put them in power.

The screening began, and continued despite bloody riots which broke out in the Communist-controlled compounds. Communist leaders carefully informed the inmates that in refusing repatriation they were choosing a life of hardship, probably even death.

The U.N. delegate at Panumunjom announced on April 18 that approximately 70,000 of the 132,000 prisoners interviewed did not wish repatriation to the Communist side. The figure was immediately turned down by Nam Il, who insisted all their men must be returned.

Already, there was ferment in the compounds between the fanatic Communists and the non-Communists, as different factions jostled for control. The ferment was only vaguely seen by the guards, and not understood at all. Communists and non-Communists were treated alike, as equals.

But the screening did have one result. The worst Communists, officers and men alike, were segregated into compounds like the soon-to-be-notorious compound 76. The segregation did not have the desired result; instead, it concentrated the die-hard Communist control.

To the Communist Chinese and North Korea leadership, the POW compounds were an extension of the battlefield. As military intelligence discovered through interrogation of prisoners and captured documents, the Communists organized a special unit to lead POWs. The unit, attached to headquarters of the North Korean Army, had two missions: to train agents who would permit themselves to be captured so they could take on specific leadership missions in the prison camps and to furnish intelligence to the Communist negotiators at Panmunjom.

Initially, the person in charge of the secret organization was Senior Colonel Lee Hak-ku, chief of staff of the North Korean 13th Division, who roused two U.S. soldiers from their sleep in Tabudong near Taegu in order to surrender on September 21, 1950. His presumed "surrender" prompted the question of whether it was a plant. The most important prisoner of all to come in by subterfuge was Senior Colonel Pak Sang-hyon, one of the original group of 36 Koreans who had been trained in the Soviet Union to set up the Communist regime with Kim Il Sung. He came into Koje-do disguised as a private using a false name, Jeon Moon-il, in early 1952, and thereafter control inside the compounds passed to him.

As documents later seized in the camp revealed, the man who organized and continued throughout the truce negotiations to direct the activities inside Koje-do was Nam Il, the same man who daily presented the Communist proposals for peace at Panmunjom. He was connected to Koje-do by means of an efficient communications network built primarily around a system for passing messages between the prisoners and Communist agents hidden among the neighboring civilians.

In February 1952, when the United Nations began screening prisoners, the Communist organization controlled by Pak and Lee was prepared to act. Leaders of Communist inmates of Compound 62 declared that all members wished to return to North Korea, and there was no reason to screen. The Communists were openly challenging, and the United Nations decided that it would need to control the Communist compounds. At about 4 a.m., February 18, a battalion from the U.S. 27th Infantry Regiment attempted to seize Compound 62, but more than 1,000 Communist prisoners streamed out of their barracks wielding spears, knives, and axes. The solders commenced rifle fire from the companies stationed outside the gate, and this was followed by a bayonet charge. The prisoners fell back, and the riot ended with American casualties of one dead and 39 wounded, as opposed to 75 prisoners dead and 139 wounded. Nam Il at Panmunjom launched an increasingly vituperative tirade.

General Dodd Captured by POWs

At 2 a.m., May 7, 1952, a message reached the headquarters of Brigadier General Francis T. Dodd, Koje-do POW camp commandant, that the leaders of Compound 76 immediately and earnestly desired his presence for a discussion.

The new base commander Dodd, completely unaware of the recent orders given to Communist agent Pak Sang-hyon by Nam Il, agreed to meet them at Compound 76, known to be under militant control. He went to see the prison leaders. As he was listening to their well-worn complaints outside an open gate, at a sudden signal, he was pulled deep inside the compound and captured by his own prisoners.

Several hours after the incident, I scored a news scoop on this incredible episode, one of the most sensational stories of the war. When I was walking along the front of the Pusan Railway Station around 11 a.m., May 7, I was accosted by an American civilian working for the U.S 2nd Logistical Command. The man, who used to greet me by saying "Hi, Scoop Shinn," asked in earnest: "What do you know about the incredible incident? Isn't it really a shame? I'm sure you know."

"Do you mean the incident that happened this morning?" I responded as if I knew. "Now I'm in a hurry. Tell me first what you've heard and then I will supplement."

"I heard that the American commandant of Koje-do POW camp was kidnapped this morning. Is it true?"

I knew that it would be really big news if it were true. "It seems to be true. If fact, I'm working on it now," I said and rushed to cover the news.

First, I asked Lieutenant Newbald, U.S. Army press officer in Pusan, but he repeated "No comment." But from his restive attitude I gathered that a very serious incident had indeed happened.

After learning from reliable sources that General Dodd was captured by his own prisoners at Compound 76, I called on South Korean Defense Minister Shin Tae-yong at his office. Because of the grave nature of the incident, I guessed that the United Nations Command had given a gag order to the South Korean authorities. So

I wanted to persuade Minister Shin as I had persuaded an army press officer to release the news of the historic Inchon landing on September 15, 1950 in the name of South Korean Army commander in chief General Chung Il-kown in spite of General MacArthur's gag order.

I told Minister Shin: "The fact that the United Nations Command has given hush orders on this incident suggests that the U.N. Command might make an important concession to the Communists at Panmunjom truce talks in order to save the life of the kidnapped American general. I think it's unwise for the South Korean government to comply with such orders because the U.N. Command is likely to make a secret concession to the Communists, at the cost of the interest of the Republic of Korea. Obviously the kidnapping was carried out under orders from North Korea. Wouldn't it be the duty of the South Korean defense minister to bring the Communist plot to light? Since I'll not reveal your name in my report, please tell me all about the Koje-do incident."

Minister Shin mused for a while, and then cautioned: "Be sure you don't disclose my name as the news source." I reassured him, "I promise you, sir."

"General Dodd was captured by the Communist prisoners in Compound 76 on Koje-do early this morning...." Shin explained the details of the shameful incident, adding that his government was requested by the U.S. Eighth Army to keep the incident "in strictest secrecy."

I hurriedly wrote the hot story after having it reconfirmed by government spokesman Clarence Ryee, and showed it to Lieutenant Newbald for his comment.

After a careful reading, he asked: "Who is the source of this information?"

"You don't have the right to know my news source. I'm only asking you if you can deny the contents of my report," I said.

"You can't send it," he said curtly.

"I wouldn't have written it if not for dispatching," I declared and ran back to my office. I phoned the story to an AP correspondent in Seoul for transmission to AP headquarters through the Tokyo bureau.

In Tokyo, U.N. Commander General Ridgway withheld the report, and was busy telephoning the Pentagon and Eighth Army Commander Van Fleet in Seoul. Meantime, an AFP reporter in Tokyo who had learned the gist of my report was about to dispatch it, skipping censorship. Immediately AP wired my story and lodged a stern protest with Ridgway for the leak while sitting on the AP scoop.

Ridgway, a few hours before the arrival of General Mark Clark to relieve him as U.S. Far East and United Nations chief on the night of May 7, sent a letter of apology to AP, saying, "Apology is mine....I had to contact the Department of Defense before releasing Bill Shinn's report."

According to witnesses, at about 3:15 a.m. Dodd was rushed inside the gate by men returning to Compound 76 after having emptied buckets of latrine sewage. Neither General Dodd nor Lieutenant Colonel Wilbur Raven, his aide, was armed. Raven saved himself by clinging to a gatepost until American guards rescued him. Dodd was hustled off with one final hoarse shout. The Communist captors hoisted signs, which said: "If our problems are resolved his security is guaranteed."

For three days Dodd was held a prisoner, and during this time, through telephone communication established between the prison compound and the camp, he instructed that no force be used or his life would be in danger. On the morning of May 10, the new camp commander appointed by General Van Fleet, Brigadier General Charles Colson, received an ultimatum from the Communists stipulating a number of conditions upon which Dodd's safe release depended. Colson met their demands. In the evening of that day, he signed a reply that was tantamount to an admission of the Communist charges:

> ...I do admit that there have been instances of bloodshed where many POWs have been killed and wounded by U.N. forces. I can assure in the future that POWs can expect humane treatment in this camp according to the principles of international law. I will do all in

Senior Colonel Lee Hak-ku (left), chief of staff of the North Korean 13th Division, surrenders at Tabu-dong on September 21, 1950. Lee's surrender is thought to have been a deception because he later led the bloody Koje-do POW camp riots in 1952.

U.N. troops quell Communist POW riots on Koje-do on June 10, 1952.

my power to eliminate further violence and bloodshed. If such incidents happen in the future, I will be responsible.

Dodd sent out a message to Colson which listed a long set of charges that U.N. guards had killed and injured prisoners. The statement — written by Communists — also contained an alleged Dodd admission that camp authorities were guilty of these offenses. The Communists haggled for even further admissions, then freed Dodd at 9:30 a.m., May 11. The next day General Clark denounced the confession as "unadulterated blackmail" and said that any concessions made by Colson "should be interpreted accordingly."

Although an Eighth Army board cleared Dodd and Colson of any misconduct, Clark convened another investigative panel that recommended reducing the brigadier generals to the rank of colonels. Major General Paul F. Yount, commander of the 2nd Logistical Command which had jurisdiction over Koje-do, was reprimanded for the laxity of supervision.

Communist Propaganda Campaign

Thus, the capitulation by the captor to his captives was one of the boldest and most successful Communist propaganda plots in history. It had given Nam Il at Panmunjom a big propaganda stick with which to beat the United Nations. He was shrieking in joyous rage:

> ...These criminal acts committed by your side under the name of voluntary repatriation thoroughly violate the Geneva Convention relating to prisoners of war and repudiate the minimum standard of human behavior.
>
> The series of cowardly acts of persecuting and slaughtering our captured personnel carried out by your side for the purpose of retaining them proves conclusively the utter bankruptcy of every fraudulent proposition of retaining war prisoners.

As soon as he had taken over from Ridgway, Clark repudiated the Colson letter; it was "made under duress," and therefore not to be honored. But far more effective than Clark's statement was the effective propaganda campaign launched by the Communists. Communist press and spokesmen were having a propaganda field day. The editor of *Pravda* in Moscow for example came forth with full and somber wrath:

> ...Koje is a whole island of death....The American hangmen are torturing, tormenting, and killing un-armed people here. They have surpassed the Hitlerites; they have turned POWs into guinea pigs and are testing on them the strength of their germ soldiers — microbes.

The "germ soldiers" alleged here was the "germ warfare" which the Communists had charged that the United States was waging against the civilian population in North Korea. This hoax was another propaganda offensive the Communists mounted against the United Nations during the stalled armistice talks at Panmunjom in 1952.

Wilfred Burchett and Alan Winnington, a Pyongyang-based correspondent of the *London Daily Worker*, also were writing condemnatory stories. Their accounts echoed propaganda reports coming from North Korea and Communist China. Western correspondents who had befriended them were dismayed by the Communist newsmen. Two decades later, Burchett was a frequent and detested visitor to American POWs in Vietnam. Winnington was almost universally hated because of his arrogant attitude.

The eyes of the world were focused on Koje-do as newsmen from the Korean front and across the world rushed to the island in droves. In the wake of the most effective Communist propaganda maneuvers, even the staunchest allies of the United States rather politely queried, "just what the hell is going on over at Koje-do?" Many would say, "Where there is smoke there must be fire."

Henceforth, until the second breakoff of truce talks in September of 1952, the Communists came to the conference table chiefly to denounce or inveigh, to spread charges which would be published and broadcast throughout the world by Communist propaganda media.

Riots Quelled

The U.N. Command now moved to break Communist control of the prison camps on Koje-do and dispersing prisoners to smaller, more secure compounds. The new U.N. commander, General Mark Clark, had empowered the new Koje-do commander, Brigadier General Haydon L. Boatner, to use force when necessary to bring the die-hard Communist POWs under control.

Boatner, with more than ten years's Asian service, decided to destroy Communist power by scattering it, and he began building smaller compounds to hold 500 men each. His tanks and soldiers were trained openly outside the tough Compounds 76 and 77. On June 10, Boatner sent a message to Lee Hak-ku of Compound 76 ordering, "Have all prisoners ready to be escorted to new compounds in exactly 30 minutes. Failure to obey will necessitate the use of force." Lee ordered his men to fight with their homemade weapons.

When the compound completely ringed by Boatner's men and tanks, a paratroop unit was to enter Compound 76. Suddenly many of the Communists brandished long spears and sharp knives made in their workshop. Behind the defensive line of trenches that they had dug in one section of the compound, the holdouts refused to surrender, screaming defiance and waving spears and knives. The paratroopers advanced, slowly pushing them back. Now there was chaos. The POWs had set their huts afire.

Then the paratroopers met the lines of the Communists, and a wild melee broke the back of their resistance. At a loss of 43 POWs killed and 135 wounded — half of their own officers — the 6,500 hard-core Communists in Compound 76 were broken down into groups of 500 and placed behind new wire. Five days after the resistance had ended, Boatner walked into the still flaming compound, and inside one hut he found a corpse, hanging by its heels — a symbol of the Communist determination to dominate, placed there as an example by the leadership. And in a ditch, the paratroopers found Senior Colonel Lee Hak-ku. They dragged him out roughly, and pushed him on his way. Also found were two sets of secret plans: a Communist resistance plan and a mass breakout plan set for June 20, 1952, which called for the POWs to cut the wire, make for the hills, and slaughter everyone in their way.

But the dedicated Communists in Compound 77 submitted without protest, thus Boatner put an end to Communist riots on Koje-do.

With both sides intransigent, but still willing to talk, negotiations on the POW issue at Panmunjom droned on through June and July of 1952. By early fall it had become obvious that the Communists were not going to accede to anything short of return of all prisoners. And it had also become plain that with the United Sates in the throes of a bitterly disputed presidential election, they preferred to stall, to continue their propaganda campaign.

Meanwhile, Admiral Joy was released from his assignment at Panmunjom at his own request. He was replaced by Major General William K. Harrison. Joy told the Communists in his parting remarks on May 22, "It has become increasingly clear through these long drawn-out conferences that your side would bring good faith to these meetings was forlorn indeed."

In the following four months, Harrison presented three different plans to break the prisoners issue deadlock while holding to the principle of voluntary repatriation with the backing of other U.N. nations. Again the Communists rejected them.

On October 8, Harrison, now a lieutenant general, stated: "The United Nations Command has no further proposals to make. The proposals we made remain open. The U.N.C. delegation will not come here merely to listen to abuse and false propaganda. The U.N.C. is therefore calling a recess....We are willing to meet with you again at any time you are willing to accept our proposals or have presented in writing the text of any constructive proposals, designed to achieve an armistice, which you may desire to make."
Thus the fifteen months old truce talks which had gone through 200 meetings entered an indefinite recess.

The United Nations Command, from Mark Clark on down, had had enough of lies, calumnies, and flaming propaganda.

In the fall of 1952, there was a stalemate at the front, with limited Chinese Communist attacks on U.N.-held hills only to be thrown back. But on October 6, the Communists assaulted White Horse Hill held by the South Korean 9th Corps with two divisions. The hill, five miles northwest of Chorwon, changed hands twenty-four times between October 6 and 15. When the enemy was finally thrown back by the stubborn, well-disciplined South Koreans, the hillsides were dotted with the bodies of thousands of Chinese; the South Koreans lost over 3,500 men.

On White Horse, and on the central front, around the Iron Triangle, the South Korean Army now proved it had come of age under the intense training program instituted by Ridgway and continued by Van Fleet. They counterattacked with stubborn courage, and time after time threw the Communists back.

The Chinese attacks on U.N. outposts were intensified as the U.S. presidential election was approaching in 1952. Inside the U.S. government there was considerable sentiment to accede to the Communist demands on the POW issue in order to achieve peace before the election.

TRUCE AT LAST

Eisenhower's Policy to End the War

Late in the 1952 presidential campaign in the United States, Dwight D. (Ike) Eisenhower, the Republican candidate, said, "I will go to Korea." The effect of this pledge was astonishing even though it had been criticized by his opposition — Democratic candidate Adlai Stevenson's camp — as "cheap politics." Ike's landslide victory demonstrated the voters' feelings about the Korean War.

The President-elect's official party flew into Korea on December 2, 1952 under tight security. The Secret Service and Joint Chiefs of Staff hit upon a scheme to conceal Eisenhower's presence in Korea until he had come and gone. He was greeted at a military airport by General Mark Clark, the U.N. commander, and James Van Fleet, commander of the Eighth Army.

He spent four days in Korea, meeting President Syngman Rhee and major field commanders, visiting front-line units, and having a happy reunion with his son, John, who was a major with the 1st Battalion, 15th Infantry, 3rd Division.

During the long day of December 4, the World War II hero witnessed a demonstration of the South Korean Capital Division, crouching over the ice-crusted battlefield. He was accompanied by aged President Rhee, who remained until the end despite the biting cold. Scores of correspondents were covering the news; I was one of them.

In the evening of December 5, the final day of the visit, Eisenhower visited President Rhee accompanied by his son and some members of the official party. Ike's visit was important to Rhee, since it would be a good chance for the Korean President to ask for further support from the U.S. government.

Eisenhower made only general comments at a press conference the day the trip ended because his press secretary James Hagerty wished to prevent him from being pressed about specific plans. So, Eisenhower permitted correspondents to ask no questions. Eisenhower observed: it would be difficult to end the fighting with a "positive and definite victory without possibly running the grave risk of enlarging the war." But he concluded, as he wrote in his memoirs, that "we could not stand forever on a static front and continue to accept casualties without any visible results. Small attacks on small hills would not end wars."

Clark and other military commanders bid farewell to Eisenhower at the Eighth Army headquarters, watching him being driven off to the airport.

Two days later, on December 7, President Rhee told me in an interview that he had urged Eisenhower to "end the Korean stalemate as soon as possible." Rhee also said he had told the U.S. president-elect that U.N. troops "could be relieved from the front lines" if the South Korean Army were built up sufficiently. He did not indicate what he thought would be a large enough South Korean Army to relieve U.N. troops from the front.

Rhee said that he made the following suggestions to Eisenhower:

1. The Korean stalemate be ended as soon as possible.

2. South Korean defense forces be increased, trained, and equipped.

3. If this is done, foreign troops could be relieved from the frontlines.

4. Korea needs help in its economy and industry, as well as military aid.

Korean government spokesman, Clarence Ryee, quoted Eisenhower as saying he would give Rhee's proposal "careful study and consideration."

With the inauguration of Eisenhower as the 34th President of the United States on January 20, 1953, the world was asking, "Can Ike end the war?"

A broad restudy of war policies was undertaken in the new administration. The generals on the Joint Chiefs of Staff and Defense Department staff officers quickly realized the new President's immediate intentions: that he would "Koreanize" the war as an alternative to the dominant U.S. role.

Eisenhower had said in one of his campaign speeches:

> There is no sense in the U.N. with America bearing the brunt of the thing, being constantly compelled to man those front lines. That is a job for the Koreans. We do not want Asia to feel that the white man of the West is his enemy. If there must be a war there, let it be Asians against Asians, with our support on the side of freedom. [3]

The consensus at the Defense Department was that the administration should increase the South Korean military to about 655,000 men with twenty army and one marine divisions. It was hoped that this expansion would enable the United States to begin withdrawing some of its own men. By March 1953 plans were well along to increase the strength of the South Koreans. It was after his return from Korea that Eisenhower openly was determined to rebuild the South Korean Army, while broadly hinting at an increased use of force.

There were now seven 20,000-man U.S. Army divisions and one even larger U.S. Marine division in Korea. The South Korean Army had twelve 10,000-man divisions. Facing the U.N. forces of three-quarters of a million, including troops from fifteen other nations, were 350,000 Chinese Communist forces and 140,000 North Koreans.

In the meantime, on February 11, Lieutenant General James Van Fleet was replaced by Lieutenant General Maxwell Taylor, then U.S. Deputy Chief of Staff for Operations and Administration. Van Fleet, after twenty-two months in Korea, announced that his Eighth Army forces had been strong enough to wage a successful offensive against the Communists. He was convinced that his troops could have beaten the Communist forces in the spring of 1951. He wrote in *Life:*

> Though we could readily have followed up our success, that was not the intention in Washington; our State Department had already let the Reds know that we were willing to settle on the 38th Parallel. Instead of getting directives for offensive action, we found our activities more and more proscribed as the time went on....General Maxwell Taylor, the new Eighth Army commander, can seize it as easily as I might have, if only our policy-makers give him the chance....I have looked the Chinese Reds in the eye and this is my verdict: If ever I should be called back to fight him again, I would go with a confident heart....If we retreat from the Communists in Asia, we are lost anyway. What are we afraid of? [4]

In mid-January, the first successful detonation of an atomic warhead of a size suitable for use in battlefield artillery, which could be used for tactical strategic purposes, was reported from the New Mexico nuclear testing ground. This prompted the Defense Department to suggest the efficacy of convincing the Chinese and North Korean Communists that the U.N. Command intended to launch a major offensive with the new nuclear warhead should armistice talks not be resumed and completed.

Secretary of State John Foster Dulles, who was on a trip to the Middle East, met with Indian Prime Minister Jawaharlal Nehru and suggested that Communist Chinese Prime Minister Chou En-lai be warned that failing an early settlement, the United States would bomb Manchurian sanctuaries north of the Yalu. Dulles also told Nehru about America's successful. testing of nuclear artillery shells, implying they might be used in North Korea.

As public evidence that he intended to change policy, Eisenhower ordered the removal of the Seventh Fleet from the Formosa Straits area, declaring: "This order implies no aggressive intent on our part, but we certainly have no obligation to protect a nation fighting us in Korea."

Although the U.S. Seventh Fleet was considered "a defensive arm of Communist China," it actually had been helping the Chiang Kai-shek government on Formosa maintain contact with guerrillas on the mainland. Eisenhower's real intention was to make the Chinese Communists fear invasion from Formosa.

Operation Little Switch

The Eisenhower Administration made one last effort to break the deadlock by taking advantage of a resolution adopted two months earlier by the Executive Committee of the League of Red Cross Societies, which called for an exchange of sick and wounded prisoners in Korea. The U.S. State Department was planning to introduce a similar resolution in the United Nations.

On February 22, 1953, Clark wrote to Kim Il Sung and to Peng Teh-huai:

> The United Nations Command remains immediately ready to repatriate those seriously sick and seriously wounded captured personnel who are fit to travel in accordance with provisions of Article 109 of the

Geneva Convention. I wish to be informed whether
you are prepared for your part to proceed immediately
with the repatriation of seriously sick and wounded
personnel....The United Nations Command liaison
officers will be prepared to meet your liaison officers
to make necessary arrangements.

There was little action on the battlefield or at Panmunjom
throughout February. Then there occurred on March 5 potentially
the most significant event: Soviet Premier Joseph Stalin suddenly
died of a cerebral hemorrhage. In his place stood Georgi Malenkov,
supported by the real power in the Soviet Russia, Nikita Khrushchev. While the Communist world was turned upside down,
Eisenhower immediately saw the Soviet dictator's death as providing
a chance for peace.

Peking and Pyongyang were congratulating Malenkov. A *Pravda*
article quoted Kim Il Sung as saying that day, "Our people are not
alone in their selfless and valiant fight. Mighty People's China has
sent its volunteers to our assistance. This aid is a good example of
Stalin's friendship for the peoples of the mighty socialist camp."

On March 28, Kim and Peng replied to Clark that they not only
agreed to the proposed exchange of sick and wounded POWs; they
suggested that the plenary session at Panmunjom, in recess since
October 8, be resumed at once.

Furthermore, on March 30, Communist Chinese Foreign
Minister Chou En-lai, returning from Stalin's funeral in Moscow,
announced that POWs who refused repatriation might be handed
over to a neutral state and that explanations be given them by the
parties concerned. Soviet Foreign Minister V.M. Molotov endorsed
Chou's statement on April 10.

The next day both sides agreed on terms for the exchange of sick
and wounded captives, and on April 20, the exchange called
Operation Little Switch began, lasting until April 26. The United
Nations handed over 5,194 North Koreans, 1,030 Chinese, and 446
North Korean civilian internees — a total of 6,670 sick and
wounded prisoners. The Communists returned 684 U.N. prisoners,
among them 471 South Koreans, 149 Americans, and 64 other
nationalities.

The United Nations Command quickly learned that there was little hope for the return of all of the 8,000 American prisoners taken by the Communists. Many of the American and South Korean prisoners came out in pitiable condition — emaciated veritably to skeleton size, their wounds untreated for months, some demented by the strain of captivity and their mistreatment. The Communist invalids, to the contrary, appeared to be full of vigor; as they drove away from Panmunjom, they threw away their U.N.-issued rations of tooth powder, soap, and cigarettes, and some tore their clothing to give the impression they had been mistreated by the U.N. Command, thus embarrassing the U.N. to the very last.

As the truce talks were reaching the final stage with the conciliatory approach by the United Nations, President Rhee's strenuous objections to the Panmunjom arrangements became further intransigent. He had insisted that the Communists must be fought to the finish and that his government would not accept any armistice which would fail to realize his life-long dream of a unified, independent Korea. Thus, the tug-of-war began between Rhee and the United States, which was now determined to end the war by all means.

The single passionate purpose of Syngman Rhee was to build a free and democratic state in Korea. That goal had nourished him during the long years of his independence movement in exile, and from 1945 onward he made it clear that he considered force the only means of unifying his homeland. When U.N. troops were fighting north in the fall of 1950, Rhee imagined that his dream of a united Korea was near. Then in 1953, Rhee hoped for a change in the U.S. approach to the war's resolution with Eisenhower's election. But now he saw the moves at Panmunjom as the final death sentence for the dream of a united Korea.

Secret U.N. Proposal Scooped

With Operation Little Switch over, hopes for real peace prevailed, and Panmunjom was crowded with correspondents again. But the U.N. Command, now resolved to put forth its final proposal that drastically conceded to Communists terms, enforced tight control on information in fear of President Rhee's obstruction.

Amidst the critical confrontation between the U.S. government trying to achieve armistice by all means and President Rhee adamantly opposing any truce that would leave Korea divided, I scored another scoop, this one on the contents of the secret U.N. proposal.

As an AP correspondent and as a Korean, I thought it imperative to report to the world the behind-the-scenes dealing that might determine the future of my country. While covering the truce talks as they dragged over twenty-two months, I had felt this sort of denouement would be inevitable.

Luckily I had a very reliable source at Panmunjom. He was South Korean Army Captain Oh Kie-chang, a young, capable press officer assigned to the office of Major General Choi Duk-shin, South Korean Army representative at the truce village. Captain Oh, well-versed in English, was in a position to have access to U.N.C. documents submitted to the Communists. (Now a professor of politics at Catholic University of America in Washington, D.C., he invited me to a dinner at his Potomac home on July 27, 1993, when I was visiting Washington for a Korean war correspondents reunion marking the 40th anniversary of the armistice signing. We were delighted to relive our Panmunjom memories forty years past.)

On the early morning of May 26, 1953, Captain Oh informed me of the hush-hush U.N.C. proposal submitted to the Communists the previous day. He said: "General Harrison handed the U.N. proposal to Nam Il, Communist chief delegate, in a closed meeting at 11 a.m. yesterday. General Choi was notified of the contents of the proposal only one hour before the meeting. Choi hurriedly wrote a letter of protest to Harrison refuting the secret U.N. proposal and boycotted yesterday's meeting. Colonel Lee Soo-yong attended instead. You can find out the details of the U.N. proposal from General Choi who is due to arrive at Yoido Airstrip at 10 this morning. He is carrying a copy of his letter submitted to Harrison." Captain Oh further explained what he had learned from Colonel Lee's report to Choi on the main points of the secret U.N. proposal.

I rushed to Yoido Airstrip to catch Choi. As he was getting off the plane, I spoke to him, "It seems apparent that the latest U.N. proposal at Panmunjom contains provisions disadvantageous to the Korean government...." Choi nodded without a word.

"Should there be any proposal that runs counter to Korean national interest, it would be your duty, as a South Korean Army representative at the truce talks, to inform the people of its contents without losing time. You should therefore make public your letter to Harrison," I said to Choi.

"If I announce the contents of the letter, it would be a breach of my promise to Harrison not to reveal it," said Choi.

I attempted a lecture: "Suppose a close friend of yours hands a secret plan that would determine your fate to your arch enemy and asks you not to reveal it, would you comply with such a request? Now is the time for you to give priority to your national interest rather than to your personal promise to another individual. Otherwise, history might brand you as a traitor."

Choi said with a blush, "You are quite right. I need your advice."

"If I were you I would telephone Harrison, saying: 'As a citizen of the Republic of Korea, I am obliged to announce the contents of my letter to you. So, I notify you that I will release it to the press.' "

Choi went to a nearby telephone booth. After telling Harrison what I had suggested, he handed me a copy of his letter. I drove my Jeep like a madman to my home with the news material I had strived to obtain so hard. I did not want to write the report in the AP office in Naija Apartment lest my "scoop" be discovered by rival correspondents.

The biggest barrier in the truce talks was the disposition of anti-Communist prisoners refusing repatriation. Communist prisoners who had insisted they did not want to be sent home included 34,000 North Koreans and 14,500 Communist Chinese troops.

As regards this thorny prisoner issue, the new U.N. proposal contained the following provisions:

1. The U.N. Command would withdraw the "But...." proviso of its previous proposal of May 13 to release North Korean prisoners refusing repatriation. (On May 13, General Harrison presented a proposal demanding that only 22,000 Chinese prisoners be turned over to the Repatriation Commission. But the 34,000 North Koreans refusing to

return home would be released in South Korea as civilians on the signing of the armistice.)

2. The 48,500 North Korean and Chinese prisoners refusing to return would be handed over to the five-nation Neutral Nations Repatriation Commission composed of India, Poland, Czechoslovakia, Sweden, and Switzerland. During a period of ninety days, explanations might be made by Communist agents to reluctant prisoners to return home. (U.N. Command's previous proposal had set the explanation period for sixty days.)

3. Those prisoners still resisting repatriation after the explanation period would be turned over to a post-truce political conference. Should there be any prisoners still left unsettled in the conference, the United Nations General Assembly would find homes in the free world for prisoners demanding political asylum.

4. All disputes within the Repatriation Commission would be decided by majority rather than by unanimous vote.

When my dispatch to AP on the secret U.N. proposal made big headlines in South Korean newspapers, the Korean National Assembly voted unanimously against the proposed truce terms, and anti-armistice demonstrations were staged in major cities — from Pusan to Munsan-ni near Panmunjom. Outside the correspondents' quarters (Naija Apartment), hundreds of Chinmyong Girls High School students sat in the dirt compound and wept. They were chanting "Give us unification, or death."

Rhee's Last Stand

General Clark visited President Rhee at Kyongmudae at 10 a.m.
May 25, to inform him of the change in the American bargaining
policy and tried to soften the blow for the old president. American
Ambassador Ellis O. Briggs and South Korean Foreign Minister
Pyun Yung-tae sat in on the meeting. Clark had flown into Korea at
2 p.m. the previous day, but waited until one hour before General
Harrison presented the new U.N. plan to the Communists in a closed
session at Panmunjom.

Clark related Rhee's reaction:

> The emotional effect of this on Rhee was profound. I
> had never seen him so disturbed. He sat bolt upright in
> his chair, the muscles of his face twitched occasionally
> and he kept rubbing the ends of his fingers, which, I
> had heard, had been burned by Japanese secret police
> in the early days of his fight for Korean independence.
> Once he broke into our recital of our plans and prom-
> ises and said: "I am deeply disappointed. Your govern-
> ment changes its position often. You pay no attention
> to the view of the ROK Government....One thing we
> must insist upon is the withdrawal of Chinese Commu-
> nists from our territory. There can be no peaceful
> settlement without that. Your threats have no effect
> upon me. We want to live. We want to survive. We
> will decide our own fate. Sorry, I cannot assure
> President Eisenhower of my co-operation under the
> circumstances." [5]

Emotionally and politically, President Rhee could not accept the
armistice terms. They left his nation and people divided. On June 7,
Rhee declared martial law, canceled the trips of fifteen South
Korean Army generals scheduled to leave for America, and canceled
military leaves for all officers and men.

Despite South Korean resistance, the U.N. and Communist
delegations met secretly at Panmunjom and on June 8 both sides

signed an agreement on the repatriation of prisoners of war, which provided, in substance:

1. All prisoners who sought repatriation would be returned home immediately.

2. Those who refused repatriation would be taken to the Demilitarized Zone between the two sides and placed in custody of the Neutral Nations Repatriations Commission — India, Poland, Czechoslovakia, Sweden and Switzerland — of which India was to be the umpire and sole provider of troops for the custodial force.

3. For the next ninety days, explanation teams from the nations involved would be allowed to talk to the prisoners in an attempt to persuade them to return home. Those who changed their minds would be repatriated immediately.

4. After this the Political Conference would try to settle the question of those still refusing repatriation.

5. If the Political Conference failed to settle the issue in thirty days, the Neutral Nations would discharge the non-repatriated prisoners as free civilians and help them settle in countries of their choice. (The U.N. Command withdrew its proposal to hand them over to the United Nations General Assembly and accepted the Communist demand.)

Upon being briefed on the new U.S. plan by General Clark, President Rhee asserted: "The United States is making a great mistake in adopting their tactics of appeasement. My government would never accept the armistice. Our Army would fight, even if it meant suicide, and I would lead them."

Rhee felt he was betrayed because the new U.S. truce plan ran counter to the U.N. General Assembly resolution of October 7, 1950 for a unified Korea; Britain presented a resolution calling for "all appropriate steps... to ensure conditions of stability throughout Korea," with a unified government elected under U.N. auspices and a prompt withdrawal of troops. The resolution passed by a vote of 47 to 5, with 7 abstentions.

He also was dismayed by the U.S. flip-flop on the anti-Communist North Korean prisoners of war issue: the U.S. withdrew its previous proposal providing that only the Chinese prisoners be turned over to the Neutral Nations Repatriation Commission and said that anti-Communist North Koreans should be released as civilians in South Korea.

President Rhee also had strenuous objections to the composition of Neutral Nations Repatriation Commission. He did not want members of the then Communist governments of Poland and Czechoslovakia on Korean soil. Moreover he disliked Indians, whom he considered to be pro-Communist disguised as neutrals.

So he told Clark that if an armistice was signed leaving his country divided, he would feel free to take any action he deemed appropriate.

Asked if this meant the withdrawal of South Korean troops from U.N. Command, Rhee said, "Not today, not tomorrow. But if it comes to that, I will discuss it with you in advance."

27,000 Anti-Communist North Korean POWs Released

The agreement on POW repatriation signed at Panmunjom on June 8 with a drastic U.S. concession dealt a heavy blow to the 34,000 anti-Communist North Korean prisoners who had anticipated to be freed soon in South Korea. The United States and the U.N. had withdrawn their proposition to free them and were now letting them go through the ninety-day process of persuasion to return home by North Korean explanation teams.

No one but President Syngman Rhee would come to their aid. Rhee himself thought now was the time for him to act. On June 9, he summoned his provost marshal, Lieutenant General Won Yong-duk, to the presidential mansion to discuss a secret plan to release anti-Communist North Koreans, who were held in POW camps guarded by South Korean MPs under General Won's Command. Just after 2 a.m., June 18, on orders from Rhee, South Korean guards at anti-Communist POW camps in Pusan, Kwangju, Nonsan, Masan, and Taegu opened the gates and some 25,000 prisoners walked out and lost themselves among the civilians. During the following day another 2,000 were released from other camps, boosting the total to 27,000 freed in a dramatic, well-planned operation. (Some 7,000 other North Korean prisoners at camps guarded by American troops could not be freed.)

General Won called on the people to "help protect these patriotic youths," while other South Korean officials broadcast the news to the country. The people were told to take care of the men from the prison camps, and the people did so: they took them into their homes.

Even those South Koreans who disagreed with Rhee and were fearful of the consequences expressed great pride in the audacious release. Later in the morning President Rhee announced: "According to the Geneva Convention, and also to the principle of human rights, the anti-Communist Korean prisoners should have been released long before this. Most of the United Nations authorities with whom I have spoken about our desire to release these prisoners are with us in sympathy and principle. But due to international complications, we have been holding these people too long." He had, therefore, ordered their release on his own responsibility. "The reason why I did this, without full consultation with the United Nations Command, is too obvious to explain."

Criticism of Rhee poured in from all over the world. President Eisenhower sent an indignant message to Rhee protesting that his action had created "an impossible situation for the U.N. Command." British Prime Minister Winston Churchill called it "treachery" and stated flatly that the U.N. had no intention of conquering North Korea on Rhee's behalf.

Significantly, the Communists directed their anger and propaganda diatribes not at the United States but at the "murderer Rhee." They still wanted a cease-fire.

U.S.-Republic of Korea
Security Treaty Concluded

Eisenhower dispatched Walter S. Robertson, Assistant Secretary of State for Far Eastern Affairs, to Seoul with a mission to persuade Rhee not to obstruct armistice. Robertson arrived in the Korean capital on June 25, the third anniversary of the North Korean invasion, and across every thoroughfare he saw anti-armistice streamers and printed slogans. Many of them cried, "Don't sell Korea," in English. Thousands of demonstrators poured through the streets. They shouted, "Pukchin! Pukchin! — March north!"

After repeated discussions, sometimes attended by General Clark, Ambassador Ellis O. Briggs, South Korean Premier Paik Too-chin, and Foreign Minister Pyun Yung-tae, the United States and the Republic of Korea jointly announced on July 12 that they had reached agreements for future collaboration.

Rhee told Robertson, in writing, that although he could not sign the armistice, "we shall not obstruct it, so long as no measures of actions taken under the armistice are detrimental to our national survival." He would "endeavor to cooperate fully and earnestly in the political and peaceful achievement of reunification of our nation."

Rhee made this promise only after he had secured the following agreements from the U.S. government:

1. Promise of a U.S.-Republic of Korea Mutual Security Pact after the armistice (such a pact having to be ratified by the U.S. Senate).

2. Agreement to expand the South Korean Army to twenty divisions,

3. Long-term economic aid, with an initial installment of $200 million for a total appropriation by the U.S. Congress of $1 billion and $9.5 million in food to the Korean people immediately after the signing of the armistice,

4. Agreement that if the post-armistice Political Conference produced no results in ninety days, the United States and the Republic of Korea would withdraw to discuss plans of their own for unifying the country,

5. Agreement to hold high-level U.S.-South Korea talks before the Political Conference.

In return, Rhee promised that he would no longer obstruct the armistice.

Commenting on the outcome of the Rhee-Robertson talks, General Clark said, "it has been proven that the Republic of Korea is not a puppet of the United States" as the Communists alleged. Rhee had succeeded in securing U.S. commitment for a huge amount of economic and military aid. The conclusion of the U.S.-Republic of Korea Mutual Security Treaty was especially important, for the stationing of American forces in Korea under the security pact was the main factor in deterring North Korean ambition to re-invade the South.

The Treaty was signed in Washington, D.C., on October 1, 1953, by U.S. Secretary of State John Foster Dulles and South Korean Foreign Minister Pyun Yung-tai, and was ratified by the United States Senate on January 26, 1954 and later by the Republic of Korea National Assembly.

On July 10, 1953, the plenary session of the truce talks were resumed at Panmunjom. Now that the U.N. Command had accepted virtually all Communist proposals except for the U.N. principle of voluntary repatriation, the talks proceeded without hindrance. But on July 13, just fourteen days before the signing of the armistice, Communist Chinese forces launched massive attacks on South Korean divisions holding the Kumsong Bulge between the Chorwon-Kumwha-Pyongyang Iron Triangle and the Punchbowl north of Hwachon Reservoir. The quick maneuver of the supporting U.S. divisions under Lieutenant General Maxwell D. Taylor, who had taken over the Eighth Army from Van Fleet on February 11, stopped any hope of a Communist breakthrough.

With the battlefront ablaze, the final negotiations went forward, disregarding the yearnings of South Koreans for reunification of their country. Thus, on July 19, the U.N. Command gave the Communists solemn assurance the Republic of Korea would not upset the truce terms already agreed upon.

After three years, one month, and two days of savage war in Korea, and after 575 sessions of truce wranglings over two years and two weeks, an armistice agreement was reached. There had been neither victory nor defeat. The war ended in a military stalemate, which continues today — forty-two years after the guns fell silent.

On July 25, American Ambassador Briggs delivered Secretary of State Dulles' reply to President Rhee, reconfirming Washington's pledge made in the Robertson-Rhee agreement announced July 12. Rhee had sent an urgent message to Dulles the previous day requesting the U.S. government's reassurance that the agreement would be implemented. Upon receiving the reply, Rhee summoned Prime Minister Paik Too-jin, Foreign Minister Pyun Yung-tai and Defense Minister Sohn Won-il to Kyongmudae and told them, "I am satisfied with it."

Now that the U.S.-South Korea agreement was firmly set, Washington felt relieved that Rhee would no longer obstruct the armistice.

Armistice Signed

The historic signing of the armistice took place on July 27, 1953, at Panmunjom. A little before 10 a.m. on Monday, July 27, Lieutenant General William K. Harrison Jr. and Lieutenant General Nam Il silently led their delegations into the T-shaped "peace pagoda" made of tar paper and straw mat. At precisely 10 o'clock, the two chief delegates sat down at a straight row of tables covered with baize cloth and signed eighteen copies of the agreement — nine covered in United Nations blue and nine in Communist red, without saying a word to each other.

At one o'clock in the afternoon, General Clark entered the U.N. Advanced Headquarters at the apple orchard in Musan-ni and sat at a long table in front of the camp theater stage. He signed the eighteen copies of the armistice agreement, and read a statement to newsmen: "I cannot find it in me to exult in this hour. Rather, it is time for prayer, that we may succeed in our difficult endeavor to turn this armistice to the advantage of mankind." To the lanky, single-minded general, the inconclusive conclusion of the long and bloody experience of Korea was infinitely distasteful.

Peng Teh-huai, commander of the Communist Chinese "Volunteers," signed the document in Kaesong for the Communist side. He was reported to have said:

"Through three years of fighting together the Volunteers forged a comradeship in blood with the North Korean people and their army — a friendship which further deepened and strengthened our internationalist feelings."

Twelve hours later, the guns were silenced on the hills and the Korean War came to an inconclusive end. To the north of these hills, the armistice already had been violated. New air fields were built, and new arms and new modern aircraft poured across the Yalu River to new fortified bases deep in the mountains. United Nations protests against these violations were unvaryingly rejected by the Neutral Nations Supervisory Commission members from Communist Poland and Czechoslovakia.

Since the armistice, North Korea has spent more than 25 percent of its gross national product (GNP) on military outlays, thus maintaining the fifth largest army in the world. It is the most fortified piece of land on planet Earth, with everything vital dug deep underground. Its formidable one million-man army is dedicated to die for Kim Il Sung's heir, Kim Jong Il. More ominous is the North Korean leader's ruthless management of a nuclear weapons program and supposed terrorist activities, including the 1983 bomb explosion in Rangoon, Burma that killed 18 high-ranking South Korean officials and the 1987 mid-air blast of a South Korean airliner over Burmese waters that killed all 115 passengers and crew on board.

Pyongyang's nuclear development threat was attenuated for now by the U.S.-North Korean pact signed on October 21, 1994, in Geneva. North Korea agreed to accept U.N. inspections of facilities under the agreement, but this isn't 100 percent reassuring because North Korea would not have to open the two suspected nuclear dump sites to international inspections for about five years. Lessons have not been fully learned that agreements are considered by the Communists merely as tactical maneuvers to gain time or other advantages.

The two Koreas technically are still at war. Across the 156-mile Demilitarized Zone, about one million armed-to-the-teeth North Korean troops are facing 540,000 South Korean ground forces, reinforced by 26,000 U.S. Army troops.

The nondecisive ending of the Korean War left Syngman Rhee and his people in the south emphatically unhappy that the United States did not achieve its once-declared goal of uniting the country. Rhee used to say, "If there must be trouble, let it be in my day, so that my children may have peace." But, even passionate Syngman Rhee was forced to flee his beloved country in 1960 at the age of eighty-five. A student uprising drove him and his Austrian-born wife, Francesca, to Hawaii. Despite all the Western criticisms of "stubborn Rhee," he was generally believed to be the only person capable of leading the war-stricken country.

Communist Chinese leaders, impervious to human loss and suffering, gloried in China's sudden leap to big-power status — for by defying the United Nations, and holding the Western armies in check, it became a great power in the East. Communist powers, notably Soviet Russia, remembered the rapid escalation from a small, almost civil-type conflict they had initiated into a large-scale action involving sixteen nations under the U.N. flag.

Though not an active participant, Japan was the only winner in the Korean War. Japan accumulated much wealth by producing a large amount of weapons for the war and acting as the service, supply and recreational base for the U.S. and U.N. troops. Thus Japan could take a giant step toward its quick economic recovery from the ruins of World War II.

On July 27, the day the armistice was signed, the sixteen United Nations allies who fought in Korea worked out a joint statement which, as it was made public two weeks later, declared:

> We affirm in the interest of the world peace that if there is a renewal of the armed attacks, challenging again the principles of the United Nations, we should

again be united and prompt to resist. The consequences of such a breach of the armistice would be so
grave that in all probability it would not be possible to
confine hostilities within the frontiers of Korea.

As the truce terms provided, within 90 days of the cease-fire all
POWs had to be screened and repatriated, or otherwise disposed of.
The prisoner exchange, dubbed Operation Big Switch, began August
5 and lasted through the first week of September at the Demilitarized Zone, Panmunjom. The U.N. Command returned 75,823
prisoners (70,183 North Koreans, 5,640 Chinese); the Communists
in turn delivered 12,773 men (3,597 Americans, 7,862 South
Koreans, and the remainder 1,314 from other allied nations).

North Korean and Communist Chinese "explainers" came to the
Demilitarized Zone to persuade their former troops to return home.
Explanations took place inside twelve tents under the eyes of the
Swedish, Swiss, Polish and Czechoslovakian members of the
Neutral Repatriation Commission, as well as the Indian umpire and
representatives from both sides. Prisoners entered the tent, were
greeted by the explainers, heard their arguments in favor of coming
home, and rejected or accepted repatriation by going out of doors
plainly marked with such destinations as "South Korea" or "North
Korea."

Some Chinese prisoners teased the explainers as they passed
through the door to South Korea, saying, "Why don't you come with
us?" Others spat at the explainers. In the end, the Communist
explanations were a staggering failure; it was a humiliating
propaganda blow against world Communism.

Of the 14,704 Chinese prisoners, only 137 opted for repatriation,
and only 325 out of 7900 North Koreans who had refused repatriation chose to go north. On January 10, 1954, 22,142 non-repatriates
(14,567 Chinese, 7,575 North Koreans) went south waving flags of
Nationalist China and the Republic of Korea amidst thunderous
cheers from crowds of South Koreans. It took 15 hours and 43
minutes for the long lines of these former Communist troops to pass
the check points toward South Korea.

The small number of Chinese and North Korean prisoners who
had remained true Communists and chose to return home led

miserable lives after their repatriation. Even Peng Teh-huai, who had fought loyally in Korea as commander of the Communist Chinese Forces, was ousted from his post as defense minister in 1959 and died in disgrace on November 29, 1974 after he was tortured by Red Guards during the Cultural Revolution. In North Korea, Lieutenant General Kim Chaek, who had led the invading North Korean Army as field commander, and other top military leaders were purged by Kim Il Sung for failing to conquer South Korea.

Of the 359 U.N. non-repatriates, 327 Koreans, 21 Americans, and 1 Briton remained with the Communists; 2 Americans and 8 Koreans chose to return home.

The returning U.N. troops were brought to Freedom Village constructed near Panmunjom, given a warm welcome, food and new clothes, and then underwent extensive questioning about life in Communist prison camps.

Their replies provided the evidence from which the U.S. Defense Department concluded that more than 6,000 American troops and 5,000 other soldiers — most of them South Koreans — had perished after falling into Communist hands.[6] As explained earlier, Colonel James M. Hanley, chief of the U.S Eighth Army's judge advocate section, caused a world-wide stir with his surprising and sensational charges on November 14, 1951, that the Communists had killed 5,750 United Nations prisoners of war — about 5,500 of them Americans — in atrocities since the start of the war.

The three years, one month, and two days of the Korean War — the first big shooting war of the Cold War fought under the United Nations banner against the Communist aggressors — wheezed to an ambiguous conclusion. The conflict's final, zig-zagging battle line generally along the 38th Parallel became a lasting demarcation, which predated the Berlin Wall by eight years and survived long after it crumbled. It has even outlasted the collapse of the Soviet Union.

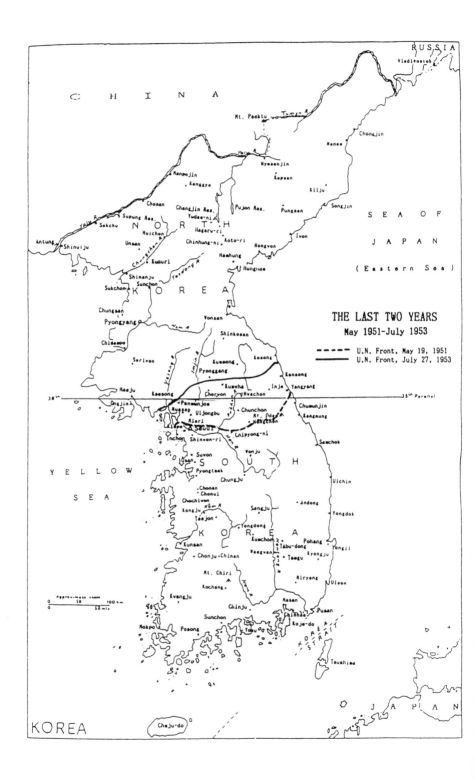

General Mark Clark, U.N. commander, signs armistice documents at his advanced headquarters in Munsan-ni three hours after they had been signed at Panmunjom by both sides at 10 a.m. July 27, 1953.

General Peng Teh-huai, commander of the Communist Chinese Forces, signs the truce documents at Kaesong.

The savage war incurred horrifying casualties. U.N. losses are recounted for all time in inscriptions at the Korean War Veterans Memorial Pool of Remembrance in Washington:

	U.S.A	U.N.
Dead	54,246	628,833
Missing	8,177	470,267
Captured	7,140	92,970
Wounded	103,284	1,064,453

Approximately 70 percent of the U.N. casualties were South Koreans.

An estimated two million North Korean and Communist Chinese soldiers had died in the battle or from disease.

According to *Thirty-year History of North Korea* (Yoo Wanshik, Kim Tae-se, Hyondae Kyongje-Ilbo-Sa, Seoul, 1975), a total of 1,410,000 South Korean civilians were victimized: 123,000 killed in Communist-occupied areas, 473,000 dead and wounded in battle zones, 84,000 abducted to North Korea, 400,000 inducted to North Korean Army, and 330,000 missing.

Thus military and civilian casualties on the South Korean side alone numbered more than 2,500,000. Victims in North Korea put together, more than 5,000,000 men, women and children were sacrificed by "the century's nastiest war," as American combat historian General S.L.A. Marshall put it.

Because they cannot look back on the Korean War with any sense of victory, despite the enormous casualties, the Americans preferred not to look back at all, thus it had been called "The Forgotten War" until the July 27, 1995 dedication of the Korean War Veterans Memorial in the U.S. capital.

Geneva Conference

The political conference provided by the armistice agreement to negotiate for a peaceful unification of Korea began on April 26, 1954, at the historic Council Chamber of the Palais des Nations at

Geneva, once occupied by the old League of Nations. Taking part were the foreign ministers of nineteen countries: those of the sixteen-nation U.N. Command, plus the Soviet Union, Communist China, and North Korea. Soviet participation was due to the Indochina question of war developments in Vietnam.

On the Korean problem, Communist and non-Communist delegates alike paid lip service to the concept of a unified, independent Korea, but East and West stood poles apart on how to achieve it. Pyun Yung-tai, foreign minister of the Republic of Korea, proposed that U.N.-sponsored elections be held in North Korea for representatives to sit in the present South Korean National Assembly, which would become a national parliament. This proposal was rejected by the Communists on the grounds that it would give control of all Korea to the Republic of Korea.

On the other hand, North Korean Foreign Minister Nam Il, mindful of the geographical realities which would permit Chinese troops to return to Korea in a matter of days, proposed that all foreign troops be withdrawn from Korea in six months, and that national elections supervised by a commission appointed by the Supreme People's Assembly in the north and the National Assembly in the south. This proposal was rejected by the Republic of Korea on the basis that it would expose Korea to further Chinese penetration after the U.N. forces were withdrawn.

On May 22, a Western counter-proposal calling for U.N.-sponsored, all-Korea elections was agreed to by the Republic of Korea, which previously had rejected the concept of all-Korea elections on the grounds that elections supervised by the United Nations had already been held in South Korea in 1948. But the concession was followed by Pyun's demand that Chinese forces be withdrawn from North Korea before any elections were held.

After seven weeks of stalemate, the negotiations broke down amid mutual recriminations. Neither side had shown a willingness to make any substantial concessions on the Korean issue, and what positive results came from Geneva concerned only Indochina.

On June 15, 1954, the Western allies broke off the negotiations with the statement that the Communists obstructed any agreement and that further discussion of Korea at Geneva was useless.

On April 27, 1954, the day after the Geneva conference convened, AP correspondent Murray Fromson called me at the Chosun Hotel where I was covering a news conference. He told me: "There were calls for you from Kyongmudae. President Rhee wants to see you. Go there right away."

I hurried to the presidential mansion without knowing what was up. The white-haired President, who was planting tree saplings in the garden, received me with a smile. He ordered secretary Kwak Yong-ju to bring a chair and let me sit next to him.

"I've received a cable from Foreign Minister Pyun Yung-tai in Geneva this morning. He said he was embarrassed that there was no South Korean correspondent at the conference site whereas many North Korea reporters were roaming around. Since there were world news agencies like AP, UP, and Reuters based in Geneva, we did not have to dispatch our own newsmen there at the expense of valuable foreign currency. But now that Minister Pyun wants them, I have decided to send just one representative Korean journalist. So I want you to go there, Bill. We will pay all expenses."

As an AP correspondent, I thought I should not do anything at the request of a certain government. Because I had twice refused President Rhee's offer to become his government spokesman (Minister of Public Information) in 1952 and 1954, I felt sorry to refuse again outright. Yet, I decided to refuse once again in a courteous way.

"I am deeply grateful, Mr. President. But other AP correspondents are already covering the Geneva conference, and I have been assigned to cover the upcoming May 20 general elections in Korea," I said.

"I will telephone to Mr. Frank Starzel [AP general manager] and get his approval for you to go to Geneva. I will be proud of having a reporter like you over there. Because there are other AP correspondents already assigned there, you do not have to file any report. Just go for a change of air," said the president.

As I had once accompanied Mr. Starzel to Kyongmudae when he was invited for a luncheon by Rhee, I was aware of their friendly relationship.

"Please allow me to inform Mr. Starzel of your kind offer and to report to you after I hear instructions from the AP head office."

"All right. You may do so."

On the following day, I called on the president and told him: "The AP head office in New York expressed deep gratitude for your kind offer to one of its correspondents like me. But I was instructed to explain to you that there is no one but me to cover the important May 20 elections in Korea. To my great regret, therefore, I am unable to go to Geneva. Please send someone else."

"It's too bad that you cannot go. But I understand AP's position, too," the president said.

Anti-NNSC Demonstrations

With the armistice signing, the Neutral Nations Supervisory Commission (NNSC) composed of members from Sweden, Switzerland, Poland and Czechoslovakia assumed the task of "enforcing" the armistice on both sides, particularly with respect to the introduction of new weapons. But in North Korea inspections were a fiasco, as the Communists flatly refused to permit Swedish and Swiss observers to visit the ten designated ports of entry into which the Communists were introducing new equipment. On the other hand, Polish and Czech members of the neutral commission sought strict application of the inspection agreement in South Korea.

It was the U.N. Command's scrupulous observance of the armistice terms — which allowed the Pole and Czech inspectors to travel freely in South Korea — that aroused Rhee's ire. In 1954 and again in the following year, violent demonstrations against the Polish and Czech inspectors were staged at the port cities of Mokpo, Pusan, Inchon, and Kangnung.

In their protests to Rhee, U.S. officials pointed out that the U.N. Command was obligated to provide protection to the inspection teams, and expressed fears that continued demonstrations would cause ill feelings between Koreans and Americans. Yet Rhee made no move to halt the demonstrations, but instead expressed indignation in a statement:

"It has been surprising — to learn that Korea and Koreans have been misunderstood and wrongfully accused in connection with the demonstrations demanding withdrawal of the Communist spies of the Neutral Nations Supervisory Commission....The people have every right to demonstrate their self-determination against flagrant international injustice. But we have repeatedly urged the demonstrators to conduct themselves in a non-violent and orderly manner...." U.N. guards had carried out the thankless task of protecting the Communist inspectors and had themselves suffered minor injuries from stone-throwing Korean crowds. The guards employed police dogs and tear gas to disperse the demonstrators, and the Korean government said one demonstrator was killed and hundreds of them injured. But finally, in the summer of 1955, the demonstrations ceased.

I filed the following dispatch on August 13, 1955:

> Seoul, Aug. 13 (AP) — President Syngman Rhee tonight lifted the midnight deadline of his ultimatum demanding for neutral nations truce supervisors to get out of Korea. He advised against violent demonstrations.
>
> Rhee said he acted on assurance from Assistant Secretary of State Walter Robertson that the United States Government "will make efforts soon" to seek peaceful withdrawal of the Neutral Nations Supervisory Commission. He said Robertson gave the assurance in a letter.
>
> "Our people at this time should be patient about everything," Rhee said in a statement. "We might be misunderstood if the demonstrations continued until all the members of the Neutral Nations Supervisory Commission leave Korea."
>
> Rhee's statement, broadcast in Korea two hours before the midnight deadline, was released by the government Office of Public Information. It followed three mob assaults on the four-nation truce team's compound on Wolmi Island in Inchon harbor. The last two attacks were stopped at a sand bag barricade thrown across a causeway linking the island to the mainland.

United States guards, reinforced by police dogs, drove back the demonstrators with smoke grenades, tear gas and high pressure fire hoses.

Rhee, charging Polish and Czech members of the NNSC were Communist spies, had demanded that they leave by midnight.

Forty-four United States soldiers and about 100 Koreans were injured in five cities where truce teams are assigned. In a statement, Rhee said representatives of the 16 Korean War allies were discussing the NNSC problem. He reported Gen. Lyman L. Lemnitzer, United States Far East commander, had issued orders to American troops to avoid shooting....

The United States soldiers guarding truce team compounds apparently have used dog units, like one dispatched to Wolmi Island tonight, for their frightening effect on attacking mobs. But no dogs actually were turned loose against demonstrators.

The Neutral Nations Supervisory Commission became virtually nonexistent after June 1991 when North Korea stopped accommodations to the once favored Polish and Czech members in apparent protest against their diplomatic normalizations with South Korea. By February 1995, they had been evicted from the North Korean territory.

FALLEN WAR CORRESPONDENTS

Eighteen Killed on Duty

About 350 news correspondents covered the Korean War on the United Nations side and 18 of them were killed, two captured and held as prisoners of war in North Korea.

Han Kyu-ho, correspondent of *Seoul Shinmun,* was killed on the fifth day of the North Korean invasion, June 29, 1950, while covering elements of the South Korean army retreating before the

Soviet-made World War II vintage T–34 tanks spearheading the Communist invaders from the north. Han's regular beat had been the South Korean Ministry of Defense.

Cpl. Ernie Peeler, 38, a correspondent for *Pacific Stars and Stripes,* with years of newspaper and World War II combat correspondent experience, and Ray Richards, 65, a veteran Hearst newspaper correspondent, who had been assigned to International News Service, were killed on July 10, 1950, when the jeep they were riding turned onto a road north of Taejon, met a Communist tank that blasted them. Each had a bullet hole in the head.

Wilson Fielder, Jr., 33, correspondent of *Time* and *Life,* was killed by Communist machine gun fire during evacuation from Taejon on July 22, 1950. Fielder, born in Chengchow, Honan, China, of missionary parents, was a World War II Marine Corps captain who had volunteered from his comfortable post in Hong Kong, leaving behind his wife and a child. He joined *Time* in 1948 and was sent to China to cover the Communist takeover, later covering the French forces in Indochina and Nationalist raids from Taiwan upon mainland China.

On July 27, a C–47 transport plane crashed into the sea en route to Korea from Japan killing four correspondents aboard. They were Maxmilien Philonenko, 33, Agence France Presse (AFP); Albert Hinton, 46, *Journal and Guide* (USA); Stephen Simmons, *London Picture Post* and Hilton Press (UK); and James Supple, 34, *Chicago Sun Times.* Philonenko, born in Russia just before the Bolshevik Revolution, emigrated to France with his family. With the outbreak of the Korean War, he was sent to the Korean front on July 7 and joined the landing at Pohang with the U.S. 1st Cavalry Division. He had pointed out in his dispatch of July 25 — two days before his death — the urgent need of immediate reinforcement and equipment. Hinton, who also represented other Afro-American newspapers, was on his way to cover the war. Simmons, born in Moscow in 1918, studied in Germany and later at King's College, London. The first article he sent to the *Picture Post* was one of the most detailed descriptions of the initial stage of the Korean War. Supple, the Chicago daily's religion editor in the Far East on assignment, was co-opted to cover the war.

William R. Moore, 40, Associated Press correspondent, was killed while covering a U.S. tank unit near Chinju on July 30, 1950. He was born in Nowata, Oklahoma, on March 26, 1910 and was a graduate of the University of Oklahoma in 1932. Moore joined the AP in Denver, Colorado, in February 1937 after serving as an Army major in World War II. In 1948, he was transferred to Tokyo staff, serving for a time in Korea and briefly in Hang Kong. He returned to Korea, at the outbreak of the war, and covered the first crucial stage of fighting along a route of retreat before onrushing heavily armored North Koreans.

Christopher Buckley, 45, correspondent of *The Daily Telegraph,* and Ian Morrison, 35, of *The Times* (UK) were killed on August 12, 1950, when their Jeep struck a land mine on the Naktong River front near Taegu. They had hitched a ride with Col. Unni Nayar, Indian representative with the United Nations Commission on Korea (UNCOK), who was also killed. Buckley was a former correspondent for *The Christian Science Monitor* and had ranged the globe for thirteen years covering World War II and the conflicts of the post-war years. He had been awarded an Order of the British Empire in 1946 in recognition of his service as a war correspondent.

Morrison, a prewar English professor at the Imperial University of Hokkaido, Japan, had joined *The Times* after Japan and Britain went to war in 1941. He was born in Beijing (then called Peiping) as a son of a famous father, "Chinese" Morrison, who was also a distinguished correspondent for *The Times* in China, where a street had been named after him in the Chinese capital. A quiet, handsome pipesmoking Englishman, Morrison was in love with Han Suyin, a famous Chinese author. She wrote a best-selling book about their romance, *Love is a Many Splendored Thing,* which later was made into a movie starring William Holden as Morrison.

Frank Emery, 23, an INS correspondent, Charles Rosecrans Jr., 30, INP photographer, and Ken Inouye, 22, a newsreel cameraman for Telenews, an INS affiliate which supplied television newsfilm, were killed on September 7, 1950, when a Korea-bound C–54 transport from Japan crashed into a fog-shrouded mountain. All died in the line of duty on their way back to the Korean front. At the news of Emery's death, Philippines Foreign Minister Carlos P. Romulo sent a message to INS from Washington where he was on an official visit: "It was with grief and sense of personal loss that I read about Frank Emery's death....He covered the Department of Foreign Affairs in Manila...and I came to know and respect him as an unusually enterprising, accurate and fair-minded reporter...." [7] Described as a "little guy but full of the devil," Rosecrans, a native of Hawaii, had been one of the INS Tokyo bureau's favorite staff members. Inouye was a young and eager cameraman, carrying his heavy 55mm newsreel camera right into action.

Jean Marie de Premonville, 30, AFP correspondent, was killed on the night of February 11, 1951, when he was struck by Communist Chinese machine gun fire while covering a U.N. raider patrol at Chipyong-ni front 37 miles southeast of Seoul. Premonville had arrived in Korea August 11, 1950 as the successor of Maximilien Philonenko who was killed earlier in a plane crash en route to Korea from Japan.

On March 3, 1951, William H. Graham, 39, correspondent of *New York Journal of Commerce,* died from injuries received when a U.S. Navy plane crashed off the eastern coast of Korea after taking off from a carrier. He had been at the Korean front only four weeks.

Derick Pearcy, 25, correspondent of Reuters, was killed on May 25, 1951, when his jeep hit a Communist landmine 10 miles northeast of Uijongbu. He had joined the Reuters staff in Tokyo a few weeks earlier on May 1.

Jorge T. Teodoro, a correspondent with U.N. Department of Public Information (Philippines), was killed when a Greek Air Force C–47 transport plane crashed on take-off at Chinhae on the night of December 27, 1952.

The Korean War, called a "police action," or America's "forgotten war," thus exacted a terrible price from the corps of war correspondents.

In addition to those 18 war correspondents killed in the line of duty, AFP correspondent Morris Chanteloup and AP cameraman Frank E. (Pappy) Noel were captured and held as prisoners of war in North Korea for three years. Chanteloup was captured by the Communists at the Chosun Hotel in Seoul on July 8, 1950, and sent to a North Korean POW camp. He returned to Paris in May 1953 via the Soviet Union and East Europe. I had strongly advised

Chanteloup to go south with other colleagues, but he chose to stay, insisting, "I would be safe because I am French." Noel became a captive of the Communist Chinese troops on November 2, 1950 at the Changjin (Chosin in Japanese) front in North Korea and returned to Panumunjom on September 4, 1953 during prisoner exchange "Big Switch."

Monument to Fallen Newsmen

A monument honoring the 18 war correspondents killed at the Korean front was erected at Munsan 20 miles northwest of Seoul by the Korean Journalists Association, and its dedication ceremony was held on April 27, 1977 with the attendance of 81 former war correspondents from abroad, including myself.

The teletype-shaped, 30-foot-high copper and granite monument stands on a small hill near the former site of the "Peace Train," which served as workshop and quarters for war correspondents covering Panumunjom truce talks. The monument is a landmark in the Unification Park facing the four-lane Unification Road, with such war memorials as "Tower of the 10 Human Bullets" and "Monument to the Loyal Dead of the Republic of Korea Army 1st Division."

The epitaph inscribed on the "MONUMENT TO WAR COR-RESPONDENTS KILLED IN THE KOREAN WAR" reads:

> Dedicated to the memory of the 18 fallen Korean War correspondents who symbolize the honor and triumph of the press. These stalwarts of journalism from here and afar joined the United Nations forces and gave their lives in this land in the course of their brave, vivid coverage of the Communist invasion that menaced peace on this peninsula and the freedom of mankind.
>
> Their pens have now run dry but their righteous spirit will live forever.

And their glorious sacrifices will always shine for
the cause of justice.

The 27th of April, 1977
The Journalists Association of Korea
On behalf of all Korean journalists

While working on the monument project, the Korean Journalists
Association (president: Park Shil) and International Cultural Society
of Korea (president: Hong Sung-chul) asked me to find out the
addresses of former war correspondents so that invitation letters
could be sent. I did what I could although it was not easy to locate
them because 24 years had passed since the armistice. Eighty-one
former war correspondents from ten countries were reunited in
Korea and shared reminiscences of "the good old days."

We indulged in our fond recollections while on our tour of
Panmunjom, Pusan, Ulsan, Kyongju, and Taegu. In Pusan, we
visited the U.N. cemetery and placed a wreath at the tomb of
Christopher Buckley, one of the fallen colleagues. During the tour,
we marveled at the rapid economic development achieved in the war-
torn country.

The following article written by Robert C. Miller of the United
Press International sums up the happy reunions of the old-time
colleagues:

> Seoul — They were fat of belly, spare of hair, a bit
> gimpy in the limbs, but naught ailed the memories and
> tongues of 81 former Korean War correspondents who
> returned to Seoul for the dedication of a monument
> honoring 18 reporters killed in the war.
>
> They came from Japan, Australia, Hong Kong,
> France, New Zealand, Colombia, Turkey, Greece,
> England and America to unveil the 30-foot-high statue
> at Munsan honoring the 17 foreigners and one Korean
> correspondent killed in the three years of the Korean
> War.
>
> Their reunions were always loud, often accompa-
> nied by Rotarian embraces, sometimes a moistened eye

and began with the merciful lie that nobody looked a day older than he did 27 years ago.

What stories they told...the scared, helpless refugees fleeing, the panicked troops — American and South Korean — the shameful retreat to the Pusan perimeter, the brilliantly executed landing at Inchon, the capture of the North Korean capital of Pyongyang, the retreat from the Yalu, the American counter offensive, the peace talks at Kaesong and Panmunjom, Little Switch and Big Switch and eventually peace.

The war stories lost nothing in the retelling. In fact they grew in dimension and excitement with repeated versions, especially when the returning correspondents were being interviewed by the Korean press.

The expensively suited returning journalists looked more like bankers and successful executives — which many of them were — than lean and tough reporters living from expense account to expense account....

The highlight of the week's visit was the dedication Wednesday [August 27, 1977] of the 30-foot-high copper and granite monument unveiled at Munsan, just across the tracks from the old Pusan-to-Paris railroad where several of the dead and most of the reporters present had lived in the parked Pullman cars that served as home and the press camp.

The olive green memorial depicts a quill and scroll of teletype paper upon which is inscribed in raised brass letters "Monument to war correspondents killed in the Korean War."

The monument is within artillery range of the North Korean front lines, and in the trees behind the monument is a nest of raucous magpies which many of the reporters felt most symbolic of their profession.

They had trouble remembering the names of many of their fellow reporters and connecting the expanded girths, shiny heads and decrepit underpins with the dashing, hard driving, romantic souls who gave the world the words and pictures of the Korean War from

the frying pan heat of Pusan to the frozen hell — if
hell can be quickly frozen — of Hungnam.

Next week they'll return home, some to highly paid
executive jobs, others to the retirement they now enjoy,
some to jobs far different than the chores of journalism
that brought them here.

They will return far richer than they arrived, with
a new supply of war stories, bigger and better lies, and
a tremendous appreciation for the new Korea and its
people....

It was suggested that maybe the monument to the
dead war correspondents — the only memorial ever
built to journalism's casualties in any war — should
have been placed at the entrance to the United Nations
building, and dedicated to all correspondents who
covered not only Korea, but the rest of the world's
wars as well. [8]

The visiting former war correspondents raised $1,400 for
planting trees in a nearby village to commemorate their reunion.
Eighteen white pines, symbolizing the 18 fallen newsmen, were
planted in the village on June 2 in a ceremony attended by John
Rich, former INS and NBC war correspondent, who had delivered
the "fund." The village was named "The Village of Eighteen Trees."

Reunions With Wartime Fellowship

Strongly bonded with wartime fellowship, 75 former Korean
War correspondents and their spouses gathered in Washington over
the weekend of May 25, 1980 to reminisce on the experiences they
shared in Korea. I flew from Tokyo to take part in the sentimental
reunions at the Key Bridge Marriott Hotel, commemorating the 30th
anniversary of the start of the Korean War, one month ahead.

James A. Michener, the novelist, led the group to Arlington
National Cemetery to lay a wreath in memory of the 18 colleagues
who gave their lives at the Korean front.

"I'm just happy that so many people survived," said Robert Pierpoint, then a CBS correspondent. "We're all survivors," said Carl Mydans, who was then a photographer with *Life* magazine. Thirteen Korean War correspondents, including myself, were again reunited on old battlefields in June 1990 when the South Korean government invited the war reporters and their spouses for a weeklong visit marking the 40th anniversary of the war's start. While a bugle sounded taps and riflemen fired a salute at Chipyong-ni, where the Communist Chinese forces suffered their first defeat, Ed Hymoff, INS, and I laid a wreath at a monument to fallen U.N. troops on behalf of the visitors, who burned incense at an altar. At Munsan, John Rich, INS and NBC, and Max Desfor, AP, placed a white floral arrangement on the monument to 18 correspondents killed during the war.

The group also included: Al Kaff, UP; Marvin Stone, INS; Joe Fromm, U.S. News & World Report; Bob Tuckman, AP; Jerry O'Leary, U.S. Marine Corps; Bob Hecox, NBC; Mike Brown, VOA; LeRoy Hansen, UP; and George Herman, CBS. (Hansen, Hymoff, and O'Leary passed away after their Korean tour. May their noble souls rest in peace!)

Some 50 writers, broadcasters and photographers from the Korean War, now in their 60s to 80s, gathered again in Washington July 23–25, 1993, to mark the 40th anniversary of the armistice that ended Korean fighting but failed to unite North and South Korea. Max Desfor, retired AP photographer and the only survivor among eight Korean War Pulitzer Prize winners, organized the three-day reunion with the assistance of his wife, Clara, and George Sweers, another AP photographer during the war.

"We are a special breed," Marvin Stone said of Korean War correspondents at a remembrance ceremony at Arlington Cemetery on June 25 honoring the 18 journalists killed during the United Nations police action in Korea. "I know of no other group such as ours that keeps meeting year after year," Marvin told the war reporters, describing why they travel thousands of miles for reunions. As he said, I had flown thousands of miles from Tokyo to see my old colleagues once again.

War correspondents — left to right: John Rich (NBC), Ed Hymoff (INS), Max Desfor (AP), the author (AP), and Mike Brown (VOA) — pose for a picture at the Naija Apartments, the foreign correspondents' quarters during the three-year war.

Seven former presidents of the Foreign Correspondents Club of Japan — (Left to right, former affiliation in parenthesis) Max Desfor (AP), Joe Fromm *(U.S. News & World Report),* John Rich (NBC), the author (AP), LeRoy Hansen (UP), Marvin Stone, (INS), and Al Kaff (UP) — were part of a group of former Korean War correspondents who visited Seoul in June 1990 to commemorate the 40th anniversary of the start of the Korean War.

Korean War Veterans Memorial in Washington

July 27, 1995, the 42nd anniversary of the armistice, was a landmark date in the history of the "forgotten" Korean War; unsung but proud veterans of that bloody conflict finally received recognition and gratitude on that day when U.S. President Bill Clinton and South Korean President Kim Young Sam dedicated the Korean War Veterans Memorial on the Washington Mall. Thousands of American veterans and Korean guests, including distinguished combat General (ret.) Paik Sun-yup, crowded the Hall in sweltering heat. Many of the Korean veterans who flew from Seoul for the ceremony said they were grateful for the Memorial.

President Bill Clinton saluted the devotion to duty and honor of the 1.5 million Americans who left homes to defend freedom in Korea. "They set a standard of courage that may be equaled but will never be surpassed in the annals of American combat," Clinton said. "When the guns fell silent, no one knew what our forces had done for the future of freedom," he said, alluding to the fact that the 1950–53 Korean War has been referred to as America's "forgotten war," even though it claimed 54,246 American lives.

President Kim Young Sam expressed the gratitude of his people for U.S. sacrifices for his now-prosperous nation. "History... has turned the Korean War from a forgotten war into a war most worthy of remembrance," President Kim, speaking through an interpreter, said. "The Korean War was the war that heralded the collapse of the Berlin Wall and the demise of Communism."

In their White House meetings earlier, Clinton had reaffirmed the U.S. pledge to keep American forces in Korea "as long as they are needed and the Korean people want them to remain." About 37,000 U.S. troops are stationed in South Korea, and the Korean peninsula remains a dangerous flash point left over from the Cold War.

Since the July 27, 1953 armistice signing, South Korea came to exemplify democratic and free-market growth, while North Korea remained a dangerous hermit state. Starving, the North begs openly for rice while clutching to forlorn hope that its nuclear threat will gain some diplomatic advantage.

The Korean War Veterans Memorial in Washington, D.C. incorporates many symbols unique to the Korean War and to the Republic of Korea. The name Republic of Korea is engraved in granite, and the hibiscus plants of the Korean national flower, rose of Sharon, are included in the landscape.

The 7-foot statues of a weary group of 19 foot soldiers are "combat ready," clad in ponchos as partial protection against the cold wintry winds in Korea. Adding to its power is a 164-foot long panoramic granite wall etched with photographic images of 2,400 support troops. At the beginning of the column of troops, the visitor ventures onto a peninsula representing Korea that extends into the reflecting pool. President Kim Young Sam planted a tree at the site of the Memorial during its dedication.

A startlingly simple motto is carved in a marble slab atop the gentle knoll under the American flag: "FREEDOM IS NOT FREE." Opposite that inscription are tallies of cost of the Korean War to preserve that freedom: "DEAD...U.S.A. 54,246...U.N. 628,833."

The long awaited and much deserved Memorial for the Korean War veterans, built at a cost of $18 million in contributed funds, is a proud salute to all who answered their country's call for the cause of freedom. A parade, mass muster, memorial services, fireworks, entertainment, film festival, and academic seminars were part of the July 26–29 dedication ceremony.

I attended the Memorial Dedication Ceremony at the invitation of U.S. Marine Corps General (ret.) Raymond Davis, chairman of the Korean War Veterans Memorial Advisory Board. (He was awarded the Medal of Honor for saving a beleaguered rifle company from complete annihilation and enabling two Marine regiments to escape possible destruction in action against vast enemy forces in the vicinity of Hagaru-ri, my hometown, from December 1 through 4, 1950, then as a lieutenant colonel commanding the First Battalion, Seventh Marines, First Marine Division.)

Stainless steel statues of 19 soldiers on patrol are the focal points of the Korean War Veterans Memorial on the Washington Mall, dedicated on July 27, 1995.

General (ret.) Colin Powell, former chairman of the Joint Chiefs of Staff, and the author at the dedication ceremony of the Korean War Veterans Memorial on the Washington Mall, July 27, 1995.

CHAPTER FIVE

A POTENTIAL FLASH POINT

NORTH KOREAN QUESTION

Military Buildup

Despite its economic hardship, ever since the 1953 armistice North Korea has been pouring more than 25 percent of its gross national product (GNP) into military buildup in a bid to maintain military superiority over South Korea. For fiscal 1993 alone Pyongyang spent $5.7 billion or some 30 percent of its budget on military outlay, according to South Korean Defense White Paper 1994–1995.

The North Korean military maintains 1.1 million troops on active duty, a huge force compared with its population of about 23 million and its failing economy. There are also 115,000 security forces and border troops and more than 3 million semi-military troops including the Farmer-labor Red Army. North Korea, with the fifth largest army in the world, is a perfect model of a garrison state operating its military forces as if it were at war. Thus the Korean Peninsula remains a potential international flash point.

North Korea has almost twice as many ground weapons and aircraft as those in the South. Its 3,800 tanks, 10,800 field artillery pieces, 12,000 antiaircraft guns and 2,500 armored vehicles far outnumbers South Korea's 1,800 tanks, 4,600 field artillery and 2,100 armored vehicles.

Pyongyang possesses 26 submarines and 454 warships, including missile boats and torpedo boats. It also has as many as 850 tactical aircraft, including fighters such as Mig–29s and bombers, and 480 support aircraft, against South Korea's 520 and 180 respectively.

North Korea has succeeded in test firing Scud-type Rodong I missiles with a range of over 1,000 kilometers (620 miles) and is

255

developing Taepo-dong missiles with longer ranges. They put the entire Korean Peninsula, Japan, and Taiwan within reach.

In its eight military factories, North Korea produces a large amount of chemical weapons and is capable of delivering the toxic weapons to all areas of the South by means of Scud missiles and Frog–5/7 rockets. Lee Chung-kuk, who had served as a chemical warfare soldier at the North's army headquarters in Pyongyang until his defection to the South in March 1993, told a news conference in Seoul that the Communist regime used political prisoners as guinea pigs in testing chemical weapons.

The North Korean military has advanced as far south as the Demilitarized Zone with Frog rockets and 170–mm self-propelled artillery, with a range of 40–50 kilometers (24.8–31 miles) and 240–mm multiple rocket launchers with a range of 70 kilometers (43.4 miles). These are capable of hitting the capital city of Seoul and Chunchon-Sokcho regions to the east.

Pyongyang is also producing Chonma tanks, a modification of the T–62 tank and TOW-type AT–4 antitank missiles. It has already produced 120 Hovercraft for infiltration and is continuing construction of underground military facilities.

In breaking up inter-Korean contacts in April 1994, a North Korean delegate went so far as to threaten a war of total devastation which, he said, would engulf Seoul in "a sea of flames." All this saber-rattling was going on as evidence of North Korea's penchant for militarism while no progress had been made in inter-Korean relations.

Meanwhile, Ko Young-hwan, who defected to the South on May 2, 1991 while serving as a third secretary at the North Korean embassy in Congo, wrote in his book titled *Wonderland:* "Military officers often emphasize the words in Kim Il-sung's directives: 'Reunify the motherland by 1995,' 'Reunification comes out of the barrel of a gun,' 'No battle, no unification.' " [1]

Another North Korean defector, Kim Nam-jun, former second lieutenant of the North Korean People's Army, told the *Sankei Shimbun* of Japan on October 18, 1992 that the Pyongyang regime was training military officers under the slogan, "Achieve South-North unification by the People's Army in 1995." While he was a cadet at the Kangkon Military Academy in the suburbs of Pyongyang, Kim said, "The instructors constantly brought home to our mind that 'We must expel the American imperialists from the Korean Peninsula and liberate the people of South Korea, the American colony. Military force is the only means.' " Kim added, "More than 99 percent of the military officers were determined to unify by force." Kim defected to the South in September 1989 when he was a platoon leader of a North Korean guard unit of the First Regiment, 6th Division, in the Kaesong district near the Demilitarized Zone.

Kim's testimony on the North Korean strategy to achieve "Communized unification in 1995" was confirmed when Pyongyang's large-scale espionage ring was rounded up in South Korea on October 6, 1992. The leaders of the Communist underground organization, "South Korean Workers Party," included cabinet-level members of the North's ruling Korean Workers Party.

Such North Korean schemes were not accomplished. Kim Il Sung died in 1994 and North Korea collapsed economically. But it is still feared that increasing desperation could prompt its military leaders to go to war.

Nuclear Threat as a Bargaining Chip

North Korea was increasingly incapable of supporting its massive army and was looking to nuclear weapons as a cheaper ultimate deterrent, *Jane's Intelligence Review,* an authoritative military intelligence magazine published in London, said in a special report. The 24-page report in its April 1994 issue entitled "North Korea — A Potential Time Bomb" said the Communist nation had become increasingly isolated, vulnerable and politically unstable. With the loss of virtually all its allies, including Russia, North Korea needed an ultimate deterrent and turned to nuclear weapons, which are "a relatively cheap form of deterrent," the report said.

Defense analyst Joseph Bermudez Jr., a New Yorker who frequently contributed to *Jane's,* said, "in the face of economic disaster and political isolation, the nuclear arsenal is North Korea's only bargaining chip and one it can be expected to continue to use both skillfully and effectively."

North Korea's suspected nuclear weapons program was brought to light early in 1991 when American nuclear specialists reported that the nuclear power reactor at Yongbyon, 56 miles north of Pyongyang, had the capacity of producing seven kilograms of plutonium a year and that a uranium enrichment facility was already in operation.

Former North Korean diplomat Ko Young-hwan, 38, who had defected to the South in May 1991, told a news conference in Seoul, "It was an open secret among North Korean diplomats that nuclear weapons would be developed within three years. Besides the nuclear facilities at Yongbyon, I heard, there was an underground nuclear test facility elsewhere."

International Atomic Energy Agency chief Hans Blix visited North Korean nuclear facilities in May 1992 and the U.N.'s nuclear watchdog agency inspected part of the facilities six times. But North Korea flatly refused subsequent IAEA requests for inspections of two other nuclear fuel reprocessing plants, and declared its intention of withdrawing from the NPT (Nuclear Non-Proliferation Treaty) on March 12, 1993.

Though it had admitted the extraction of "a fraction of plutonium" from the Yongbyon nuclear power facilities, Pyongyang was adamant that the other two plants were never to be subjected to IAEA inspections on grounds that they were "military facilities."

On May 11, the U.N. Security Council adopted a resolution calling for North Korea's reconsideration of its withdrawal from NPT by a vote of 13 with two abstentions (China and Pakistan).

But both the renewed IAEA inspection and the inter-Korea working-level contacts at Panmunjom ended in an utter fiasco with North Korea continuing its tactics of rejection and delay. The whole slow-moving drama involving the suspected nuclear program had served merely to give Pyongyang more time for continuation of its nuclear scheme coupled with diplomatic maneuvers for direct contact with the United States.

IAEA Suspends Aid to Pyongyang

Meanwhile, the IAEA declared on June 3, 1994 that North Korea had made it impossible to select fuel rods for tests to see if there had been any diversion of fuel from the reactor for a suspected nuclear arms program. North Korea and IAEA traded their first hostile blows on June 11 as a global crisis over Pyongyang's secretive nuclear program intensified: IAEA voted to suspend technical aid to North Korea as a penalty for its refusal to grant access to the agency's inspectors. The rare decision to impose a penalty was prompted by North Korea's refusal to allow inspectors to take samples of spent fuel rods from a nuclear reactor.

North Korea officially withdrew from the IAEA on June 15, 1994, further raising the crisis. Pyongyang, which joined the IAEA in September 1974, was the first member to withdraw from the U.N. nuclear watchdog agency of its own accord, reducing the number of member states to 121.

Because the prospect of conflict with unpredictable Pyongyang — another Korean War — was so horrible, U.S. and South Korean governments for more than a year had gone through a tortuous process of dealing with the North in the evolving nuclear row.

Many experts said a determined, unified, and toughened international approach was the only way to convince Pyongyang that the world community was serious about curbing its suspected nuclear weapons program. But the Clinton administration in Washington decided to settle the dispute with Pyongyang by means of a diplomatic approach rather than mild punishment of the intransigent Communist regime.

Under these circumstances, the glad tidings that former U.S. President Jimmy Carter brought back from Pyongyang obscured North Korea's real intentions — whether they are truly interested in peace or merely buying time for sinister nuclear plans. Carter volunteered to go to Pyongyang. He met for hours with Kim Il Sung and concluded that "the crisis is over." Carter said on June 20, 1994 that Kim Il Sung was ready to freeze the nuclear program, allow IAEA inspectors to stay in Pyongyang, hold a summit with South

Korea, reduce South and North Korean troops, and account for American troops missing from the Korean War.

In exchange, the United States would resume formal talks on diplomatic and economic contacts, suspended the previous year over North Korea's nuclear intentions, and help North Korea develop a light-water nuclear reactor that does not produce plutonium that could be used for weapons.

But Kim, 82, had made these and other promises before, while continuing to turn his isolated nation into an economically deprived military camp primed for battle with its hated enemies, South Korea and the United States.

Critics predicted the Clinton administration might be duped by the North Korean Communists if it backed off a tough policy against an international outlaw. The White House, said critics such as Republican Senator John McCain, had done nothing toward North Korea but "extend carrot after carrot, concession after concession."

Retired Colonel William Taylor of the Center for Strategic and International Studies, who had visited North Korea several times, said Kim was "accomplishing exactly what he wants" by undercutting the U.S. government's resolve for sanctions with a facade of conciliation. "The whole thing with Carter is deja vu," Taylor said, recalling Kim's meeting with U.S. lawmakers in 1991, evangelist Billy Graham in 1992 and Taylor several times in the 1990s. During those sessions, he said Kim made conciliatory remarks that were never followed by action.

U.S.-North Korea Nuclear Pact Signed

The United States and North Korea on October 21, 1994 signed a nuclear agreement in Geneva aimed at easing tensions over Pyongyang's nuclear program and perhaps establishing full diplomatic relations between the two countries.

A dispute between North Korea and the international community over unfettered outside inspections of its nuclear energy sites had raised global tensions, and the United States pushed for international sanctions against Pyongyang. North Korea threatened war with South Korea if U.N. sanctions were imposed.

In discussing details of the accord, U.S. chief negotiator Robert Gallucci told newsmen that North Korea would not have to open two suspected nuclear dump sites to international inspectors for about five years. Gallucci defended the arrangement, saying, "Those radioactive waste sites aren't going anywhere." He called on critics of the pact to think very carefully about its significance in terms of international security.

Despite Gallucci's insistence, International Atomic Energy Agency (IAEA) chief Hans Blix expressed concern that a delayed special inspection would undermine the credibility of the global nonproliferation system.

North Korean First Deputy Foreign Minister Kang Sok-ju, who had signed the agreement with Gallucci, declared at a separate press conference that his country would eventually scrap its graphite reactors, which sparked international suspicions over its nuclear development program. Kang said the agreement should resolve "once and for all" nearly two years of tension over his government's nuclear ambitions.

In the agreement, the United States pledged to assemble an international consortium to help North Korea achieve its "legitimate energy objectives." The consortium would finance construction of two light-water reactors by 2003 and supply heavy oil to meet North Korea's energy needs in the interim. The switch to light-water reactors was estimated to cost $4 billion. South Korea agreed to put up more than two-thirds of the money on condition that South Korean-made reactors be installed in the North. The consortium, named the Korea Energy Development Organization (KEDO), would also finance the cost of shipment to a third country and disposal of the 8,000 spent uranium fuel rods stored in North Korea.

President Clinton said in a statement to reporters, "North Korea has agreed to freeze its existing nuclear program and to accept international inspections of all existing facilities." He hailed the pact, saying, "This agreement represents the first step on the road to a nuclear-free Korean peninsula."

Yet the agreement leaves unanswered a big question: Was North Korea already nuclear armed? Earlier in 1994, the Clinton administration had threatened to push for United Nations economic sanctions against North Korea to force an answer to that question.

But now Washington was willing to wait up to five years. Many analysts were clearly unconvinced that Pyongyang would adhere to the agreement given its record of reneging on promises under dubious pretexts.

Despite Pyongyang's denials, many sources suggested that the Communist north had already developed nuclear weapons. An article in the June 24, 1994 issue of the Russian daily *Izvestia* cited KGB documents asserting that North Korea had an explosive nuclear device in 1990. The *Izvestia* article disputed Russian Foreign Minister Andrei Kozyrev's remark that Pyongyang had yet to develop a nuclear bomb, quoting the text of a February 1990 document from the KGB archives, written by former KGB Director Vladimir Kryuchkov. The article quoted the Kryuchkov document as saying, "The KGB has learned from reliable sources that the DPRK (Democratic People's Republic of Korea) is actively continuing scientific and constructive work on the creation of nuclear weapons" and that "work has been completed on the creation of [North Korea's] first nuclear device." [2]

In an interview with Seoul's independent MBC TV on September 27, 1994, North Korean defector Lee Chung-kuk, 23, said he had witnessed North Korea's military testing detonators in 1993 near the Communist state's nuclear complex at Yongbyon. Lee said he had worked for years as a staff sergeant at a nuclear warfare unit under the control of the North Korean Defense Ministry until he defected to South Korea in March 1994. He said his unit helped scientists develop nuclear weapons. Assisting senior officers of his unit, Lee said, he participated in major tests and had access to classified information. He made similar claims at a news conference right after his defection, but was more specific and graphic in the TV interview.

On July 27, 1994, another defector Kang Myong-do, claiming to be the son-in-law of North Korean Premier Kang Son-san, told a news conference in Seoul that the hardline Communist country already had five nuclear warheads. Kang, 36, carried a passport and identification card supporting his identity. Kang said he had obtained his information from conversations with an intelligence chief responsible for the Yongbyon nuclear complex.

Quoting a South Korean government source, the *Chosun Ilbo*, a leading Seoul daily, reported on August 7, 1994 that North Korea extracted sufficient plutonium to make "three or four" nuclear weapons from spent fuel removed by temporarily shutting its 5-megawatt reactor three times in 1989, 1990 and 1991.

A Reuters dispatch from Vienna on September 14, 1994 said that North Korea appeared to have halted reprocessing nuclear fuel by 1992, but the U.N. atomic safeguards agency, IAEA, suspected plutonium was still being hidden from inspectors. "What did they do before inspections began? How much plutonium had they squirreled away? How much raw material for making plutonium did they still have on hand when our inspections began?" an IAEA official told Reuters. He said, "We are perfectly convinced they have got more, but we can't prove it."

The New York Times reported on March 11, 1993 that a classified CIA document concluded that North Korea probably had developed one or two nuclear bombs. The CIA's assessment represents the collective judgment of U.S. intelligence agencies, the *Times* said. CIA Director James Woolsey said on March 22, 1994 it was the best estimate of U.S. intelligence services that North Korea had diverted enough material to build at least one nuclear bomb.

In the U.S.-North Korea nuclear agreement, North Korea pledged to freeze its nuclear program and allow resumption of international inspections at sites suspected of developing nuclear weapons. But it would not have to open two suspected nuclear sites to the U.N. nuclear watchdog agency for about five years after the signing, as U.S. chief negotiator Robert Gallucci explained.

Through its nuclear strategy based on intimidation of war threats, playing on fears that they would lash out if they were pushed too far, Pyongyang succeeded in achieving most of what it had wanted from the United States. Critics pointed out that the U.S. concessions to North Korea, America's decades old enemy, branded as a terrorist state, was inconsistent with its human rights policy applied to countries like Cuba and China.

North Korea — which denies its nuclear work is intended to make bombs — would receive two modern nuclear power plants of light-water reactors for the protection of electricity. The North also would be given new diplomatic links to the United States, which it had long longed for in an attempt to drive a wedge between America and South Korea and press its demands for the withdrawal of U.S. forces from South Korea and unification of the Korean peninsula under the Communist term.

Highlights of the U.S.-North Korean Accord:

- The United States will undertake to make arrangement for the provision to North Korea of a light-water reactor project by 2003.

- The United States will organize under its leadership an international consortium to finance the $4 billion cost of two light-water reactors that do not generate weapons-grade plutonium.

- The United States will make arrangements to begin deliveries of heavy oil within three months of the signing and ship to North Korea 500,000 tons annually.

- North Korea will cooperate in moving out of North Korea fuel rods that the United States says hold enough pluto-nium to make about four nuclear weapons.

- Within three months of the date of the document, both sides will reduce barriers to trade and investment, includ-ing restrictions on telecommunications services and financial transactions.

- Upon receipt of U.S. assurances for the provision of light-water reactors and for arrangements for interim energy alternatives, North Korea will freeze its graphite-moder-ated reactors and related facilities and will eventually dismantle these reactors and related facilities.

- Each side will open a liaison office in the other's capital following resolution of consular and other technical issues through expert level discussions.

- As progress is made on issues of concern to each side, North Korea and the U.S. will upgrade bilateral relations to the ambassadorial level.

- North Korea will consistently take steps to implement the North-South Joint Declaration on the Denuclearization of the Korean Peninsula.

- North Korea will remain a party to the Treaty on the Non-Proliferation of Nuclear Weapons (NPT) and will allow implementation of its safeguards agreement under the treaty.

South Korean Role Spelled Out

After months of wrangling over Pyongyang's almost hysterical attempt to exclude South Korean technology from the project that will give it a new nuclear power system, the United States and North Korea on June 13, 1995 reached a written agreement in Kuala Lumpur, Malaysia, spelling out how South Korea will provide North Korea with new light-water reactors while Pyongyang freezes its nuclear program. South Korea will pay 60 percent to 70 percent of the $4-billion cost of the two light-water reactors that are planned to replace the Soviet-supplied reactors whose used fuel rods yield weapons-grade plutonium. Seoul rightly insisted that unless it is the prime provider it will have nothing to do with the deal.

Pyongyang's resistance to accepting South Korea as its lead nuclear patron was almost wholly a matter of pride. To rely on a bitter ideological rival whose remarkable economic growth and political development mock Communist North Korea's staggering failures would be humiliating. The Kuala Lumpur agreement, therefore, never specifically names South Korea as the provider of the new reactors. But the description in the agreement of the technology to be provided leaves it clear that the source can only be South Korea. Prior to the signing of the agreement, U.S. President Bill Clinton guaranteed in his personal letter to South Korean

President Kim Young Sam that South Korea will be the sole provider of the new reactors.

The Geneva accord specified that the new reactors would be supplied and financed by an international consortium, the Korean Energy Development Organization (KEDO) — the three key countries in this consortium being South Korea, Japan and the United States.

Under the Kuala Lumpur agreement, Washington nailed down two crucial elements left hanging after the Geneva accord of October 1994:

- Pyongyang in effect agreed to accept nuclear reactors from South Korea to help make up for energy it is losing by closing and eventually tearing down existing, more dangerous facilities, plutonium-producing nuclear reactors.

- North Korea went along with having a South Korean firm serve as prime contractor in building the reactors. But an American firm will be named program coordinator, and Americans will lead multinational delegations handling the huge construction project. That will let Pyongyang deal primarily with Washington, thus minimizing its contacts with Seoul. Equally it will advance North Korea's long-time interest in establishing direct and continuing relationship with the United States that, Pyongyang hopes, will weaken the alliance between Washington and Seoul. But Pyongyang should be left with no illusion that it will be able to undercut those ties.

KIM IL SUNG DIES

The Last Hard-liner

Kim Il Sung, who ruled the world's most reclusive country for 46 years and built a slavish personality cult that made him a god in an officially atheistic state, died of a heart attack on July 8, 1994. He was 82.

In announcing Kim's death on July 9, Pyongyang radio eulogized: "The Great Leader Comrade Kim Il Sung was the greatest of the great men who had all the qualities and traits of a great man on the highest level and enjoyed deep reverence and respect from all of our people and the world people."

Propagandists churned out millions of words of praise for the "Great Leader," but revealed little truth about the man himself.

Kim was the world's longest-reigning ruler, with a tenure as long as his country's history. Exercising a mixture of his own brand of Stalinism, Oriental despotism and an unabashed personality cult, Kim became a skillful master of North Korea, with decades of political maneuvering interspersed with bloody purges after being installed by Soviet occupation authorities.

Throughout the country, massive statues of him were erected, including a heroic 64-feet gold-plated statue gracing central Pyongyang, and numerous buildings were created to celebrate his birthday or mark his achievements.

His portraits hang in nearly every household and public building. Most of the adults in this nation of 23 million people wear tiny ceramic portraits of Kim on their lapels.

Even the word "Communism" was replaced with "Juche (self-reliance), the thought of Kim Il Sung." But critics dismiss the Juche ideology, which took form when Kim started purging one political rival after another after the 1950–53 Korean War as a means of consolidating his grip on power.

While officially revered at home, Kim in his final years became increasingly isolated internationally. His hardline Communist nation seemed like an outpost from another era as the Cold War ended. The Soviet Union, one of North Korea's patrons, stunned Kim by establishing diplomatic relations in 1990 with his arch enemy, South Korea, a testament to Seoul's growing economic punch. Communist China, which fought the Korean War on the North's side, followed the Soviet's suit in 1992. Virtually all former Communist states except Cuba have normalized relations and strengthened economic ties with the capitalist South.

Although Kim was widely accused of severe human rights violations at home, his official biographies — probably no other national leader has had so many — are fabricated hagiography.

The official story of his life goes like this:

He was born Kim Sung Ju on April 15, 1912, in Mankyungdae, a village near Pyongyang that became a shrine known as "the Cradle of the World Revolution." His father was an anti-Japanese fighter tortured to death in prison by the Japanese in 1917. All his close relatives were ardent revolutionaries.

At the age of 13, Kim took part in anti-Japanese struggles in Manchuria.... As a general, he commanded the Korean People's Revolutionary Army, fighting 100,000 battles.... In August 1945, he ordered the Korean People's Revolutionary Army to attack the Japanese Army and liberated the fatherland.

The real story is that at 18, Kim started to follow various bands of Chinese-Korean guerrillas fighting the Japanese Imperial Army in East Manchuria, eventually commanding an independent guerrilla unit. As the Japanese forces crushed the guerrillas, Kim was among the survivors who fled to Russia in 1941.

In Soviet Russia, he married a woman partisan named Kim Jong-suk who bore him a son on February 16, 1942 at a village in Khabarovsk. Kim joined the Soviet Red Army in July 1942 and commanded a Korean unit of the Khabarovsk 88th Brigade as a captain. The son was named Yura in Russian, Jong Il in Korean.

Official North Korean biographers refuse to mention junior Kim's Chinese and Russian connections, calling Kim a top Korean independence fighter and insisting that he was born at a log cabin in a secret guerrilla camp on Mt. Paekdu, Korea's highest and most sacred peak on the border with China.

Kim Il Sung was picked as the prospective leader of North Korea by Stalin at the end of World War II. Kim returned to Korea with the Soviet occupation army in August 1945. Kim's first public appearance was not until October 1945, as chairman of the October Revolution Memorial meeting in Pyongyang. As the fleshy 33-year old was introduced to the gathering by his assumed name "Kim Il Sung," the crowd whispered, "Kim Il Sung? Didn't the famous general die fighting the Japanese in Manchuria years before?" The original Kim Il Sung was a legendary general who had been adored by Koreans for his patriotic guerrilla exploits against the Japanese in Manchuria in the late 1930s.

With Soviet help, he became premier of the Democratic People's Republic of Korea in 1948, and was named president in 1972. From the start, Kim's avowed goal was a united Communist Korea. Thus he invaded South Korea in June 1950 with Soviet planes and tanks.

When he failed to conquer the South by his initial target date of August 15, 1950, the fifth anniversary of Korean liberation from Japan, Kim passed the buck to his military leaders. In December 1950, he purged Lieutenant General Kim Moo-jung, the top military leader of the Yonan Faction from Communist China who commanded North Korea's 2nd Army during the invasion, and in January 1951, Lieutenant General Kim Chaek, field commander of the invading North Korean forces. Both men were led to mysterious deaths.

Kim's ruthless purges against prominent political and military leaders, whom he feared as his potential rivals, continued until 1970 to consolidate his autocratic power base. He purged the leaders of the South Korean Workers Party faction and Soviet faction in 1953, and the Yonan faction from Communist China during 1956–58. A partisan faction was purged in 1969 on the ground of its failure in underground operations in the South, and minor internal factions were purged in 1970.

In August 1953, Lee Sung-yop, secretary of the ruling Workers Party's Central Committee, and 11 other party and government high officials were convicted of "betraying the people in connivance with American espionage agents." Ten of them were executed and two were sentenced to 12–15 years imprisonment. Most conspicuous was the execution of Park Hun-yung, Korea's top-ranking Communist leader who was serving as vice premier and foreign minister in the Pyongyang regime, in March 1956 on charges of spying for "the American imperialists."

Kim Il Sung formulated his "Juche" philosophy of political and economic self-reliance, which cut off the nation from much of the rest of the world. As Moscow and Seoul opened a new chapter in history by establishing diplomatic relations at the ambassadorial level on September 30, 1990, Pyongyang began talks with Japan on normalizing relations in January 1991 and said it would improve relations with Washington. Pyongyang was dealt another heavy blow when Beijing and Seoul opened full diplomatic ties on August 24, 1992.

Pyongyang continued to send agents southward to capture and sink South Korean fishing boats, and to blast South Korean aircraft. North Korea had kidnapped 438 South Koreans, mostly fishermen and airline passengers, since the end of the Korean War in 1953, and 429 of them are still held in the North, according to the Seoul government's National Unification Board.

Amnesty International announced in October 1993 that during the previous 30 years North Korea had either tortured or executed several thousand political prisoners, and taken several tens of thousands, including former Korean residents in Japan, into custody in concentration camps. U.S. Congressman Steven Solars, who had visited North Korea several times, reported in July 1992 that political prisoners charged with anti-Kim Il Sung thoughts and incarcerated in concentration camps numbered 100,000 to 150,000. There were seven types of concentration camps in the Communist state, and those classified as "Strict Guard" took custody of political prisoners. Four of 12 such camps were opened after Kim Jong Il had consolidated his power as the heir apparent.

For a time in the 1960s, Kim Il Sung's younger brother, Kim Yong-ju, seemed to be heir apparent. But in 1971, propagandists began praising his son, Kim Jong Il. Boosted in party ranks, he was dubbed "The Party Center," "Respected Leader" and "The Future Sun of Communism." His portraits appeared in public with his father's. Newspapers reported his words in blue ink (red was used for Kim Il Sung's speeches.) In 1980 he was named to three top party posts, making him the obvious heir apparent.

Kim Il Sung suffered from arthritis, hearing problems and sporadic cardiac trouble. He also had a disfiguring lump on the right side of his neck. Nonetheless, he remained in good health well into old age. One of the secrets purportedly was his fondness for stew made from 500-year-old ginseng.

Kim Jong Il Takes Over

In the wake of the sudden demise of "The Great Leader," a god-king to his own people, a monster to those on whom he waged war, world attention was focused on his first son, Kim Jong Il, heir to the Communist world's first dynastic father-son succession. The junior Kim had been called the successor to his father for more than 20 years.

When Kim Jong Il was born on February 16, 1942 in Bayatsk, Khabarovsk, in the Soviet Far East, he was given the Russian name Yura. But North Korean propagandists preferred to hide that "unpatriotic" nativity, claiming that their "Dear Leader" was born on the sacred Mount Paekdu — the site, according to legend, where Korean civilization sprang into existence 4,300 years ago.

Referring to Kim Jong Il's birth, North Korean propaganda organs fabricated numerous legends and anecdotes. For example: "At the birth of Kim Jong Il at dusk, the frozen lake at the top of Mt. Paekdu split into two pieces and brought about a double rainbow in the sky." "At the birth of Kim Jong Il, there began to grow mountain ash trees (symbolic of righteousness, succor, goodness, and beauty) around the secret camp in Paekdu after the land and sky were covered with a red aurora and lightning." Thus, "The guiding star of our future" was born. [3]

Kim Jong Il's childhood was hardly a settled one. He was only seven when he lost his mother, Kim Jong-suk. She died in 1949 at the age of 30 just after her husband was anointed leader of North Korea by Stalin. Then, the Korean War, waged by his father, engulfed the peninsula, and junior Kim spent its duration in northeast China and in Russia. Back home, he transferred from school to school before graduating from Kim Il Sung University in Pyongyang in 1964. He studied political economics.

Until 1975 Kim Il Sung's younger brother Kim Yong-ju was heir apparent. Then, suddenly, Jong Il was publicly hailed as the "party center;" soon afterward, he became "Dear Leader," wielding more power than any other in the North Korean hierarchy apart from his charismatic father since the early 1980s. He became a member of the Standing Committee of the ruling Workers Party's Politburo and of its Military Affairs Committee in 1980.

Though without military training, he was promoted in 1991 to succeed his father as commander-in-chief of the country's 1.1 million-man armed forces and was deemed to have been in charge of the daily running of the world's most secretive country. He moved another step closer to taking over the reins of leadership from his father when the North Korean rubber-stamp legislature appointed him head of the National Defense Committee in April that year.

On April 13, 1992, two days before Kim Il Sung's 80th birthday, the senior Kim was named Great Marshal, and on April 21 Jong Il, then 50, was given the title of Marshal. Thus the junior Kim firmly established his power base as the heir apparent, and Kim Il Sung spared nothing to burnish his son's reputation.

But Kim Jong Il, lauded by his country's propaganda machine as "Dear Leader," had remained highly secretive and an enigma whose ability to govern North Korea was questionable. Mercurial and erratic, he rarely met foreign diplomats.

More ominous was Kim Jong Il's reputed ruthless management of Pyongyang's nuclear weapons program and terrorist activities. He was suspected to have engineered the October 7, 1983 bombing at Rangoon, Burma, that killed 18 top officials of the South Korean government, including four cabinet ministers: The obvious target was visiting President Chun Doo Hwan, but he was not at the disaster site when the explosion occurred. Kim Jong Il also was blamed for his alleged involvement in the November 29, 1987 mid-air explosion over Burma that destroyed a South Korean airliner (KAL Flight 858), killing all 115 aboard. North Korean defectors depicted Kim as a cruel individual who was held responsible for the axing to death of two U.S. soldiers at Panmunjom in 1976.

Meanwhile, an unseen but severe conflict among Kim's family members was intensifying. The origin of the family feud is traced back to the death of Kim Jong Il's mother. According to defectors, he was suspicious about his mother's death and his father's role. It was said his mother Kim Jong-suk had died while delivering a stillborn infant. But the Russian newspaper *Komsomolkaya Pravda* said in its December 19, 1991 issue that Jong Il's mother "committed suicide because Kim Il Sung was in love with Kim Sung Ae, his second wife who was then his secretary."

Kim Jong Il eliminated the power bases of his stepmother Kim Sung-ae and her children, especially his half-brother Kim Pyong-il (now ambassador to Finland). A tall and good-looking retired military officer, Kim Pyong-il was popular among certain groups of army officers. His mother Kim Sung-ae was officially the chairperson of the Women's League, but had little power: the League existed only within the Central Committee of the Workers Party and did not have any local structures in cities and provinces.

The only relatives Kim Jong Il trusted were his sister Kim Kyong-hi, of the same mother, and her husband Chang Sung-taek. Kim Kyong-hi was the head of the ruling Party's Light Industry Department of the Central Committee. She was so powerful that her role was often likened to that of the First Lady.

Her husband, Chang Sung-taek, acting as the right-hand man of Kim Jong Il, played the dual role as the chief of the powerful Operations Department of the Three Revolution Division and Youth Department of the Central Party.

Jong Il idolized his mother, Kim Jong-suk, who was just a cook when Kim Il Sung was engaged in guerrilla operations in Manchuria. Her grave, located on the highest point at the Revolutionaries Memorial Cemetery in Daesung-san, was the center of all memorial services.

A fanatical movie fan, Jong Il was said to own a large stock of films which he watched in his private viewing rooms. South Korean actress Choi Eun-hee was abducted in 1978 and held in North Korea for eight years, reportedly on Jong Il's order.

According to North Korea watchers, Kim Jong Il was in poor health. Some said he was suffering from cirrhosis of the liver as a result of heavy drinking and smoking. Even after one and a half years had passed since his father's death on July 8, 1994, he had not stepped forward as official leader of North Korea.

In the face of severe food and energy shortages, a sharp upsurge in defectors and possible social disorder, the seemingly erratic and desperate regime of Kim Jong Il may not survive long, at least not without some drastic change.

Facing a Painful Future

Kim Il Sung, the Great Leader, bequeathed to his people one of the greatest political messes to face any society. His son, the Dear Leader, was not likely to save them from a painful future. What factions might exist in the leadership, who would control them and what they stood for could only be guessed by most intelligent analysts. What was said about Kim Jong Il was itself a mass of contradictions: terrorist and war monger, or would-be economic reformer. North Korea had been organized so tightly into a pyramid of power with Kim Il Sung at its apex that the possibility of a cataclysmic social implosion could not be ruled out.

When hardline Communism collapsed all around the world, Kim Il Sung's ruling philosophy of Juche, or self-reliance, became exposed as a total failure and fraud. The Pyongyang regime had been preaching to its 23 million people that South Korea was a brutally poor, miserable place as "an American colony." But, not only was the South's economy 16 times stronger than the North's, but the ideological game seemed all over.

North Korea's economy had been shrinking by more than 5 percent during the previous decade. In 1993, it harvested only two thirds as much grain as it needed to feed its population. It would have only one direction to turn for help in the long run — and that would be toward the South.

According to defectors from North Korea, Pyongyang's relentless ideological campaigns included calls for people to eat only two meals a day and fast one day a month. Kim Il Sung had been promising North Koreans boiled rice, meat soup and silk clothing since 1962. Now his son, Kim Jong Il, would have to deliver at least enough to satisfy a military complex that gobbles up more than 25 percent of North Korea's gross national product — at a time when the GNP was declining by about 5 percent a year.

To feed the hungry soldiers of the world's fifth largest army was a serious problem for the Pyongyang regime. To supplement the food shortage, the government set the period between mid-August and late September as the "acorn collecting period." It mobilized the soldiers and citizens to collect acorns to make acorn soy sauce and acorn bean paste.

A quota for a platoon of 30 to 40 men was 800 kilograms (1,760 pounds), collected during more than 20 days in the mountains. When the quota was met, the acorns were cooked for preservation and then sent to the corps level food factory. Those in the military units located in the Demilitarized Zone (DMZ) areas were treated better than those in other areas. Still the food situation was so serious that some hungry soldiers sneaked into the villages around their barracks and stole domestic animals. [4]

To ensure his survival at the head of a leadership elite that reportedly ranges from old revolutionaries to technocrats impatient for reform, Kim needs the ability to control the aggressive military, and at the same time, to guide his country toward economic reform with something like the skill of China's Deng Xiaoping.

But some analysts aren't counting on Kim's ability. They believe that he is disliked by some elements of the military, and that he will not be able to reform North Korea's deep-rooted, helpless economic fabric based on his father's Juche (self-reliance) ideology. Credit is given to Kim Jong Il for such wasteful spending as the building of Pyongyang's Monument to Juche — a tower 13 feet higher than the Washington Monument in the United States.

QUEST FOR UNIFICATION

Transcending Ideologies and Political Systems

Koreans have been suffering the agony of national division for half a century. Breaking down the 38th Parallel barrier and paving the way for a unified and prosperous homeland is a duty history has imposed on every Korean alive today. Even though the division was not brought about by Koreans' own volition, it is their responsibility to achieve national unification through their own efforts.

Peaceful unification can be achieved only through reconciliation between the South and the North transcending conflicting ideologies and political systems. A pragmatic assessment of the Korean unification question suffers from the marked contrast that exists today between the divided halves. While the North has a closed and unicentered society under the personality cult of the late autocrat Kim Il Sung and his heir Kim Jong Il, and its people suffer from a mechanical discipline and uniformity in attitude, expression, thought and way of life, the South is an open, free society with global contacts and its people have achieved a democratic way of life under a freely elected government.

In order to overcome mistrust and suspicion caused by a long period of separation and the fratricidal Korean War waged by the North, a pragmatic and realistic approach with an attitude of conciliation and confidence will be helpful in gradually eliminating obstacles that stand in the way of achieving national unity. The memories of the Korean War are still alive in the political and social psychology of those who fought it. It is especially acute for the 10 million members of families separated between the South and North, as in my own case. The promotion of a cordial atmosphere between the conflicting halves, therefore, is an essential prerequisite to the gradual process of winning mutual confidence. Now that the competition between the South and the North over which can build a better society has been decided, it is high time to use all Koreans' determination and energies to find a breakthrough toward lasting peace and unification on the Korean peninsula, which is still threatened with the danger of war.

In an effort to end hostility and promote cooperation between the two Koreas, a number of inter-Korean prime ministers' talks have been held alternately in Seoul and Pyongyang since September 4, 1990, when North Korean Prime Minister Yon Hyong-muk led a seven-member delegation to Seoul for the first time ever. During the sixth round of the high-level talks held in Seoul on December 13, 1991, South Korean Prime Minister Chung Won-shik and his North Korean counterpart, Yon Hyong-muk, signed a landmark "basic agreement" on reconciliation and cooperation, which will be further explained in later pages.

In the wake of the unprecedented signs of thaw between the hitherto hostile South and North, Kim Dal-hyon, North Korean deputy premier in charge of external economic cooperation, made a tour of South Korean industrial facilities July 19–25, 1992, and met

President Roh Tae Woo to discuss South-North economic cooperation.

Thus inter-Korean dialogue between Seoul and Pyongyang seemed to be on a right track. However, the dialogue hit an impasse in December of that year when Pyongyang began boycotting various subcommittee meetings to discuss implementation of the reconciliation agreement. On December 19, 1992, Pyongyang issued a statement calling off the scheduled December 21–24 ninth round of inter-Korean prime ministers' talks, blaming the South "for making it impossible to open the talks in Seoul as scheduled by persisting in its decision to resume the Team Spirit military maneuvers" conducted jointly by U.S. and South Korean military forces.

Out of the problematic issues that are involved in the quest of national reunification, the most embarrassing for the Communist society in the North, is that South Korea represents a model example of economic progress, vis-a-vis Communist North Korea. The ever increasing contrast in the well-being of the people in the South and poverty in the North makes the Marxist society and its leadership suffer from an inferiority complex. Advocating its Juche philosophy, the North fears that its people may aspire to the material comforts and freedom enjoyed in South Korea and may rise up in revolution. Thus Pyongyang appears to be stepping up its last-ditch effort to protect its own form of socialism from collapsing and being absorbed into economically-superior South Korea.

Arduous Course of Reconciliation

The first step toward realizing peaceful unification should be to build mutual trust through bilateral commitments to reconciliation translated into action. Though a number of important agreements on reconciliation between the South and the North have been signed since 1972, none of them was realized because of dubious pretexts put forth by North Korea. North Korea's breach of agreements centered around insistence on repealing the National Security Law in the South, or stopping U.S.-South Korean joint military exercises.

On July 4, 1972, the South and the North announced a historic agreement to end a quarter century of hostility and york together

toward peaceful unification of the nation. In a seven-point communique, the two sides agreed on the following three principles for
unification:

(1) Unification shall be achieved through independent Korean efforts without external imposition
or interference;

(2) the unification shall be achieved through peaceful means and not through the use of force
against each other; and

(3) as a homogeneous people, a broad national
unity shall be sought above all, transcending
differences in ideas, ideologies, and system.

The two sides also agreed:

(1) Not to slander or defame each other, not to
undertake avowed provocations so as to prevent
inadvertent military incidents;

(2) to carry out various exchanges in many fields;

(3) to cooperate peacefully with each other for
early success of the South-North Red Cross
Talks;

(4) to install a direct telephone line between Seoul
and Pyongyang;

(5) to establish and operate a South-North Coordi-
nating Committee; and

(6) to pledge before the entire Korean people that
they will faithfully carry out these agreements.

The Joint Communique was signed by Director Lee Hu-rak of the Central Intelligence Agency of Seoul and Director Kim Yong-ju of the Organization and Guidance Department of Pyongyang. The Joint Communique was an important landmark from the point of view of establishing peace on the Korean peninsula. However, the environment of mutual confidence and optimism was dealt a severe blow to South Koreans when they discovered, with the help of the United Nations, that the North had dug tunnels under the truce line toward Seoul. The tunnels were believed to have been constructed for the purpose of an armed invasion from North to South. On March 14, 1990, during the 455th session of the Military Armistice Joint Commission investigating the fourth tunnel, North Korea, in a shocking move unprecedented in over 40 years of tense inter-Korean confrontations, admitted tunneling underneath the Demilitarized Zone (DMZ) into South Korea.

Another landmark move, as we have seen earlier, was the South-North prime ministers' signing on December 13, 1991 of an Agreement on Reconciliation, Non-aggression, and Exchanges and Cooperation between the South and the North.

The agreement said in its preamble:

> Whereas in keeping with the yearning of the entire people for the peaceful unification of the divided land, the South and the North reaffirm the unification principles enunciated in the July 4, 1972 South-North Joint Communique; Whereas both parties are determined to resolve political and military confrontation and achieve national reconciliation; Whereas both recognize that their relations constitute a special provision as both pledge to exert joint efforts to achieve peaceful unification, therefore, the parties hereto agree as follows:
> "Both sides shall respect each other's political and social system without interfering in each other's internal affairs, without slandering and vilifying each other; both parties shall not attempt in any manner to sabotage and subvert the other and shall endeavor together to transform the present armistice regime into

a firm state of peace between the South and the North and shall abide by the present Military Armistice Agreement [of July 27, 1953] until such time as such a state of peace has taken hold; both parties shall cease confrontation on the international stage and shall cooperate and endeavor together to promote national interests and esteem; to ensure close consultations and liaison between both parties, a South-North liaison office shall be established at Panmunjom within three months of the effective date of this Agreement; South-North political subcommittees shall be established within one month of the effective date of this Agreement with a view to discussing concrete measures to ensure the implementation and observance of the accords on South-North reconciliation."

The five-article South-North Nonaggression Agreement provides that both parties shall not use armed force against each other and shall not make armed aggression against each other, and that differences of opinion and disputes arising between the two parties shall be peacefully resolved through dialogue and negotiations. It also states that a South-North Joint Military Committee shall discuss and carry out steps to build military confidence and realize arms reductions and a telephone hotline shall be installed between the military authorities of both sides to prevent accidental armed clashes and avoid their escalation.

In the South-North Exchanges and Cooperation Accord, both sides pledged to promote an integrated and balanced development of the national economy and the welfare of the entire people through economic exchanges and cooperation. It also guarantees residents of both sides free inter-Korea travel and contacts, free correspondence, reunions and visits between family members and other relatives dispersed south and north and take other humanitarian measures. Furthermore, both parties promised to reconnect railroads and roads that have been cut off and open South-North land, sea and air transportation routes, to link postal and communications services, and to cooperate on the international stage in economic, cultural and other fields.

With the conclusion of these epochal South-North agreements, it appeared that at long last a new chapter of the history of the long-divided land had been opened and would bring to an end intra-Korean confrontation and mistrust. The widespread assumption was that North Korea felt that it was running out of time. Its economy was no longer propped up by aid from the Soviet Union, which now demanded that its former ally deal in hard currency, or not at all. It was Koreans' conviction that exchanges and cooperation in the more mundane realms of economy and daily routine should and could come earlier to build mutual confidence and understanding. Indeed, the provisions of the agreement covering economic exchanges between the two Koreas was the most likely to be carried out quickly.

However, all these hopes and expectations were betrayed as none of the agreements have been implemented while Pyongyang's rattled sabers with nuclear threats. The road to reconciliation is indeed an arduous course, but it is the only road toward peaceful unification.

Denuclearization Accord

On December 31, 1991, South and North Korea reached an agreement on a nuclear-free Korean peninsula, which was signed by their prime ministers and put into effect February 19, 1992 during the sixth round of their talks held in Pyongyang. On that day, South Korean Prime Minister Chung Won-shik and North Korean Prime Minister Yon Hyong-muk, in a nationally televised ceremony, exchanged copies of the Agreement on Reconciliation, Nonaggression, and Exchanges and Cooperation, and the Joint Declaration for a Nuclear-free Korean Peninsula. The denuclearization agreement bans development, manufacture, possession or deployment of any nuclear arms on the peninsula.

But only a day after the South and the North put into effect the accords, North Korea refused to set a date for inspection of its nuclear-energy facilities in Yongbyon, 56 miles north of Pyongyang, which South Korea and its allies suspect are used to develop weapons. Meeting the South Korean delegation on February 20, North Korean President Kim Il Sung denied that his country was making nuclear arms, but failed to give a timetable for resolving the nuclear dispute by allowing inspections. Discord on how to carry out mutual inspections of suspected sites on each side under the South-North nuclear ban accord threatened to derail implementation of the historic inter-Korean peace accords.

Officials of the South and the North met 25 times in the next two months, including 10 times on nuclear issues, but failed to make significant progress. On May 6, South Korean Prime Minister Chung warned North Korea that the previous accords could become meaningless if they kept disagreeing on how to carry them out. He said, "We should no longer remain stuck in a Cold War rut. We must join the mainstream of the emerging new world order of progress."

The North warned on June 22, at a Panmunjom meeting, that it might call off the recently-agreed dispersed families reunion plan if the South continued to insist on nuclear inspections as a condition for better relations. The South had said that no progress in inter-Korean relations would be made unless the North agreed upon mutual nuclear inspections in addition to those of the International Atomic Energy Agency.

IAEA experts, headed by Director General Hans Blix, made their first visit to North Korean nuclear facilities at Yongbyon in mid-May 1992 and found that a plant was being built to reprocess nuclear fuel into plutonium usable in nuclear arms and had already produced some of this substance. North Korea's record of secrecy, violence, treachery and deceit made this discovery cause for international alarm.

Seoul and Pyongyang clashed again over the nuclear issue at the fifth South-North Military Commission meeting in the border village of Panmunjom on June 19. At the closed-door talks at Tongilgak in the northern sector of the truce village, South Korea demanded North Korea dismantle the controversial Yongbyon facility but the North maintained its nuclear program was for peaceful purposes.

There were unwelcome signs that inter-Korean relations were cooling, even before they bore any tangible fruit, because of the negative stance of North Korea in implementing its international and inter-Korean commitments related to nuclear arms development program. Both the renewed IAEA inspections and the inter-Korea working level contacts at Panmunjom ended in utter fiasco, with North Korea continuing its tactics of rejection and delay. Breaking off Panmunjom meetings in March 1993, North Korean delegates went so far as to threaten a war of total devastation.

North Korea's whole strategy on the nuclear issue was based on intimidation playing on international fears that it would lash out if pushed too far. Using all this saber-rattling tactics, Pyongyang succeeded in obtaining substantial concessions from Washington as evidenced in the U.S.-North Korea Nuclear Agreement.

What is most disturbing to Seoul is the fact that Pyongyang, besides its nuclear threats, has taken steps that indicate its intent to neutralize the all-important Armistice Agreement of 1953. On February 28, 1995, North Korea evicted Polish members of the Neutral Nations Supervisory Commission (NNSC) from their camp on the North Korean side near the truce village of Panmunjom. The Poles were the sole NNSC members left on North Korean soil after Pyongyang had forced the Czech members to leave their NNSC camp in March 1993. Pyongyang had always barred Swiss and Swedish members of the 4-nation truce watchdog body from entering its territory.

North Korea also boycotted senior officers' meetings of the Military Armistice Commission (MAC) starting in March 1991 when its chief American delegate was replaced by a South Korean army major general. In the absence of Chinese delegates who had unilaterally withdrawn from MAC, Pyongyang is maneuvering to negotiate a separate peace treaty with Washington to replace the July 27, 1953 Armistice Agreement, excluding South Korea. Pyongyang's ultimate goal is to realize its long-sought withdrawal of U.S. troops from South Korea, whose presence was a critical factor in deterring North Korean invasion during past decades. On March 5, 1995, Pyongyang revealed its intention through the government organ *Minju Chosun,* which said in a commentary, "The issue of setting up a new peace structure on the peninsula is a bilateral matter between the United States and us and, therefore, no other forces are allowed to intervene."

Pyongyang's long-hidden design was also indicated in North Korean Prime Minister Yon Hong-muk's keynote speech after the December 13, 1991 signing of the inter-Korean basic agreements on reconciliation, nonaggression, and exchanges and cooperation: "Since the South-North agreements have been adopted and come into force, there is no ground to hesitate about the question of withdrawal of foreign forces. We think that time has come to resolve the question of withdrawal of foreign forces and completely stop the joint military exercises with the United States."

Closing the South-North Economic Gap

The growing economic disparity between the South and the North is a matter of grave concern to South Koreans, the main players in the drive to reunify the Korean peninsula. If impoverished North Korea were suddenly to collapse, South Korea would need to spend $1.53 trillion over the next 10 years to bring the North's economy up to par with the South's, according to a report of the Korea Development Bank released in September 1994.

If, however, the two Koreas were gradually to merge, with unification occurring in year 2000, the 10-year cost would be even greater, at $2.22 trillion, the report said. It said the increase in cost is the result of the growing economic disparity between the two Koreas as time passes, and assumes that North Korea would fail to significantly close the economic gap through industrialization on its own before 2000.

North Korea's gross national product in 1994 was estimated at $21.12 billion, one-sixteenth of South Korea's $330.8 billion, according to a Bank of Korea report. The North's economic troubles have steadily worsened since 1991, when the Soviet Union and Communist China began demanding hard currency for goods instead of barter trade. Since then, Pyongyang has suffered from energy shortages that have idled the majority of factories and from poor harvests that fill only 60 percent of the nation's needs. Defectors to South Korea have painted grim pictures of widespread starvation, with some of them saying they were reduced to eating tree bark to survive.

The capitalist south, however, has rapidly industrialized, becoming the world's 12th biggest economy. According to statistics of the South Korean National Statistical Office, the South's average economy grew at the rate of 7.26 percent between 1991 and 1994, which was higher than any member country of the Organization for Economic Cooperation and Development (OECD). In trading, South Korea recorded the world's 10th largest volume of exports as well as imports with $83.2 billion and $83.8 billion respectively in 1993. North Korea's two-way trade came to $2.7 billion in 1992, one sixtieth of South Korea's in the same year.

Food shortages in North Korea became so critical by May 1995 that the Pyongyang government, breaking its taboo on admitting a food crisis, openly requested an early supply of rice from Japan and South Korea. Meeting with Japanese coalition government leaders in Tokyo on May 25, North Korean Chairman of International Trade Promotion Commission, Lee Song-rok, asked for prompt shipment of surplus rice from Japan, and at the same time he requested Tokyo to inform Seoul that "We are ready to accept unconditional rice assistance from South Korea." Lee said he was authorized to make the request by North Korean Foreign Minister Kim Yong-nam and Prime Minister Kang Song-san. Although Pyongyang has quietly purchased rice from capitalist nations in the past, this request marked the first time it had openly asked for aid.

The Seoul government was quick to respond to the North Korean request. Seoul's position was that the food crisis in the North should be tackled as an intra-Korean problem, with South Korea playing the major role in helping its starving brethren in the North. In their vice-ministerial talks in Beijing, the Seoul and Pyongyang governments reached an agreement on June 21, 1995 for the unconditional supply of 150,000 metric tons of free rice from South Korea.

Early on the morning of June 29, a South Korean vessel, the *Sea Apex,* unloaded the first shipment of 2,000 tons of rice at the northern port of Chongjin, but was forced to hoist the North Korean flag. Under the landmark Beijing deal, the two Korean governments agreed that no flags would be hoisted on the southern ships.

South Korean Unification Minister Rha Woong-bae demanded an apology, ordered two more ships en route to the North to turn back, and threatened to call off shipment of the rest of the 150,000 tons of free rice. On June 29, Pyongyang sent a formal letter of apology promising the flag incident would not happen again. On July 3, South Korean Deputy Unification Minister Song Young-dae announced that Cabinet ministers decided to accept the North's apology and to resume rice shipments.

And then South Korean President Kim Young Sam, who had agreed to supply rice to Pyongyang, was humiliated when the ship providing it was seized on spying charges at a North Korean port. The ship was later returned to the South.

Already plagued by acute agricultural problems, North Korea suffered heavy flooding in some areas in August. Both U.S. and South Korean officials say that Pyongyang has exaggerated the impact of the floods because it prefers to blame its food shortages on a natural disaster rather than on chronic structural problems in its agricultural system. They pointed out that North Korea's estimate of $15 billion in economic losses from the floods would represent about three-quarters of the country's gross national product, which in recent years has been about $21 billion a year.

Unification Scenarios

There are a variety of scenarios projected for North Korea's future, each of which would affect reunification of the Korean peninsula. Some observers have predicted that, sooner or later, North Korea will undergo upheaval due to economic and political factors, with either a protracted factional struggle for power or a collapse in the fashion of the old East European regimes.

Another possible scenario for the North would be to abandon efforts to adopt an open-door policy and perpetuate the old order, with its reliance on isolation, Stalinism, "Juche" economic strategy, and the existing ruling elite.

If the present course continues, North Korea is likely to evolve into an authoritarian-pluralist system, with politics still highly constrained but a civil society gradually developing apart from the state and a mixed economy, with market forces increasingly prominent.

The crucial question would be: How does a tightly closed Communist society accommodate itself to the rapidly evolving free society in the South? How does it adjust without chaos or collapse?

This is the question which the North Korean leaders must ponder in the months and years ahead.

The issue of peaceful unification of the Korean peninsula, which is basically a bilateral one in character, suffers from the heterogeneity of the Communist society in the North, which does not suit the will and aspirations of the majority of the Korean people. It is a problem of political and strategic mechanics of totalitarianism on the one hand and the defense of freedom and democracy, human rights and improved economy on the other. Whenever or however it happens, national unification must begin with the restoration and development of the presently divided and heterogenous elements of Korean society into a unified national community.

North Korea is now in a state of flux following the death of Kim Il Sung, its only leader for the past half century. This should offer an unprecedented opportunity to take a new initiative and actively transform South-North relations. To this end, it has become imperative to re-examine and redefine the South's unification policy, as well as its policy toward the North in order to set clear-cut guidelines for future endeavors toward unity.

The thrust of the new policies is to outgrow the past passive and defensive policies toward North Korea, as well as a well-defined and forward-looking unification formula designed to ensure well-being and prosperity for all Koreans.

In a nationally-televised speech on August 15, 1994, marking the 49th anniversary of national liberation from Japanese colonial rule, South Korean President Kim Young Sam redefined the Republic's unification policy, as well as its policy toward North Korea, in light of the changing situation on the Korean peninsula. He made it clear that the philosophy behind the Republic's unification policy was rooted in the values of freedom, democracy and well-being for all, rather than on any ideology narrowly focused on a specific class or group.

The Korean National Community Formula enunciated by President Kim envisions the following three phases:

(1) Reconciliation and cooperation phase: The present hostility and confrontation between the

South and the North will be replaced with a relationship of reconciliation and cooperation,

(2) Korean commonwealth phase: Peaceful coexistence and coprosperity will be secured and the two parts of Korea will be joined in a single socio-economic community,

(3) Single nation-state phase: A single nation-state is to be completed by fully integrating the South and the North.

The initial version of the Korean National Community Unification Formula was laid down by then President Roh Tae Woo in his August 15, 1989 speech. For many past centuries, the homogeneous Korean people lived in a single national community until they were divided by the artificial 38th Parallel demarcation line imposed by the United States and the Soviet Union at the end of World War II. This age-old sense of community still binds all Koreans together. This explains why Korea must be reunited and is indeed the motivating force for reunification.

While the North's formula for unification, Democratic Confederation of Koryo (an old name for Korea), which is based on the Juche ideology (a variation of Stalinism), proposes a conference of delegates from all political and social organizations, the South's formula calls for democratic general elections in both the South and the North under the constitution of a unified Korea.

The South's national community concept is focused on enabling the entire people under one roof, with one system and one government, ensuring freedom, democracy and well-being for all, while the North's confederation concept is based on the interests of a specific class and groups, with two states, each with its own system and government.

Unification no longer remains in the realm of a pipe dream or wishful thinking; it has now become a realistic goal, a feasible task. This calls for greater preparedness on the part of the affluent South for unification, including the buildup of its capabilities to accomplish the task, as well as its more active efforts to improve intra-Korean relations.

Although the South Korean government has been pursuing a policy of progressive South-North integration, it would be unwise to rule out the possibility that unification can take place abruptly and unexpectedly depending on developments in the North. All possible scenarios must be examined and sufficient preparations made for any turn of events. For this matter, South Korean Prime Minister Lee Hong-koo rightly said in a special lecture on unification on August 8, 1994, that his government would immediately unify the divided peninsula by absorbing North Korea "if such an opportunity is given." Lee said such an opportunity would include the collapse of the North Korean government. But he added: "I oppose the opinion of some people that we have to take active steps to advance the collapse of North Korea."

What needs to be considered, in this context, is that if the process of unification is delayed with the passage of time and appearance of a new generation, which has never experienced life in a united Korea, the desire for unification may not be as intense as it is with the present leadership. The memories of the Korean War which are alive with the present generation, provoking aspiration for national unification, may become mere lessons of history for upcoming generations.

It should be remembered that more than 10 million family members separated between the South and the North are especially anxious to bring down the 38th Parallel barrier to realize their half-century dream of reuniting with their loved ones.

Fruitless efforts to facilitate mutual visits of the separated families have been made through on-again, off-again South-North Red Cross talks. While the South based the discussions on humanitarian reasons, the North linked them to political issues, invariably arguing that there was no way of solving the problem of separated families so long as there remains the National Security Law and U.S. troops remain in South Korea.

Also, those in the South are troubled by the question of duplicity of the North Korean leadership on the unification issue. North Korea has talked peace and made public pledges of peaceful reunification but has never renounced its strategy for "Liberation of the South by military means." The basic theme was set forth by Kim Il Sung on February 28, 1968 in his article on national unification published in *The Unification of the Homeland:* "Political power is to be gained through military struggle...Among the ways of struggle, the most active and decisive one is the national liberation struggle in the form of organized violence, armed struggle...." [5] Indicating the North's political-military scheme in this regard is the fact that a full withdrawal of U.S. troops from South Korea has been set as prerequisite to the proposed North Korean formula for unification — creating a Democratic Confederation of Koryo.

Pyongyang still sticks to its "One Korea Principle" policy disregarding the existence of the Republic of Korea. While Seoul deals with North Korea on the basis of coexistence, Pyongyang treats South Korea as its southern half or "unliberated territory still under American colonial rule." North Korea should know that such a preposterous stance does not square with its joint admission with South Korea to the United Nations on September 17, 1991.

The United States, now engaged in direct dialogue with the Pyongyang government in an effort to prevent North Korea from developing nuclear arms and to open doors of the reclusive country, should be wary of its record of deceit and treachery as experienced in the two-year haggling of the Korean truce talks. In its overtures to the Communist regime in Pyongyang, Washington ought to make its position clear on the question of reunification of the Korean peninsula to forestall North Korean maneuvers to estrange South Korea from the United State. With the United States providing the stabilizing security factor, North Korea will have to drop its political-military goals and respond to South Korea's call for an early implementation of the landmark South-North basic agreement on reconciliation, non-aggression, and exchanges and cooperation, signed on December 13, 1991, as well as the denuclearization accord put into effect February 19, 1991.

Though the unification of the Korean peninsula must be achieved through the Korean people's own efforts, genuine cooperation from the United States, China, Russia, and Japan — doing away with their self-interests — will be indispensable.

EPILOGUE

By any reasonable measure, Kim Il Sung's invasion of South Korea on June 25, 1950 was an unprovoked act of raw aggression, which the South lacked the means to resist. Whereas North Korea was armed with Soviet-made tanks, planes, and heavy artillery, the Southerners had been deliberately denied by the Americans the means of war for fear that a strong South Korean army would be tempted to seek reunification of the country by an attack on the North.

However, President Harry S. Truman's response to the invasion was quick and decisive. The decision to pour American armed forces into the war was greeted with a standing ovation from Congress. The American assistance was motivated by its goal of checking Soviet hegemony in the Far East.

Following 1,095 days of warfare and unprecedented destruction, an "armistice without victory," as U.N. Commander Mark Clark called the inconclusive end of the war, left Korea with unfinished business.

"In war, there can be no substitute for victory," said General Douglas MacArthur in 1991. Many American career officers were deeply dismayed by the precedent Korea established: the United States had failed to fight a war to a victorious conclusion. Lieutenant General Arthur Trudeau, commanding the U.S. 7th Division, spoke of "that odious armistice...when we let the Russians and the Chinese off the hook in Korea, we opened the door for their victory over the French in Vietnam. We should have let MacArthur go to the Yalu and bomb the piss out of them on the other side."

Lieutenant General James Van Fleet, after 22 months in Korea as U.S. Eighth Army commander, announced on February 11, 1953 that his forces had been strong enough to wage a successful offensive against the Communists. He wrote in *Life:* "Though we could readily have followed up our success, that was not the intention in Washington; our State Department had already let the Reds know that we were willing to settle on the 38th Parallel. Instead of getting directives for offensive action, we found our activities more and more proscribed as the time went on...."

Thus the bloody Korean War ended inconclusively on July 27, 1953. Many United Nations veterans came home from Korea to discover that their experience was of no interest whatsoever to their fellow-countrymen. The war seemed unsatisfactory, inglorious, and thus it became a forgotten war.

The men and women who fought the forgotten war finally took their place in history on July 27, 1995, when the Korean War Veterans Memorial — a long-overdue tribute to their achievements in Korea — was officially dedicated in Washington.

As the sense of frustration and stagnation that attended the armistice faded as time passed on, soldiers and politicians became disposed to think more favorably of the Korean War's value as a demonstration of the West's commitment to the arrest of Communism. If the United Nations failed to achieve the reunification of Korea, they had prevented North Korea from imposing its will by force to Communize the South.

The hardest price South Korea has paid for the war is that, even today, it remains a society under siege. The threat from the North has never receded. North Korea's constant efforts to undermine the South by subversive activity, and periodically by guerrilla and terrorist operations across the border, intensify tension between the divided halves. Pyongyang maintains a constant propaganda war with formidable military capability.

South Korea, meanwhile, has become the world's 12th economic power, now under a freely elected democratic government. The South Korean people, like the phoenix, arose from the ashes of their burned-out cities and ruined industries into a new day of freedom and progress. "I guess the best monument we've got is the free people in South Korea," said Win Scott, former Marine Corps private first class. Thousands of Korean War veterans who visited South Korea are deeply moved by the gratitude that South Koreans still display for the salvation of their country from the Communists 43 years ago. In contrast, the people in North Korea have paid the bitterest price of all for Kim Il Sung's adventure in June 1950. To this day, they remain the prisoners of the teachings of the "Great Leader" in his wretched self-created prison camp. North Korea exists in pitiful isolation, a society dominated by poverty and the cult of Kim Il Sung and his heir Kim Jong Il.

Who can doubt, looking at Korea today, that the 45 million South Koreans enjoy incomparably more fulfilling lives than those of the 23 million inhabitants of the North who are on the verge of starvation?

Despite its failing economy, North Korea has been pouring more than 25 percent of its gross national product (GNP) into military buildup, now with 1.1 million troops on active duty — the fifth largest army in the world. North Korea has succeeded in test firing Scud-type Rodong 1 missiles with a range of over 1,000 kilometers (620 miles) and is developing Tae-dong missiles with longer ranges.

In the face of economic disaster and political isolation, North Korea has been using its suspected nuclear arsenal as a bargaining chip skillfully and effectively. The October 21, 1994 nuclear agreement signed in Geneva between Pyongyang and Washington was a landmark success for Pyongyang which had long sought a direct dialogue with Washington, excluding South Korea; not only for a favorable settlement of the nuclear issue but for establishing diplomatic links with the United States; the North Korean strategy was seen in South Korea as its scheme to drive a wedge between America and South Korea, and press its persistent demands for the withdrawal of U.S. forces from South Korea and unification of the Korean peninsula under the Communist term.

North Korea, in exchange for freezing its nuclear weapons program, is scheduled to receive two light-water reactors by 2003, along with 500,000 tons of heavy oil annually from the United States and its allies. Pyongyang felt festive because, under the agreement, the long-disputed international inspections of its two suspected nuclear facilities were ruled out for about five years. On

June 13, 1995 North Korea reluctantly reached a written agreement with the United States in Kuala Lumpur, Malaysia, on the provision of two South Korean-made light-water reactors that do not generate weapons-grade plutonium. South Korea will pay more than 60 percent of the $4 billion project financed by an international consortium. Thus Pyongyang succeeded in achieving most of what it wanted through its nuclear threat.

The Geneva accord leaves unanswered some important questions: was North Korea already nuclear armed? What if Pyongyang refuses to open the two disputed nuclear facilities for international inspections after the five-year term of agreement? Critics say they are clearly unconvinced that Pyongyang will adhere to the agreement given its record of reneging on promises with arbitrary excuses. During the two years of haggling in truce talks at Panmunjom, the United Nations Command learned the bitter lesson that agreements are considered by the North Korean Communists merely as tactical maneuvers to gain time or other advantages.

During the past two years, the important question of Korean unification has been overshadowed by the more immediate crisis over North Korea's nuclear weapons program. The submerged questions of particular importance about the future of the reunification of the Korean peninsula are: will South and North Korea ultimately join together once again, as West and East Germany did after the fall of the Berlin Wall? Will the affluent South absorb the impoverished North? How will the unified Korea operate?

Bringing down the 38th Parallel barrier dividing the country would affect the four major powers involved in northeast Asia — the United States, China, Russia and Japan. The truth is that all these major powers have their own hidden interests in how these questions are resolved.

Japan is said, contrary to its official statements, to have the strongest interest in keeping Korea divided for fear that a reunited Korea could threaten it militarily and economically. Japan could attempt to develop close ties to North Korea and give the Communist state plenty of aid, in an effort to keep it alive as long as possible. It has made moves in that direction before, such as when the late Kanemaru Shin (former deputy prime minister) led a Liberal Party delegation to Pyongyang in 1990. And, while Russia for now doesn't seem to have any reason to oppose the reunification of Korea, the Chinese, with an army of about four million, would not face the same potential threat from a reunified Korea that Japan would. But on the whole, China seems to prefer things the way they are now with ties with both Koreas.

It is believed that a reunited Korea would be a natural ally for the United States. But that raises the most delicate question of all: What about the U.S. bases and the 37,000 American troops in South Korea? Would they stay?

The official statement of the Pentagon issued in February 1995 notes that American forces are in South Korea not just in defense against the North Korean threat but also "in the interest of regional stability." In other words, the United States would want its troops in Korea, even if there were no North Korea. As if endorsing this viewpoint in his White House meetings with South Korean President Kim Young Sam on July 26, 1995, U.S. President Bill Clinton reaffirmed the U.S. pledge to keep American forces in Korea "as long as they are needed and the Korean people want them to remain."

Since lasting stability on the Korean Peninsula is the key to maintaining peace in northeast Asia, it should be the foremost interest of the four major powers — which had been involved directly or indirectly in bisecting the Land of Morning Calm — to facilitate peaceful reunification of the divided Koreas transcending their individual self-interests.

American MPs and North Korean guards at their posts in the truce village of Panmunjom in 1993.

Kim Il Sung (right) and Kim Jong Il, his son and successor, are seen taking a stroll in Pyongyang in April 1982.

CHRONOLOGY

June 25, 1950 — North Korean forces invade South Korea. U.N. Security Council, in the absence of the USSR, adopts a resolution calling for the withdrawal of North Korean forces to the 38th Parallel.

June 27, 1950 — President Truman orders U.S. air and sea services to give support to South Korean forces. U.N. Security Council asks member nations to give aid to South Korea in repelling aggression.

June 28, 1950 — Seoul falls; South Korean army defeated.

June 30, 1950 — President Truman orders U.S. ground troops into Korea.

July 5, 1950 — First U.S. ground troops go into action at Osan; forced to retreat.

July 7, 1950 — U.N. creates United Nations Command; General Douglas MacArthur named supreme U.N. commander.

July 13, 1950 — Lt. Gen. Walton H, Walker, commander of Eighth Army, assumes command of ground forces in Korea.

July 21, 1950 — Taejon falls; Major General William F. Dean, 24th Division commander, missing in action. (He was taken prisoner by North Korea on August 26.)

August 4, 1950 — Pusan Perimeter established.

Aug. 27-Sept. 15, 1950 — Perimeter battles, heaviest of war.

September 15, 1950 — U.S. X Corps makes successful amphibious landing on Inchon, enabling U.N. forces to break out of Pusan Perimeter and push toward the 38th Parallel.

September 26, 1950 — Seoul recaptured.

October 1, 1950 — South Korean troops cross the 38th Parallel.

October 7, 1950 — U.N. sanctions defeat of North Korea, reunification of country. U.N. forces cross the 38th Parallel.

October 15, 1950 — Truman and MacArthur meet at Wake Island.

October 19, 1950 — Pyongyang, North Korean capital, taken by U.N. forces.

October 26, 1950 — U.S. X Carp lands at Wonsan on east coast.

October 30, 1950 — President Syngman Rhee visits Pyongyang.

November 1, 1950 — Communist Chinese Forces ambush 1st Cav. Div, at Unsan.

November 10–26, 1950 — X Corps advances toward Yalu in east, Eighth Army in west.

November 27, 1950 — Chinese forces strike 1st Marine and 7th Divisions in east.

Nov. 27-Dec. 10, 1950 — X Corps fights back toward port of Hungnam in east. Marines retreat from Koto-ri.

December 5, 1950 — Eighth Army withdraws from Pyongyang; Chinese occupy the North Korean capital.

December 23, 1950 — General Walker killed in jeep accident; Lt. Gen. Mathew B. Ridgway takes command of Eighth Army.

December 24, 1950 — X Corps withdraws from Hungnam; North Korea evacuated.

January 4, 1951 — U.N. forces evacuate Seoul.

February 15, 1951 — Communists defeated at Chipyong-ni.

Feb. 17-March 17, 1951 — U.N. forces continue offensive, move north.

March 15, 1951 — U.N. forces retake Seoul.

April 11, 1951 — Truman relieves MacArthur; Ridgway succeeds him.

April 15, 1951 — Lt. Gen. James Van Fleet takes command of Eighth Army.

April 22, 1951 — Chinese begin spring offensive; Gloucesters hold on at Imjin.

May 23, 1951 — Eighth Army begins offensive.

June 23, 1951 — Yakov Malik, Soviet ambassador to the United Nations, calls for a ceasefire.

July 10, 1951 — Truce talks begin at Kaesong.

November 27, 1951 — Truce talks resume at Panmunjom; ceasefire line agreed upon, at line of contact.

Nov. 1951-April, 1952 — Stalemate along battlefront during truce talks at Panmunjom.

April 2, 1952 — Screening of U.N. POWs begins; Koje-do riots commence.

May 7, 1952 — Brig. Gen. Francis T. Dodd, Koje-do POW camp commander, captured by Communist prisoners.

May 12, 1952 — General Mark Clark succeeds Ridgway.

October 8, 1952 — Truce talks recessed at Panmunjom; complete deadlock.

December 2, 1952 — President-elect Dwight Eisenhower arrives in Korea for four-day visit.

February 11, 1953 — Lt. Gen. Maxwell Taylor replaces Van Fleet at Eighth Army.

February 22, 1953 — U.N. Command again proposes exchange of sick and wounded prisoners.

March 5, 1953 — Joseph Stalin dies; Georgi Malenkov succeeds him.

April 20–26, 1953 — Exchange of sick and wounded prisoners at Panmunjom.

April 27, 1953 — Resumption of plenary sessions at Panmunjom.

May 25, 1953 — U.N. negotiating team presents its secret proposal to the Communists. President Rhee angered.

June 8, 1953 — Rhee orders South Korean guards to release 27,000 North Korean prisoners who do not wish to be repatriated.

June 25, 1953 — Walter S. Robertson, U.S. Assistant Secretary of State for Far Eastern Affairs, arrives in Seoul to persuade Rhee to accept armistice.

July 12, 1953 — Rhee and Robertson jointly announce that South Korea would not obstruct the armistice in return for U.S. promise to sign mutual defense pact and provide vast economic aid.

July 27, 1953 — Armistice signed at Panmunjom. Fighting ends.

August 5, 1953 — Screening and repatriation of war prisoners begin at Freedom Village, Panmunjom.

BIBLIOGRAPHY

The principal sources for this book have been the notes I took while covering the Korean War as an AP correspondent, relevant files of my AP dispatches and newspaper clips, preserved memories indelibly etched on my heart, as well as my book *Bringing Down the 38th Parallel Barrier* published in Japanese. I have also drawn upon the contemporary files of major American and Korean newspapers and magazines.

The bibliography given here represents those which I found to be particularly helpful or pertinent.

Chung, Il-kwon, *Chonjaeng-Gwa Hyujon (War and Truce)*, (Dong-A Ilbo, Seoul, 1986)

Chung Kyung Cho, *Korea Tomorrow*, (The Macmillan Company, New York, 1956)

Cumings, Bruce, *The Origins of the Korean War*, (Princeton University Press, Princeton, New Jersey, 1990)

Dean, William F., *General Dean's Story*, (The Viking Press, New York, 1954)

Fehrenbach, T. R., *This Kind of War*, (The Macmillan Company, New York, 1964)

Goulden, Joseph C., *Korea: The Untold Story of the War*, (Times Books, New York, 1982)

Hastings, Max, *The Korean War*, (Michael Joseph, London, 1987)

Kang, Man-kil, *Hanguk Hyondaesa (Contemporary History of Korea)*, (Koryo Sorim, Tokyo, 1985)

Kim, C.I. Eugene/Kim Han-kyo, *Korea and Politics of Imperialism*, (University of California Press, Los Angeles, 1968)

Khrushchev, Nikita, *Khrushchev Remembers*, (Little, Brown, 1971)

Knightley, Phillip, *The First Casualty: From the Crimea to Vietnam*, (Harcourt Brace, New York and London, 1975)

Ko, Yong-hwan, *Wonderland*, (The Institute of North Korean Affairs, Seoul, 1994)

Korea Annual, (Yonhap News Agency, Seoul, 1995)

Leckie, Robert, *Conflict, The History of the Korean War,* (G. P. Putnam's Sons, New York, 1962)

Media History Digest, Vol. 10/No. 2, (Editor & Publisher, New York, 1990)

Middleton, Harry J., *The Compact History of the Korean War,* (Hawthorn Books, New York, 1965)

Neillan, Edward, *One Korea,* (Si-sa-yong-o-sa, Seoul 1990)

Oliver, Robert T., *Why War Came In Korea,* (Fordham University Press, New York, 1950)

Poats, Rutherford M., *Decision in Korea,* (The McBride Company, New York, 1954)

Stone, I. F., *The Hidden History of the Korean War,* (The Monthly Review Press, New York, 1952)

Srivastava, M.P., *The Korean Conflict,* (Prentice-Hall of India, New Delhi, 1982)

Tsunoda, Fusako, *Minbi Ansatsu (Assassination of Queen Min),* (Sinchosha, Tokyo, 1993)

Yoo Wan-shik/Kim Tae-se, *Thirty-year History of North Korea* (Hyondae Kyongje Ilbo-sa, Seoul, 1975)

NOTES

CHAPTER ONE

1. Tsunoda Fusako, *Minbi Ansatsu (Assassination of Queen Min)*, (Shinchosha, Tokyo, 1993), P. 401
2. Robert T. Oliver, *Why War Came In Korea*, (Fordham University Press, New York, 1950), P. 43
3. C.I. Eugene Kim/Han Kyo Kim, *Korea and Politics of Imperialism*, (University of California Press, Los Angeles, 1968), P. 130
4. *Korea Herald*, (May 13, 1992, Seoul)
5. Teresa Watanabe, *Los Angeles Times*, July 20, 1995.
6. Chung Il-kwon, *Conjaeng-Gwa Hyujon (War and Truce)*, (Dong-A Ilbo, Seoul, 1986) P. 19
7. AP dispatch from Seoul, (June 22, 1992).
8. Joseph C. Goulden, *Korea, The Untold Story of the War*, (Times Books, New York, 1982), P. 61
9. *Ibid*
10. Max Hastings, *The Korean War*, (Michael Joseph Ltd, London, 1987), P. 52

CHAPTER TWO

1. John Toland, *In Mortal Combat, Korea 1950-1953*, (William Morrow and Company, New York, 1991), P. 34
2. *Ibid*, P. 53.
3. Joseph C. Goulden, *Korea, The Untold Story of the War*, (Times Books, New York, 1982), P. 64.
4. *Media History Digest*, Vol. 10/No.2, (Editor & Publisher, New York, 1990), PP. 17-18
5. Chung Il-kwon, *Chonjaeng-Gwa Hyujon (War and Truce)*, (Dong-A Ilbo, Seoul, 1986), P. 126
6. *Ibid*, P. 86
7. *Ibid*, P. 88

CHAPTER THREE

1. Chung Il-kwon, *Chunjaeng-Gwa Hyujon (War and Truce)*, (Dong-A Ilbo, Seoul, 1986) PP. 131-132
2. Rutherford M. Poats, *Decision in Korea*, (The McBride Company, New York, 1953), PP. 67-69.
3. Chung Il-kwon, *Chonjaeng-Gwa-Hyujon (War and Truce)*, (Dong-A Ilbo, Seoul, 1986)), P.131
4. Phillip Knightley, *The First Casualty, From the Crimea to Vietnam: the War Correspondent as Hero, Propagandist, and Myth Maker*, (Harcourt Brace, New York and London, 1975), P. 341

5. Chung Il-kwon, *Chonjaeng-Gwa-Hyujon (War and Truce)*, (Dong-A Ilbo, Seoul, 1986), P. 201
6. T. R. Fehrenbach, *This Kind of War*, (The Macmillan Company, New York, 1964), P. 287
7. *Ibid*
8. Joseph C. Goulden, Korea, *The Untold Story of the War*, (Times Books, New York, 1982), P. 268
9. *Ibid*, P. 269
10. Harry J. Middleton, *The Compact History of the Korean War*, (Hawthorn Books. New York, 1965), P. 154
11. *Ibid*, P. 164
12. *Ibid*, P. 165
13. *Ibid*, P. 172
14. T. R. Fehrenbach, *This Kind of War*, (The Macmillan Company, New York, 1964), P. 436
15. Harry J. Middleton, *The Compact History of the Korean War*, (Hawthorn Books, New York, 1965), P. 176
16. Joseph C. Goulden, *Korea, The Untold Story of the War*, (Times Books, New York, 1982), P. 262
17. Max Hastings, *The Korean War*, (Michael Joseph, London, 1987), P. 270
18. Robert Leckie, *Conflict, The History of the Korean War, 1950-53*, (G. P. Putnam's Sons. New York, 1962), P. 292
19. *Ibid*, P. 294
20. Joseph C. Goulden, *Korea, The Untold Story of the War*, (Times Books, New York, 1982) P. 554

CHAPTER FOUR

1. John Toland, *In Mortal Combat, Korea 1950-1953*, (William Morrow and Company, Inc., New York, 1991), P. 494
2. *Ibid*, P. 295.
3. Joseph C. Goulden, *Korea, The Untold Story of the War*, (Times Books, New York, 1982), PP. 627-8
4. John Toland, *In Mortal Combat, Korea 1950-1953*, (William Morrow and Company, Inc., New York, P. 556
5. Robert Leckie, *Conflict, The History of the Korean War, 1950-53*, (G. P. Putnam's Sons, New York, 1962), P. 379
6. *Ibid*, P. 388
7. *Media History Digest*, Vol. 10/No. 2, (Editor & Publisher, New York, 1990, P. 20
8. *Korea Herald*, (Seoul, May 1, 1977)

CHAPTER FIVE

1. Ko Yong-hwan, *Wonderland*, (The Institute of North Korean Affairs, Seoul, 1994), P. 187
2. UPI dispatch from Moscow, *(Korean Herald*, Seoul, June 25, 1994)
3. Ko Yong-hwan, *Wonderland*, (The Institute of North Korean Affairs, Seoul, 1994), PP. 71, 72
4. *Ibid*, P. 148
5. Edward Neilan, *One Korea, (Si-sa-yong-o-sa*, Seoul, 1990), P. 28

ACKNOWLEDGMENTS

I am deeply indebted to my old friends who read critically this book in manuscript form, correcting typos and grammatical misfortunes. They are Al Kaff, former United Press correspondent who covered the Korean War and later served as a vice president of United Press International; Edward Neilan, former foreign editor of *The Washington Times* and now a Tokyo-based columnist; and Mary Ann Maskery, former reporter for ABC News in Tokyo. I owe a grateful debt to Ed Reingold, former Tokyo bureau chief for *Time Magazine*, now co-director of the Center for International Journalism at the University of Southern California, who patiently read the galley proofs. They made their contributions solely on the basis of friendly interest and I am anxious to express my gratitude to all of them. Without their valuable help, this book would not have seen the light.

Thanks are also due to Frank Won, who was chief of the Press Liaison Office of the U.S. Eighth Army during the Korean War, and Dr. Kim Joon-yong, former professor of Seoul National University, for their cordial assistance. I would like to express special thanks to Mr. Gene S. Rhie, a librarian at Kean College of New Jersey, for his favorable evaluation of my manuscript and warm support for its publication in the United States.

Acknowledgment is hereby made, and gratitude expressed, to the bibliographical sources cited in this book for permission to quote portions of their work, I also gratefully acknowledge that the photographs in the book, excepting those in my private possession, are the courtesy of the Associated Press, National Archives, and Lim In-sik, former South Korean Army photographer.

The Author
Los Angeles

INDEX